f**P**

Salvador Minuchin
Michael P. Nichols

FAMILY
HEALING

Strategies for Hope and Understanding

THE FREE PRESS
New York London Toronto Sydney Singapore

THE FREE PRESS
1230 Avenue of the Americas
New York, NY 10020

Copyright © 1993 by Salvador Minuchin and
Michael P. Nichols

First Free Press Edition 1998

Published by arrangement with The Free Press, a
division of Simon & Schuster, Inc.
THE FREE PRESS and colophon are registered trademarks
of Simon & Schuster Inc.

Manufactured in the United States of America

3 5 7 9 10 8 6 4

Library of Congress Cataloging-in-Publication Data is available.

ISBN: 0-684-85573-9

Contents

Preface

After thirty years as a family therapist, I proclaimed myself an elder. After all, I was there when family therapy began. I was one of the ones who helped it grow, and I have seen it move, for better or worse, from being a radical new departure, a novel way of looking at people and helping them, to its present secure position within the mental health establishment.

In the best tradition of storytelling, the elder, seated on a low bench, regales his audience with the exciting adventures of his youth. So I wrote four autobiographical chapters. But when I began to look at cases that could represent a universe of families and describe the way I work, I felt overwhelmed by proximity. I realized that one of the barriers to an honest account of therapy would be the tendency to read my own theories into my client families, recreating them in my own image. The collaboration with Mike Nichols began at this point. Together we reviewed dozens of cases to select ones that would illustrate various stages of family development and the issues that crop up to bedevil all families. Although we included some exceptional and unusual families, most of the stories in this book are about ordinary human beings learning life's painful lessons. Mike took on the thankless task of transcribing the tapes of the sessions and brought fresh eyes to encounters that had become so much part of me that I was in danger of imposing my bias on what actually happened. As you will see, I have tried to help the reader understand some of the critical issues that families wrestle with and some of what was going on in my own mind as I tried to help them solve the problems that brought them to therapy.

After Mike sent me the transcripts, I went over them to reduce them to manageable size and to add my thoughts about the meaning of the therapeutic encounter. We met on numerous weekends, going over the material together, pruning the superfluous content, and rechecking the tapes to ensure complete accuracy. It was a rich and satisfying collaboration.

Because I wanted to let the family members tell their own stories, we limited our selection to cases for which I had tapes. For that reason we could not include some long-term treatment cases. We also excluded the whole body of my work with poor and welfare families. I felt that the characteristics of this work would require a description of institutions and larger systems than could be encompassed in the format of this book. Naturally we changed the names and identifying characteristics of the families, but otherwise the stories you read are told exactly the way they happened.

I want to thank my wife, Pat, who has been an integral part of my life for more than forty years and now shares more than half of my memories. She read and reacted to the stories, but her participation in the autobiographical chapters was even more essential: She brought flavor and accuracy to my description of the events we lived together. I thank her for the past and for the present.

As with all my previous books, I want to thank Fran Hitchcock, who has become indispensable in my writing. She is my grammarian, editor, sounding board, critic, and friend. Mike and I would also like to thank Joyce Seltzer of The Free Press for expert guidance and encouragement.

PART ONE

THE MAKING OF A FAMILY THERAPIST

1

Family Roots

I am in a state psychiatric hospital to do a consultation with Tony, age ten, and his family. Before I see the family, the staff tells me about Tony. I listen attentively. When he was eight his mother took him to a prestigious university hospital, where he remained for ten months. His diagnosis was attention deficit disorder, a variation on the previous label, minimal brain dysfunction, that replaced his first diagnosis, hyperactivity—all of them meaning pretty much that the child has poor impulse control and a short attention span. In the university psychiatric ward, doctors tried to find the appropriate dose of medication that would make him fit to return home. After trying a variety of doses and medications, they decided

to refer him to a state psychiatric hospital. Tony has been here
for a year, so he has spent 20 percent of his short life in
psychiatric wards.

At the state hospital Tony has individual, group, recre-
ational, and sundry other therapies. He attends a highly structured school and lives in a cottage with other children in a
token-economy milieu, meaning that they earn stars for good
behavior that can be exchanged for special treats later on.
Focusing not on Tony but on his neurological system, the
psychiatrist rattles off a long series of pharmacological trials.
He says that at the university hospital, Tony was given Ri-
talin and Mellaril, with the focus on aggression and the attention problems, while here the issues of separation anxiety
are the focus of the medication efforts. To that effect, he says,
Tony was tried on and then off Clonidine, showing clear differences on and off medication. Toward the end of December
he was begun on copharmacy of Lithium with the antidepres-
sant: "We are a long way, I would say, from expecting self-
control in a home situation that can still destabilize, which
destabilizes Tony when it does."

The precision with which the ten people talking with me
cover up the narrowness of their point of view impresses me.
When I ask about Tony's future, the answer is a vague hope
that he will spend less than another year in the hospital, and
then something like a lifetime in what the psychiatrist calls
parallel institutions. I assume that these are day hospitals or
less restrictive settings. And Tony is only ten years old!

I talk to Tony. I expected a monster. Instead I find a boy
who is impulsive but alert, making contact with me without
difficulty. I wonder if anybody connects the experts' statements
to life, or even to cost. Tony's hospitalization costs the state
more than one hundred thousand dollars a year. For two years
this child has been separated from real life and institutionalized in a hothouse where his pathology has been observed
while it expanded in the absence of significant, age-appro-
priate activities. The staff is wedded to an ideology that says
Tony lives only inside himself: not even that—inside his nervous system. Couldn't we do better?

Later I meet with Tony and his mother. I ask her why
Tony is here. "I can't control him," she explains.

"Well, then, why aren't *you* here?"

Tony and Mother laugh. Though it is a strange question, I don't think it's funny. Mother looks at me, puzzled. "Tony will remain here as long as you and he don't fit," I say.

"That's a very different way of looking at things," Mother replies, and she is right. My view of Tony is that he exists not only inside himself but also in the interaction between him and his family.

During the session Tony throws a tantrum. I point out that he is not acting his age and ask his mother to help him be ten. She sets limits; he calms down; and I congratulate them both for their competence. Later I talk to the staff again. I am indignant because this child, who faces life imprisonment, could be living at home, treated in an outpatient facility. His family would need support and help in managing him, but outpatient treatment would be more efficient, less painful, and less costly.

Tony's life and future are organized by a very narrow view of people. This book is about a new way of looking. It is partly about me, partly about my theories and therapy, and always about the dynamics of families. It is a book of stories, because therapists are always storytellers. We are like anthropologists, exploring other people's lives. And like anthropologists, we are inevitably guided by our own experiences in describing others. The observer, however impartial, necessarily selects what seems important, shaping what is observed in ways that make sense.

I want to begin with my own family story. You need to know who I am, since I am the observer of the family dramas that follow. If I describe who I am, the family I grew up with, my family today, and how the world has changed during my lifetime, I will be telling you something about the transformations within all families, about the ways in which we all resemble each other.

Later I will be telling stories about families who have come to see me in therapy. I am concerned that these stories—with their family stresses, their difficulties, and their deviances—may titillate. But these people should not be seen as psychiatric specimens. They are people, like us.

First my family will appear very similar to yours. Then it

will become clear how little it differs from the families described in this book. Professionals tend to draw the line that separates therapist and client with heavy strokes. We center on difficulties and problems, but that is a highly artificial distinction.

Let me take you to my hometown, the setting of my early life. It was a shtetl, a small, tightly interwoven Jewish enclave, turning inward for protection and continuity within a majority society that was very different. My village was in rural Argentina, but it was nonetheless a shtetl.

Main Street Number 11 was one of seven streets in San Salvador, a small town in the province of Entre Ríos, Argentina. The "11" reflected the optimism of our town planners, who had hoped for a brighter future.

Our home—three large bedrooms, two dining rooms (one for guests), a newly installed bath, an outhouse, a detached kitchen, a maid's room, and a chicken coop—was connected to my father's company store: "Everything for the farmer, from tractors to espadrilles." The store had a large zinc-lined warehouse in which grain was stored until it was sold to Bunge y Born or Dreyfuss—large corporations that sold Argentinean grain throughout the world.

Four thousand people, one-fourth of them Jewish, lived within six blocks. I knew everybody in those six blocks, and they knew me. We were an important family in town. The neighbor to the left was my cousin Paulina, *La Gorda* (the Fat One). Between her house and the corner was my Uncle Elias's pharmacy. My father worked there as a bottle washer when he was eleven years old. To the right were my Aunt Ester and Uncle Isaac, with their hardware store. My father's parents, Jose and Jaiatable, lived next to them; by then they were supported by their children. Across the street was my Uncle Bernardo, my mother's brother, who was married to my Aunt Jailie, my father's sister, and their seven children. They owned a clothing store. My Uncle Isaac's mother and his older brother also lived in the same block. While we didn't live in an actual compound, membership in this extended family was in the air we breathed.

Let me open one of the doors in Main Street Number 11

and tell you its story. It is a hardware store. He is thin, she tends to fat; he is neat, she is flabby and unkempt. They yell at each other, but it is her voice that carries. Everybody in town knows she shacks up with the salesmen who come from out of town. I wonder what the attraction is, but I never wonder whether the rumor is true.

Another door: The pharmacist is an older, unmarried man. He lets his hair grow long like a Romantic poet, though his speech is as abrupt as the language of medical prescriptions. He carries on a love affair with the beautiful, married schoolteacher, who is some ten years his senior. Theirs became a Greek drama—by Sophocles or Aristophanes, depending on your perspective—when, fifteen years later, the pharmacist, still thin, married the schoolteacher's beautiful daughter, twenty years his junior. Whom would she select to avenge her father? It was only a matter of time.

Another door: Maria, the wife of Perez. She underwent a false pregnancy. We all waited for months while she grew bigger and bigger, waiting for the child who never came.

There were many stories. One man killed himself. One family had a retarded child, who was always hidden inside to conceal the family shame. Everybody knew these stories. But for us children, it was the sexual stories that were heard and amplified, and they have remained most vividly in my memory.

When in memory I enter the barbershop, the two butchers, the bakery, the movie, the pharmacies, and the grocery, I realize that all the stores are Jewish. Other than the two banks, I have no images of non-Jewish businesses. Perhaps only Tenerani, the publisher of the weekly newspaper. I had a big fight with his younger son. We fought until we could end with honor—when blood gushed from somebody's nose. I suppose whose was important then; it's not now.

I lived, my family lived, in a Russian shtetl transported, modified, and improved by the Argentine culture. We Jews stuck together, shopping in each other's stores. We coexisted in this checkered Argentinean town, but each community was self-sufficient. We even had our own drunkards. Goodson, who was Jewish, would shove his pushcart full of fish through the town once a week. He got drunk on grappa and insulted his customers, canceling sales by blustering: "If you want a fish, wet your ass." We children thought this was screamingly funny. Spindola, the gentile drunkard, was a housepainter. When he got drunk on cheap wine he would yell at the top of his lungs: *"I am Salvador Spindola!"* It was a challenge to the world, with a cadence resembling that of dogs barking at the moon, when he lay on the sidewalk with his finger lifted to the skies.

I grew up Jewish in a town in which graffiti read: "Be patriotic; kill a Jew." But I got drunk on the Argentinean music, learned the local ghost stories, fought if another child stepped on a line I drew in the earth or if somebody wet my ear, just like other rural Argentinean children. In issues of defiance we had no alternatives. I fought and was beaten "with honor" by children older and stronger than me. I grew up Argentinean, but without knowing it. My sense of pride and honor, the need to keep my good name even if it meant challenging windmills, had little to do with Russian Jewry—it was authentically Hispanic. Part of a despised minority, I learned to despise my Jewishness, to try to pass, and to hate myself for it. I grew up divided, internalizing the prejudices of the Argentinean majority and fighting the unfairness of prejudices both inside and outside myself.

Who was I at three? At five? At eight? I have snatches of memories, disconnected phrases that I thread into a plot I make continuous. The demands of storytelling always construct a childhood that wasn't. But, for want of any other perspective . . .

I am the oldest of three. My sister, Sara Dina, whom everyone called Chola, is two years younger than I; and my brother, Rogelio, known as Kelo or Kelito, is eight years younger. My aunt Ester, father's younger sister, had children the same age. They lived in the next house. We climbed the fence instead of walking the twenty yards to the front door. My father was important. He worked hard and was successful. My mother elaborately created space for him: "Be quiet, Father is sleeping . . . Father is eating . . . Father is working . . . Father is tired. . . ." Mother was the overseer who made my father's life an organized and predictable little world.

My father was a loving parent; he cuddled and kissed us a lot. But he was also involved in the store, always trying to solve important issues in a large enterprise that bought grain from the farmers and sold them plows, tractors, and clothing and often advanced credit until the next harvest. He had a reputation for being just. Employees and clients alike knew they could rely on Mauricio. Business agreements were sealed with a handshake. They were written in a ledger for accuracy's sake, but the real contract was in the handshake. I was in awe of my father. I wanted to be just like him—fair, honest, and just.

Mother worked too. We had a full-time maid who cooked, a woman who came twice or three times a week to do the laundry, and a hired girl who helped with the children, among other things. They all helped in the house, but Mother was always dusting, cleaning, knitting, mending, and organizing what had to be done. She was always protecting something: father, the dining room, the furniture, the children. Someone had to stand against illness, dirt, and disorder.

This view of my father as loving, fair, and often distant, and my mother as protecting, controlling, and always involved with us, was constructed, reinforced, and confirmed in millions of transactions throughout my childhood and adolescence. Of course there were also many other exchanges that might have challenged this view. But families are conservative organisms. They develop certain pathways that at first are only preferred. Over time they become comfortable, until finally they become so familiar that variations will make family members uncomfortable. In time pathways become ruts, which can be very difficult to get out of.

Discipline was strictly enforced in our house. Father was the disciplinarian. Mother might get angry if I broke a rule. She might spank me, twist my ear, or slap me. But I was never afraid of her. With her I could get angry back, run away, argue, or repeat my offense just to spite her. Father was something else. When he got upset an involuntary tic on his left cheek would begin to flash a warning. But his spankings were methodical, reasoned, and rather calm. I knew he would spank me if I did something wrong, particularly if I lied. He would simply beckon to me, and I never disobeyed his command. He would explain exactly why I was to be punished, take off his belt, tell me to lie across his knees, and whip me. If I thought he was in the wrong I absolutely would not cry, in spite of the pain. I would move away from him, tight-lipped, in silent protest. I was a stubborn child, and clearly my father was a stubborn man—though I couldn't see that then. Once, in third grade, when I was nine, I brought home poor grades. I had had a nine in history; this time I got a seven. Afraid of what Father would say, I wrote over the seven to make it a nine. My forgery was crude, and Father immediately asked if I had done it. I said no. Father said yes, I said no. The next act in the drama was all too predictable. After every whack he asked if I had done it. "No." Another whack—"No." Another whack—"No." Father was afraid he was hurting me; he begged to me to say yes. "No."

Mother tried to intervene. "Say you did it," she implored. "No."

"Mauricio, please, you are hurting him!" By now my Aunt Ester, my mother, and my seven-year-old sister were all pleading with Father, and he was pleading with me. I didn't give in. By then I couldn't; I was too busy *not* giving in, defending myself against parental authority. By now both my father and I were trapped. His duty as a father demanded that he punish my wrongdoing. For me it had become a question of pride; I would not submit.

Sixty years later I have only to close my eyes to see this scene. I can hear my mother crying, pleading. I don't remember the pain, but I can still feel a nine-year-old's rebellion and challenge.

In today's world that whipping would have constituted child abuse. The belt left me black and blue. But I never experienced my father as abusive, and neither did anyone else. His whipping was just. He was doing what he knew was right, and everybody else knew it too.

To me, well into adulthood, my father was always larger than life. But in that place and time, a father's authority was simply one of the givens.

One of my earliest memories is of being on his shoulder, watching a parade of Jewish flags. I was three, and it was the fifth anniversary of the Balfour Declaration, establishing a homeland for Jews in Palestine.

I was five when he bought me my first horse. We kept the pony, Petiso (Shorty), on the farm, but if Chas the farmhand let him loose, he would come to the house to find me. With

Petiso I joined the Argentinean rural culture. Like the other children I was almost a centaur, and I joined them in many escapades and on Sunday outings.

I liked to go with my father when he supervised the warehousing of grain at the railroad station. He discussed business with me and asked my opinions as if they really interested him. He was sometimes asked to arbitrate conflicts among other Jews, who were reluctant to bring their problems to the gentiles' justice, and I was proud of him. I was proud of his negotiating with the president of the bank—to me the most powerful non-Jewish authority after Mr. Lopez, the chief of police. I still see all these memories from the height of about three feet, looking up.

My parents ruled different worlds. My father went to the store in the morning. My mother organized the house. We children walked to school and returned at noon. Lunch was a family event. It was the main meal and the family council. Father sat at the head of the table, Mother to his side. It was time together. We talked, discussed school, or listened to my parents talk about adult issues.

Then in 1930, when I was nine, the Great Depression took away my father's power. Suddenly we were very poor. There were no more maids, no more store; food was scarce. My mother prepared polenta and told us to eat it with bread. Now the memory of my father attains mythic stature. With a friend, one of my uncle's brothers, he became a gaucho, driving horses from Entre Ríos to Corrientes, hundreds of miles away. There, with a loan from one of my uncles, they bought cows to be herded home and sold in the province. For a year in fact and fantasy I saw him sleeping under the open skies, his saddle for a pillow, fishing in small rivers, herding cows in a never-ending scene in which my father, Tom Mix, and Gene Autry alternated in the saddle.

Meanwhile I was becoming an adult. I helped my mother sell potatoes and kosher salami. Every morning we cleaned and burnished the potatoes. I suppose it was to prevent spoilage, but I also knew that my mother's aesthetics simply prevented her from selling dirty potatoes. Today I wonder how it was that my father became a hero to me but my mother did not become Mother Courage in my eyes. Only after many years did I recognize her strength.

As we grew older, things changed. When my uncle Pablo came to town from Concordia, a nearby city, he would sit at the head of the table. He was the principal partner of the company, and my father's superior. When he came, we all felt the change. I could not understand my father's subservience to him or why my father insisted that he also act the head of the household, and I disliked Uncle Pablo intensely. My mother resented his autocratic ways, too, and this became one of our secret coalitions.

After my grandmother died my grandfather came to dinner every Friday, the beginning of the Sabbath, and he sat at the head of the table. My mother lit the candles, blessing the Sabbath. My grandfather's absolute authority was never, ever questioned. He looked patriarchal, with his large frame, his white beard, and his skullcap. He used a cane that—since he walked straight and firmly—was mostly an aesthetic artifact. He died at eighty-six with a full set of teeth.

One Sabbath, on a hot summer evening, my mother served him a glass of tepid beer. Grandfather stood and spat the beer at my mother, the table, the world. I remember it as a gesture of regal indignation: "You don't do that to *me!*" My mother froze; my father's tic pounded; time stood still. But did Grandfather leave the house? Did my mother apologize, wipe the table, and bring another beer? The images have vanished. I only know that it would have been impossible in our family for my father to challenge his father, even in defense of his wife.

I remember my parents as a very close couple. When they had conflicts my mother would withdraw, unhappy and silent, nursing her grudge. My explosive father would apologize, persevere, expressing affection until my mother gave in. I remember listening at night as they read each other romantic novels, like José Mármol's *Amalia*. Then I would hear muffled giggles that I refrained from interpreting. Their strength as a couple lay in their need for each other and their clarity about their own turfs. Embedded in a huge extended family within a rigidly hierarchical society, they supported each other by carrying out roles and functions that were clearly defined. They were comfortable in traditional roles, with my father the vital breadwinner—demanding the respect of wife and children—and my mother the vital caretaker. I think Mother saw her tasks in life as first to support him and then to protect her children, and I don't think she ever questioned these priorities. She saw herself as dependent on my father, and to her that was as it should be.

A helpful person, committed to doing things for others, often sacrificing herself for others, dependent on their dependency, my mother was frequently sad. But it would never have occurred to any of us that her sadness had anything to do with her family life. The death of her nephew Abraham, who was a noncommissioned officer in the Argentine army (unheard of for a Jew), kept her crying for more than a year. We simply ascribed this to a naturally sensitive nature. Today I can see my mother as the youngest daughter of a very close family, very beautiful, very close to her mother, very protected by her six siblings. When she married my father she moved to a town more than a hundred miles away—a four-day journey on horseback. She was very nearly absorbed by my father's family, in which she held a position subservient to my father's blood relatives. But at the time, all of us, including my mother, would have felt very uncomfortable with the idea that a proper wife might not find complete happiness in wife- and motherhood. To us, my mother was simply "sensitive."

The harmony of my parents' marriage was based on their neatly fitting complementarity. Each developed an expertise that supported the other. Both served the needs of the couple. This extremely functional way of being can also be limiting, however, and in fact, when my father died, at the age of seventy-five, my mother was inconsolable. She had dedicated her life to making his life easier. Now she was alone, nobody needed her, and she had no other way of being. For two years she remained depressed, wedded to the memory of their life together. She needed the skills that had been assigned to my father, but they had atrophied in her. Yet as she moved slowly out into a life alone, she surprised everybody—including, I am sure, herself—with the strength and variety of her resources. During the last fifteen years of her life, as a widow, she evolved into an extraordinarily vital and complex person. She rediscovered her competence in the tasks my father had carried out and found she could do them in ways he had never thought of.

When a couple functions harmoniously there is no need for

competition; the sense of self is compatible with the sense of being a couple. This can be both efficient and rewarding, but it can also make development of a new sense of self—necessitated by widowhood—that much more difficult.

Puerto Rican healers say that every child is born with an invisible aura that defines his or her future. I was the oldest son (in Hebrew, the *b'chor*). As in other cultures, I would inherit the mantle. I grew up responsible. I remember my father quite deliberately creating situations that gave me a sense of autonomy and responsibility. When I was eleven and my father was selling a used car, a 1928 Chevrolet, to a farmer, he told me that, as a selling point, I was to teach the farmer how to drive the car. When I was in high school he opened a store that sold car parts, and I worked with him. He told me that the money in the cashbox was ours, and I could take whatever I needed. Of course I never did.

My mother gave me the full treatment as the firstborn. She made sure that the white tunic I wore to school was starched, that I ate enough, and that I was well groomed. She cut my meat for me. If I learned from my father to be thoughtful and responsible, I learned from my mother that people always need help. They were preparing me for an adulthood as a doctor who would need at least two secretaries or as an absent-minded Talmudic scholar married to a *balabosta* (a competent, order-loving person). I made some modifications and innovations of my own, but—as they say—the acorn didn't fall very far from the oak.

Psychological pigeonholes work like a cast on a broken bone. The wet plaster is flexible and malleable, adjusting itself to the body. But then, as it hardens, it becomes an external skeleton, governing the bone's growth. In my family the construction of our respective identities worked with memorable simplicity. Most of the things I did were considered "responsible." If I did something irresponsible, I would just be labeled "clumsy," "forgetful," or "dreamy"—but never irresponsible. So, slowly, I grew up to be a responsible man. It's not that pigeonholes are bad, it's just that they restrict freedom of movement—like trying to play tennis without bending your elbows.

My sister had a vivid imagination. Chola's observations were extraordinarily perspicacious, as was her ability to make use of them. But she was a girl, and a second child, so her talents were labeled "cute" or "beautiful." She used to wander to neighbors' houses to tell stories. Once, having told a neighbor she'd been given no dinner, she got an extra dessert. The neighbor knew the story was a child's fantasy, but my sister told it so well. Of course the neighbor couldn't resist telling my mother, who was horrified, but nonetheless it became a family joke. This is one of the advantages—and tragedies—of psychosocial identities. Once you are defined, those definitions color and label all your actions. Chola was "cute," thus anything she did was so defined. The fact that she was also very smart and imaginative went unrecognized; it would have disturbed the harmony of her aura.

In my brother Rogelio's life, responsible actions became invisible or surprising. The expectation was that he always "almost tried," but preferred easy living. He was so much younger that he and I didn't share childhood. He was only three when I left home (at eleven, because school in my hometown ended at fifth grade). It is from our later experiences that I know the pigeonhole my family constructed for him.

He was born in 1929, a time of great upheaval for my family. The Depression had left my parents confused, penniless, and powerless. It was not a time for indulging in dreams of the future. The concern was for daily survival. I think Rogelio grew up with fewer expectations, but as the youngest child he was nurtured more and controlled less: Whatever he did was more or less okay. I was Father's son; Chola was Mother's companion; I think Rogelio felt like the runt of the litter.

Of course this description of character formation is incomplete. Many other aspects of our lives as children were observed, supported, and rewarded, and they are part of the resources we carry with us. Clearly, like calculators, we carry most of our potential under the surface, but it is available.

All three of us married, had children, and became successful professionals. My sister is a medical anthropologist living in Israel, and my brother is a professor of political science there. I think this says something about our undereducated parents' determination about our future. But it is also true that family labels become our calling cards, and we use them like Japanese corporation men exchanging cards and determining from them the proper depth of their respectful bows. Our labels become the way we preferred to present ourselves. The label became us.

Psychoanalytic mythology has reinforced this view in the last half century, and it has sent millions of people on complicated treks through the past in search of their true being. But the "I am" grows even if the calling card does not. As I married—became a father, a therapist, a teacher, a writer, an elder—I entered into new relationships, which required different and complex responses. Sometimes I kept separate parts of myself for different contexts, like an impersonator selecting the identity for a particular con game. But slowly, in twists and turns, I became a three-dimensional being.

I never developed much manual dexterity. I was a klutz, and I accepted that. But when my wife, Pat, and I came back from Israel, when our son Danny was one year old, we lived on the Upper West Side of Manhattan in a very modest neighborhood. We were poor, living mostly on Pat's salary as a psychologist at the Bank Street College of Education. We bought three chairs for our living room with wrought-iron legs and skimpy upholstery. I decided, with Pat's support, to build a couch. I got a door from a lumberyard, put on four legs, and added a piece of wood to each end. A mattress, varnish, polish—and suddenly I no longer had the ten thumbs my mother had always teased me about.

Human beings are snails. We carry our shells of memory with us, and we are them. I grew up knowing that we are all responsible for each other. Loyalty to the family, the clan, to others, was part of my daily experience, and at the same time I simply expected to be protected by others, because I belonged, and they owed me the way I owed them. This gave me a sense of a predictable and reasonably safe world, so that even though our lives were profoundly shaken by the Depression, I knew that the future was mine. There was a place for me; all it needed was hard work.

That sense of hierarchy and interdependence was fundamental to my growing up. I think that even my cognitive style—paying scant attention to details, working well with connections, comfortable with discontinuous leaps that can be creative but are sometimes disastrous—grows out of an assumed intersection with someone who takes care of the details. In my world, cognitive styles were gender related. The caretakers were women. Of course I expanded, edited, and corrected this world of my childhood. I have incorporated many new truths and relabeled the naive truths of the past. But roots still grow from my toes into the world I walked as a child, and certain ideas from my shtetl form part of my style of therapy.

I carry from these beginnings a sense of responsibility and leadership, of human interdependence, of strong identification with just causes—from the Zionism of my early youth to political prisoners, minorities, and the poor. And from these same beginnings springs some knowledge about the workings of families, extended and nuclear, about family subsystems and boundaries, and about ways of helping that lead people who think of themselves in individual terms to discover that, as members of their families and other significant social groups, they have more possibilities than they know.

2

From Individual to Family Therapist
A Journey of Transformation

A journey of transformation has no real beginning, but I have the usual human weakness for logical coherence, so I have given my story a beginning in the traditional fashion, starting with childhood. Of course, memories of childhood are colored by the perspective of later years. As we grow, and grow older, our images acquire different hues and multiple meanings. Like the Sistine Chapel, with its layers on layers of paint and glue, the result is mysterious in its shadings and emotional resonance.

Mental health professionals, fascinated with the individual and the past, have greatly overemphasized the power of childhood, as though learning and experiencing were limited to early life. This seems to fit an apparently self-evident truth: that the self is inside the individual. The realization that the self is fluid and includes interaction with other people is acquired rather than self-evident knowledge.

Like most people, I suppose, I started with the idea that I was inside me. My cousins Paulina and Juana, who were my constant teachers, told me that there is a part of the brain called the cerebellum, in which there is a bird that creates songs and music and poetry. This concept was fascinating to a six-year-old, and I still retain the sense that, somewhere inside me, I have the capacity to create songs. At some level I am sure that that bird is the source of the poetry I wrote as an adolescent, and for the metaphor, the imagery, and perhaps the humor that I use in therapy today. But I have also learned that if "I am the singer, you are the song." Each person I encounter elicits different aspects of me.

Learning to move beyond the natural focus of the self-contained individual, to a more complex view of the individual rooted in contexts, was a journey of some years. I decided quite early that I would help juvenile delinquents. This was due to my high school psychology teacher—a bright, enthusiastic, engaging man who sometimes talked about people, although his subject was nineteenth-century studies of memory and perception. He taught us about Rousseau's ideas of the nobility of uncorrupted innocence and taught us to see juvenile delinquents as victims of society. Something in me responded to the idea of defending society's victims, possibly the victim in me. Then and there I decided that I would become a lawyer so I could be a psychologist. Today this would seem a circuitous route, but at that time in Argentina psychology was part of "philosophy and letters," and was considered a career for women.

When I entered the university at eighteen, I forgot about law and psychology. My grandfather was an immigrant farmer, my uneducated father a successful businessman. What else would the oldest son study? My mother gave me a shield to bear into medical school—a new notebook on whose front page she wrote: "A place for everything, and everything in its place." It seemed a poor substitute for her concerned care and loving control, but I packed it and caught the train for the two-day journey to Córdoba.

My first three years in medical school were predictable and uneventful. But in 1944 Juan Perón, the Argentinean dictator, took control of the country's universities. Students rebelled. We took and held buildings of the university, and we marched against mounted policemen. We armed ourselves with powerful slogans. We were young and courageous, noble and naive. Firemen tried to break up our demonstrations with powerful waterhoses. Exhausted and drenched, we unfurled a huge banner: BARBARIANS! YOU CAN'T DROWN IDEAS!

I learned to take a gun apart and reassemble it blindfolded—considered a necessary skill for a revolutionary in those days—even though I never learned how to shoot it. I carried my gun with pride and fear, filled with a sense of heroic sacrifice in the service of ideals, a sense that we belonged to each other and to the future.

With the turn of events I was jailed and put in solitary confinement. The tiny cell had no windows and no light. The hours dragged. But I had read once about a Brazilian political prisoner, in solitary for years, who spent his lonely days writing and organizing a newspaper. He wrote in his head about news that never happened, composing daily editorials about the various problems of the country. His anger at the corrupt government gave him the tools for psychological survival. So I spent my time building my own defenses. I spent a lot of time remembering my elementary school. Details brought other details. I would select a starting point, like my first-grade teacher, Miss Sere, with her shapeless black dress and her hair in a bun. I could see her at the blackboard, drawing blue and white ducks in a pond to illustrate simple arithmetic problems. I would muse, move on, find a detour or a side road, and return to an enlarged or modified point. I didn't know what was genuine memory and what was fiction, but it protected me from fear. From time to time, always in the middle of the night, I was called by the Special Section (the political police). They would ask me whether I had a sister named Sara or a cousin named Samuel (both were true), then return me to my cell. I was never threatened. They never asked me questions that might endanger my friends—they already knew more about the leaders of the student movement than I did. It was just a sadistic game.

After a week, without explanation, I was moved to a different jail with political prisoners of much greater importance. We were kept at the disposal of the "President of the Nation" (which made due process nonexistent). Although it was certainly a period of anxiety and uncertainty, what I remember best are moments of bold and raucous humor. We used to say that we were the only safe people in Argentina—nobody could put *us* in jail! I learned to play chess and devoted a lot of strategic thought to finding the best spot in the food line. Making sure that the level of the thin soup was low enough to contain a few vegetables when they ladled out your share was well worthwhile. I learned about friendship and loyalty, and how a shared sense of powerlessness and hate could cement disparate lives.

I remained in jail for three months. During Christmas 1944, just as capriciously as we had been imprisoned, all the political prisoners of Córdoba were freed. I had originally become an activist as a member of the Jewish student movement, but my time in jail had expanded my identity. I was now political. The sense of loyalty and belonging that had been the hallmark of my clan, and had expanded to include the Jews of my village and of the world, now included new vistas. As a political prisoner I had become a symbol for many of my friends. So, timidly at first, feeling like a fake, I began to live up to the persona of the challenger. I began to see and study the unfairness of the establishment and the rigidity with which institutions protect themselves. If I draw a straight line denoting my journey from my twenty-first year to my seventieth birthday, the line will be heavily marked by challenges to the injustices and lies of established truths. It is this orientation that sustains the healthy skepticism about all assumptions and seeming certainties that, in my practice, becomes a source of hope.

When I finished medical school in 1946, I took a residency in pediatrics with a subspecialty in medical psychology. Unfortunately, training in psychology was fragmented and poorly supervised. I read books on child development, and I interviewed children who came to the clinic. Training as a pediatrician was supposed to prepare me, magically, for talking with children, but of course it didn't.

As I was opening a pediatric practice in 1948, Israel became a state, and a nation at war. My plans changed abruptly. I suppose I must have had doubts, but I don't remember them. In retrospect it seems to me that I simply sold my brand new medical equipment, took a month's training in emergency procedures and transfusions at the Jewish hospital in Buenos Aires, and set sail with a group of about thirty other young Argentinean men and women. The journey itself was a lesson in perspective. When the boat stopped in Bahia, Brazil, the Jewish community was waiting for us, and suddenly we were heroes. When we stopped in Genoa, we were transported to a camp with Holocaust survivors, and suddenly we were refugees. In Israel we went to Negba, a besieged kibbutz near the Egyptian border, and now I was a member of a collective. Eventually I was assigned as a doctor to the Fourth Regiment in the Palmach, an elite unit of the army whose officers wore no insignia of their rank. They received the same salary as the men: three pounds a month, if memory serves. I didn't speak Hebrew, but my nurse, Yitzhak, spoke Hebrew and a German Yiddish that bore some relationship to my Spanish Yiddish. Together we managed to understand a population of seventeen- and eighteen-year-old soldiers who spoke Romanian, Bulgarian, Hungarian, Czech, Spanish (thank goodness), Ladino, and of course the Hebrew of the Sabras. In a very short time I had moved from the routine certainty of a small medical practice in Buenos Aires to the life-and-death responsibility for young soldiers in a war. I was overwhelmed, frightened, and terribly aware of the limitations of my medical knowledge.

This period of my life, like my childhood, has many layers. Small details have special resonance, like a moment in the Negev at dawn, alone, waiting for the wounded, four miles from the front. I tried to find the ends of the roots of a wild bush and dug deeper than four feet, only to find them attached to the universe.

It is hard now to remember that in those days, Israel was the David fighting the Goliath of the Arab conglomerate. The nation's survival was in our hands. We were the future, and the future belonged to us—to all of us. We were making something important happen, and we were together. People from all over the world, with different languages, cultures, dress, and memories were my brothers and sisters. Suddenly the Jewishness that in Argentina had been a mainstay of my identity disappeared. The sense of belonging without ambivalence made me not more Jewish but more human. I didn't have to defend myself. I could join others. This became the other main strand of my theories and of my professional practice. Interwoven with my challenge to ossified patterns was my acceptance of the inevitability of our commitment to others, of the need to search for the tenderness of belonging.

When the war ended I left the Israeli army, and in 1950 I came to America to study psychiatry, planning to return to Israel as a child psychiatrist. I had been accepted to study with Bruno Bettelheim, but when I arrived in New York the distance to Chicago overwhelmed me. So, like many an immigrant, I remained where I landed.

I trained simultaneously in two settings that could not have been more different. As a part-time psychiatric resident at Bellevue Hospital, working with psychotic children under the direction of Lauretta Bender, I learned to look at highly disturbed children's behavior, and to assign labels. Faced with chaos and pain, we fall back on the human impulse to label as a way of distancing ourselves while giving ourselves the illusion that we are doing something. But there was little understanding of the development of psychoses, and no attempt at psychotherapy. Our contacts with the children were not seen as part of a therapeutic problem solving. Our job was to diagnose.

My other placement was as a fellow in child psychiatry at the Jewish Board of Guardians. I lived and worked at its residential center, Hawthorne Cedar Knolls. I lived with twenty disturbed children in a cottage, where we created a therapeutic milieu and intervened actively in the children's lives. There were individual therapy sessions, guided by psychodynamic concepts. Other interventions were less traditional. I remember bringing the case of a promiscuous seventeen-year-old girl, who was intent on seducing me, to my supervisor, Dr. R. Sobel. I was confused and embarrassed by my response to her and asked him what I should do.

"Tell her that you are a pushover," he advised me. "Tell

her that she doesn't have to work so hard, because you are interested in her, but that it would not be helpful to her if you let yourself go." This freed me from my sense that I had to remain unresponsive to her charms, but it was certainly different from the ideal noninvolvement of the therapist behind the couch.

My training was psychoanalytic. We read Freud, and I was entranced by his writings. But I had trouble connecting the learning in the main office to my work in the cottage. The idea that there was somehow a budget of psychic energy seemed to relate more to hydraulics than to children.

The experience of having to deal with theory in the classroom and reality in the cottage challenged established truths for me. Bouncing different ideas against each other confused me, but having divergent ways of thinking created a dynamic tension that forced me to reassess my training.

I married in 1951, and my wife and I emigrated to Israel. I became codirector of five residential institutions for disturbed children for Youth Aliyah, an organization that brought surviving children without families from Europe and later expanded to children from other parts of the world. I tried to apply my American training to the Israeli context and found myself floundering in ignorance. My codirector, Shulamit Klebanoff, was an educator with a broad grasp of group dynamics and a lot of experience in developing educational settings for adolescents. My puny understanding of individual children was continually confronted by her vast knowledge of child life in different cultures.

We were working with European orphans of the Holocaust, but also with children from India, Yemen, Iran, and Morocco. The residential institutions were all directed by people embedded in the culture of Israel's agricultural units—kibbutzim and moshavim (cooperative farms)—and they felt comfortable handling groups.

It was there that I really began to look at the significance of culture and context in the lives of people. I had always seen Jewishness as a unity—forming a protective group against a hostile outside. But now I began to see internecine struggles between different ethnic groups. Ashkenazim engaged in racial struggles against Sephardim; Yemenites fought Bulgarians; Moroccans fought everybody. This was more than diversity—it was bigotry.

I began to attain a better understanding of people within diverse contexts. When a fourteen-year-old Moroccan girl shrieked, *"Mustafa!"* at a butterfly in my office and then explained that it was the soul of her father, who had not closed his mouth at the moment of death, I knew this was not a psychotic response but a cultural one. When I saw children who had spent the war being moved from hiding place to hiding place, I realized that their need for rigidly structured groups was not a matter of individual pathology but rather the need of fragmented and depleted victims for an external skeleton, a kind of psychological plaster cast. I was beginning to understand more about human adaptability and about the power of groups to provide support and the potential for growth. But I also felt increasingly ignorant. In those days ignorance could be cured by psychoanalytic training. So I returned with my wife to the United States, in search of wisdom.

Between 1954 and 1958 I was in training at the William Alanson White Institute of Psychoanalysis in New York City. I selected this program because I was attracted by the ideas of Harry Stack Sullivan, the creator of interpersonal psychoanalysis. He saw the psychoanalyst as a participant observer, and his ideas of human development and pathology included an understanding of the individual set in his circumstances. I was attracted too, then, by the writings and teachings of Erich Fromm, who also saw man rooted in culture, and by the other cultural psychoanalysts, like Karen Horney, Abraham Kardiner, and Erik Erikson. I was taught to sit behind my reclining patient, attentive to verbal and paraverbal utterances, listening and watching for meaning, restraining my impulse to respond. Because I am by nature an active participant in dialogues, maintaining such silence was a burden for me, but I followed the prescribed procedures, producing occasional noises to confirm my presence to the analysand. From time to time I spoke, and my pronouncements achieved profound significance by virtue of the silence that preceded and followed them.

While I was still in training at the psychoanalytic institute, I began to work with juvenile delinquents at the Wiltwyck School for Boys, returning in fact to my adolescent dream of helping troubled young people. This was a very different population from the articulate middle-class adults who usually came to analysis—one that required a very active form of therapy.

As I began practicing family therapy at Wiltwyck, I kept up a private psychoanalytic practice, repeating the schism that had characterized my early training and that is still the reality for many professionals. The two forms of therapy arose from two very different sets of assumptions, and for a time I maintained a strict separation between them. But slowly the power of my experiences in family therapy took over, and it became impossible for me to rely solely on the information that an individual patient produced about parents, spouse, and siblings. I began to want to hear from the others directly.

During the period when I was doing both individual and family therapy, my approach to individual therapy changed. I focused more on the interaction of people with other people, rather than on individual inner dynamics and pathology. I think I began to realize that this was the case when an Italian widow in her late sixties came to me for help with acute paranoia, for which a psychiatrist had recommended hospitalization. She was in a period of profound mourning for her older brother, who had been very significant in her life. During this difficult period, she came home one day to find that the apartment where she had lived for a quarter century had been robbed. She decided to move, called in a moving company, and entered a nightmare. The movers tried to tell her where to move. They purposely misplaced her precious belongings. They chalked cryptograms on her furniture. When she went outside people followed her, making secret signals to each other behind her back. At this point the woman began to realize that she was overreacting, and she went to a psychiatrist. He gave her tranquilizers and referred her to an inpatient unit. She refused hospitalization and, through a friend of a friend, came to see me.

As I heard her story, I commented to her that she had lost her shell: everything that was familiar and that had protected her. Just after losing her brother, she had left her home, the apartment where she had known every corner, each object, and the people in the neighborhood. Now, just like any molting crustacean, she was vulnerable.

I assured her that these problems would disappear when she grew a new shell, and we discussed how to speed that growth. We decided that she was to unpack all her belongings, hang her pictures, shelve her books, and organize her new apartment so that it would become familiar to her. I had been reading about the way the writer Georges Simenon organized his life when he was writing a new book. He made each day resemble the previous day, moment by moment. With his external life totally routine and predictable, it could become invisible. That was what this woman was to do. All her movements were to be routinized. She was to get up at a certain time, shop at a certain time, and go to the same stores and the same checkout counters. She was not to try to make new friends in the new neighborhood for two weeks.

She was to go back to visit her old friends. But in order to avoid their becoming concerned about her, I told her that she was not to describe any of her frightening experiences. If anyone inquired about her problems, she was to explain that they were merely the problems of illogical, fearful old people. As her experiences began to become familiar, her symptoms disappeared rapidly. She continued living in her new apartment, with the independence she desired.

In this situation I saw the woman as a normal person in a crisis of transition, a person whose symptoms were rooted not in an inner pathology but in her life circumstances. By viewing her as a person in a normal period of mourning, for whom the experience of moving had triggered a crisis that resembled a paranoid state, I had been able to help her move back to a position of controlling her world. I protected her by taking over the situation, guiding her while she "grew a new shell."

The same developing sense of working with the person in the context of everyday life guided my experiments in seeing the families of institutionalized juvenile delinquents. Working with displaced children from a wide variety of ethnic backgrounds in Israel had oriented me to both cultural and social issues, so that when I began to work with black and Puerto Rican children and their families in New York City, my sense of their "pathology" was framed by a broader view of the pathology of the social contexts that had disorganized their lives.

The Wiltwyck residents were delinquent adolescents who had been removed from the ghettos of New York, from black and Spanish Harlem, to live at Wiltwyck for one or two years and then be returned to their families. I worked with a lively group of professionals in the aftercare program: Dick Auerswald, Charlie King, Braulio Montalvo, Clara Rabinowitz. But we found that we shared an overriding sense of impotence. We followed up on these adolescents who had been wrested from their context, treated at the institution, and returned to the compelling pressures of Harlem, and we realized that the benefits of our contact with them were questionable.

So we began to see the children and their families together. We had read a paper by Don Jackson* in which he argued persuasively that the individual was an artificial construct "produced" by the simple process of ignoring his or her connections to the members of significant social networks. We began to see families all in the same room at the same time, working both with aftercare families and those with children still in the institution. We built a therapy room with a one-way mirror, so we could watch each other's sessions with families and study the dynamics of these encounters. We declared ourselves family therapists.

I was in psychoanalytic training at the time and had experience in group dynamics and therapy. The other members of the team were also grounded in individual and group psychodynamic therapy, so we considered ourselves prepared to do family interviewing. We were soon jolted into a different reality. The experience of sitting with an individual or groups of adolescents had nothing to do with the impact produced by an encounter with a family.

We had been trained to look for a set of invisible internal dynamics regulating the visible behavior of individuals. We were certain that if we were curious, careful, skillful, and patient, sooner or later the patients would provide us with an Ariadne's thread to lead us through the labyrinths of the mind. With our population of youngsters, we expected to mine the roots of aggression, fear, and anxiety in their early memories so that we could understand their present view of the

* D.D. Jackson, The question of family homeostasis, *The Psychiatric Quarterly Supplement 31* (1957): 79–90.

world. We were deep-sea divers searching for motivation inside people, helping our patients to "own" their behavior and to see how they were the builders of their lives.

Now, in family sessions, we were suddenly unsure about the beginnings of behaviors or feelings since we could see them as responses to behaviors or feelings of other family members, who were in turn responding to behaviors and feelings. We began to see all behavior as action, but also as reaction, a response that was also a point of departure. We also developed new perspectives from which to observe behavior and deduce meaning—for example, an impossible, aggressive, disruptive youngster could be seen as the only protector of an inept, depleted, and abused mother. The memories of the individual family members were now challenged by the experience of all of them, interacting in the present. We were forced not only to listen but to look. There were invisible codes, shared signals, that seemed to mobilize a number of family members, not only one, to respond in patterned fashion. We began to predict such events and to discover an underlying structure directing patterns of family functioning.

But this new understanding was gained slowly, in fitful bursts. In the sessions we didn't have time to reflect. In other modes of therapy the therapist has some control. He or she can respond to the patient or not, selecting the nature of the response and its level of intensity. In our sessions with families we felt anything but in control. We felt like foreigners, visiting a group of people with their own common culture and history, their own ways of communicating, and their own well-established loyalties and rivalries. We needed to learn how to join them, to gain their trust, and demonstrate our usefulness. Above all, we needed to develop new ways of intervening that reflected our new understanding.

Thoroughly trained in a more reflective kind of therapy, we found ourselves pushed and pulled by the families with whom we worked to become active participants in the therapeutic process.

We had no models, and there was no literature to guide us. We had only working hypotheses. But we thought it would be useful to see whether the relationship of family members changed in different contexts. So we developed a three-stage interview, in which the therapists met with the family in different groupings. First we saw the whole family together. Then one therapist would meet with the mother, or both parents, and the second would meet with the children. Then the family and therapists regrouped. Each session was observed by two other members of the team, and we debriefed after each session. This gave us insight into the family interactions and also into the way we ourselves were interacting with the family.

As we struggled to hear, and learn how to help, these families, we began to develop techniques that became part of our repertoire of skills. Working with a population that was not introspective, we focused on behavior and communication. If a family member asked a question, he or she had to wait for an answer. We had to teach that interruptions must be signaled, so that they could be constructive instead of disruptive. In some families we passed an object to the person who wanted to talk, and made the others stay silent until it was their turn. We used space as a concrete metaphor for emotional proximity and distance. We asked people to change chairs, moving them physically apart to indicate greater psychological distance or, to indicate psychological closeness, moving them to sit next to someone they had to talk to. We encouraged continuity of dialogue and respect for the individual point of view, and we pushed for a recognition of individual differences in family members.*

As a result we developed a very active form of therapy. Passionate advocates, we wanted desperately to help. We lent our own indignation to people who had no expectation of personal rights. We were highly critical of the prejudicial way the judicial and welfare systems responded to the families of our children, alienating and disempowering family members, but in the excitement of our new discoveries about the family we didn't explore the possibilities of challenging the larger social systems. We were applauded for our insights and our efforts, and we became visible advocates of the so-called multiproblem family, demonstrating that if the therapist learns to hear and speak a language that is meaningful to these clients, the development of a therapeutic system is as possible with the "unreachable poor" as it is with any other families.

* S. Mınuchın, B. Montalvo, B.G Guerney, B.L. Rosman, and F. Schumer, *Famılıes of the Slums* (New York· Basıc Books, 1967).

In 1965 I moved with my wife and two children to Philadelphia. There I became simultaneously director of the Philadelphia Child Guidance Clinic, director of psychiatry at Children's Hospital of Philadelphia, and professor of child psychiatry at the University of Pennsylvania School of Medicine. Those eighteen years were full of interesting developments. But because I am constructing a coherent story out of a life that was lived in bits and pieces, jumping around in response to circumstances, I will select the segments relevant to my professional journey.

I made myself very unpopular in the Department of Psychiatry at the medical school by insisting that child psychiatry was family psychiatry. Child psychiatry at the time had nothing to do with families. I had been recruited because of my visibility at Wiltwyck, working with the type of poverty-stricken family that had become a major concern to the Philadelphia Child Guidance Clinic. But that type of therapy—"family therapy"?—was, of course, for the poor. My insistence that it also had value for middle-class children stepped on many toes and, to the psychiatric establishment, felt like betrayal of the guild. The Pennsylvania Council of Child Psychiatry initiated an investigation aimed at taking away from the clinic the right to train child psychiatrists, and the investigators of the Department of Psychiatry of the University of Pennsylvania stated: "Dr. Minuchin's ideas are dangerous for the Department."

Today I see that I provoked this response. I insisted on making my total nonacceptance of the usual way of working highly visible, forcing the establishment to challenge me. I suppose I could have been more accommodating, moving one step back for each two steps forward. But by now a lifetime of challenging rigid assumptions had become a personal and professional necessity, and I was unbending in my zeal. In retrospect I think that to have elicited such an attack was something of an accomplishment.

In the meantime our professional horizons for family therapy were expanding. One day I picked up a neighbor, Robert Kaye, and gave him a ride to Children's Hospital of Philadelphia, the affiliated institution of the Child Guidance Clinic. Bob, head of the diabetic study section, told me about four diabetic girls who required hospitalization, again and again, for coma or impending coma. Since their lack of response to excellent medical management was believed to be psychosomatic, they had been referred—with no effect—for individual psychotherapy. Would I see them?

My response was automatic: Yes, I would see them, *with* their families. I assumed that a biological symptom in a child should be seen in the context of family relationships. In fact, we learned later that in the hospital these girls responded normally to insulin. Only at home did they fail to respond as predicted, though the insulin they were taking had been checked and rechecked and found to be of normal potency. The pediatricians were firmly convinced that their difficulties were psychosomatic in origin. But a year of individual psychodynamic therapy, to build up "fragile ego strength," had produced no change.

In the course of therapy with these girls, and others suffering from psychosomatic illnesses, we discovered that their families all had one highly unusual feature: They invariably described themselves as normal, happy families—families without conflict. Their only problem was the severe illness of this one child. We discovered that when we probed for conflict in the family, it was "detoured" through the psychosomatic child. In inaccurately simple terms, psychological conflicts elicited physical symptoms, to which the family could readily respond with protection and care, meanwhile never negotiating or even acknowledging those conflicts.

In time we developed a research project that focused on these "brittle diabetic" children but also included anorectics and asthmatics and their families. Our research with psychosomatic families,* which was later broadened to include presenting problems of sickle-cell anemia, ulcerative colitis, and other psychosomatic complaints,† provided physical evidence of the effectiveness of family therapy. Brittle diabetics began to respond as predicted to medical management, instead of

* S. Minuchin, L. Baker, B. Rosman, R. Liebman, L. Milman, and T.C. Todd, A conceptual model of psychosomatic illness in children, *Archives of General Psychiatry, 32* (1975): 1031–1038.

† S. Minuchin, B. Rosman, and L. Baker, *Psychosomatic Families. Anorexia Nervosa in Context* (Cambridge, MA: Harvard University Press, 1978).

suffering bout after bout of ketoacidosis; "intractable" asthmatic children could be weaned from cortisone, and one even took up the flute.

During that same period, in the late sixties and seventies, we began to explore not just family therapy but the social context in which families are embedded. This was, of course, a natural development for a systemic thinker who is continually pushed to look at connections with larger systems, but it also seemed a natural continuity in my life. I had been a member of a minority in Argentina, an immigrant in Israel and the United States. I had spent sabbaticals living in Amsterdam, London, and Rome. The impact of multiple social contexts had shaped me, and I was aware of being different in different cultures. In retrospect it seems surprising that for so long my focus and enthusiasm for exploring different groups of families had handicapped my perspective and obliterated my view of their social connections. But the sixties insisted that we look at all social constructs anew. An ecological awareness was increasing our understanding that we were misspending our resources because we were blind to our connections. "Spaceship Earth," "Small is Beautiful"—slogans spoke of a new consciousness of interconnections.

In South Philadelphia, the community, mostly poor black families, claimed a voice in the delivery of mental health services by the Philadelphia Child Guidance Clinic. We were a clinic staffed predominantly by middle-class whites, with a sprinkling of minorities. We tried, but it was difficult at that time to recruit minority professionals. We decided to train naturally talented people without academic credentials. We got a five-year grant from the National Institutes of Mental Health (NIMH), and developed one of the most exciting training projects I had ever participated in. But we were unprepared for the rigidity and negativism of the larger administrative bureaucracy.

The staff included Jerome Ford, a black psychologist; Jay Haley; Braulio Montalvo; Marianne Walters; Rae Weiner; myself; and others—the most qualified trainers we had in the clinic. The trainees, who had a stipend for their apprenticeship, received intense supervision as well as theoretical training. At the end of the project, when our funding ended, we had about thirty trained minority family therapists. We hired almost all of the first graduates, but when we tried to help others get jobs in other clinics, we realized how naive we had been. The family therapists we had trained with government funds could not find jobs that acknowledged their expertise. Lacking college degrees, they didn't fit the categories that were reimbursable by the city or the state. We had to get the Commonwealth of Pennsylvania to create a special category for them, which we finally did through lobbying and connections. But it was a valuable lesson from the mental health establishment about the penalties that accrue to those foolish enough to try change. Like Pogo, we had met the enemy and he was us.

But by now the awareness of the significance of larger systems to the lives of individuals and families had become a major focus of my professional life. It is also the area in which I feel the greatest sense of frustration.

Although during the past decade I have returned to my early work with poor families, now I focus not only on the problems inside families but also on the destructive power of the institutions that control their lives—how the practices of "protective services" in their blind arrogance persist in "protecting" children while destroying their families. Trying to move institutions out of the established practices toward an understanding of systemic alternatives is a Sisyphean labor. The ease with which established practice reinstates the comfort of old routines is astounding. I am getting older, but I am also wiser and have more ways of trying. In any case I know I shouldn't give up.

3

Families and Family Therapy

From San Salvador to today has been a seventy-year journey, and for the last thirty of those years, I have been a family therapist. Family therapy can be thought of as an approach to treating human problems by bringing together the members of a family to help them work out conflicts at their source. But it is also a new approach to understanding human behavior as fundamentally shaped by its social context.

Family therapists recognize the pull of the past and that, to some extent, people live in the shadow of the family that was. But family therapy also recognizes the power of the present and so addresses itself to the ongoing influence of the family that is. Therapy based on this framework is directed toward changing the organization of the family, on the grounds that when family organization is transformed, the life of each family member is altered accordingly.

Naturally I was not the only person making the journey from individual to family therapy in the decades of the fifties and sixties. There were many explorers, coming from many different disciplines, in many settings. Family therapy was a child of the 1960s: one of the many flowers of that time of change, when "If you're not part of the solution, you're part of the problem," "Black is Beautiful," and many other challenges to the established order of things were beginning to be heard. What did family therapy challenge? Nothing less than the fundamental conviction that the individual is the center of the psychological universe.

The focus on the hero—the self against all odds—that seemed so self-evident to our grandparents had been undermined by Freud, who challenged the cherished belief in rationality by opening our eyes to the witches' brew of the unconscious. But Freud left intact the notion that the self is self-contained. Family therapy challenged the equally cherished belief in self-determination by illuminating the power of the family. It recognized men and women as parts of a larger whole—as subsystems, albeit significant ones, of larger systems. For the family therapist the family was a unit, and when one or more members of the system posed a problem, the family was the site of intervention.

It seems strange in retrospect that family therapy grew out of a field that had traditionally seen the family as a repressive force. David Levy's 1940s description of the "overprotective mother" strongly influenced the thinking of the fifties. Frieda Fromm-Reichmann's "schizophrogenic mother" was popularized in attacks like Philip Wylie's *Generation of Vipers,* which indicted "Momism" as the direct cause of the United States' withdrawal from Korea and the triumph of Communism there. Adelaide Johnson and S. A. Szurek described "superego lacunae": blaming the child's destructive behavior on the projection of the parents' deficient superegos. Bruno Bettelheim, at the Orthogenic School in Chicago, was prescribing "parentectomy"—the removal of the parents from the child's life—as a solution for severely damaged children.

Early family therapy, consistent with this prejudice

against parents, approached families with a view to protecting patients from them. R. D. Laing, the British psychiatrist and cult hero, experimented with a nonpsychiatric, nonhierarchical residence for severely disturbed individuals, Kingsley Hall. The purpose was to organize a setting in which adults could repair the damage they had suffered in their families. Another pioneer of family therapy, Murray Bowen, working with psychotic patients under the auspices of NIMH, hospitalized the patient's entire family in order to study the mutual influences of family members and patient in the maintenance of the illness. He encouraged individuals to differentiate themselves from the "undifferentiated family ego mass"—a kind of psychological quicksand in which family members lose their capacity for autonomous action. Nathan Ackerman's early papers dealt with the child as the "family scapegoat," seeing the family as a persecuting force. Gregory Bateson's double-bind theory, postulating that parents mystify the psychotic child by sending contradictory messages whose contradictions they deny, similarly expressed the period's mistrust of parents. It took many years for the family therapy movement to accept families' errors and weaknesses.

Nevertheless, as clinicians began to see families together, we began to understand. Though family therapy had no central discoverer, I like to spotlight two visionaries who had very different views of human nature.

Gregory Bateson, then in Palo Alto, was an English don, an anthropologist, a philosopher, a man of ideas. He imported theories from cybernetics, Russellian logic, systems theory, and mathematics and grafted them onto mental health. Bateson was a strange guru for mental health. It was not his field; in fact, being an anthropologist, he was extremely uncomfortable with the idea of inducing change. Nevertheless, here was this passionate explorer of ideas, in love with the view of people as carriers of concepts, at the forefront of a clinical, interventionist way of working with people. I always see this tall man as Don Quixote, challenging windmills. His influence on the field, which until then had been dominated by ideas of individual psychology, was highly productive. But it hampered family therapy too, because in truth Bateson was more interested in people's concepts than their lives.

On the opposite coast, in New York, was Nathan Acker-

man, a child analyst who was the director of an institution for
children with serious psychological disorders. Increasingly
uncomfortable with psychoanalytic practice in working with
children, he began slowly to include the mother, and then the
father, in the treatment of children and then to experiment
with seeing the total family. Challenging the notion of searching for the real truth of human nature in the depths of the
individual psyche, Ackerman looked instead at the interpersonal aspects of family life and the ways in which individual
behavior related to the family unit.

Ackerman was short and round, with a potbelly and a
small beard, though he stood tall in the clinical encounter. I
see him as Sancho Panza to Bateson's Don. When Ackerman
tilted at windmills, he was also concerned with the people who
lived there: the miller, his wife, and their children.

These two approaches to the family were very different. To
Bateson, the man of ideas, the family was an object of scien-
tific curiosity, a study in logical paradoxes and patterns of
communication. To Ackerman, the therapist, the family was a
set of living relationships with the capacity to stifle or en-
hance the full range of human experience. We are still struggling with this dichotomy between the ideological and the
clinical. It is not a clear division, however, and there are many
family therapists, myself included, who would not feel comfortable if pigeonholed in only one or the other category. They
must coexist, because they are different perspectives that complement each other.

Our group at Wiltwyck was one of several that worked through
trial and error to put this systemic view into practice. We saw
and studied families, all together and in subsystems. We observed each other's sessions, analyzed the effects of our interventions on the families and ourselves, tried again, and
observed and analyzed some more. We also began to comb the
literature, looking for other people who were working with
families.

As a result Dick Auerswald, the medical director, and I
traveled to observe some of these people at work. We went to
Palo Alto, hoping to see a session with Gregory Bateson. Jay
Haley suggested we attend Virginia Satir's class instead, because Bateson's anthropological approach made his sessions

more a matter of gathering information than of attempting change.

Virginia was the first family therapist outside our group I ever saw in action. Though she was to become one of the most influential teachers of family therapy, at the time she was working with a very limited communicational theory whose idea was that every message conveys both content and relationship. I remember her telling a student to imagine that a woman offers her husband a cup of tea. The husband says: "This is good tea." If by that he means only that he likes the tea, and there is no hidden message about their relationship, a lot of misunderstanding in the family can be avoided. Later her theories developed a more useful complexity.

We went to New Haven because the Yale group (Theodore Lidz, Stephen Fleck, and Alice Cornelison) had written some interesting papers about the families of schizophrenics. But we learned there that they had not yet interviewed any family; their descriptions of family dynamics had been based only on individual interviews. Lyman Wynne, whom we visited at NIMH, was interviewing schizophrenics and members of their families. But his interviewing was still tied to psychodynamic tradition, focusing on the individual patient's dynamics.

Although we might be new kids on the block, we nonetheless realized that we were on the cutting edge of meaningful explorations. The family therapy of the sixties was characterized by enormous competition between various practitioners: All of them rejected psychoanalysis, but all enthusiastically explored their own small corners of the new world. Different schools of therapy appeared, each convinced that a particular exploration of a grain of sand carried more truth and more complexity, and was more efficient, than the others. Names like *structural, strategic, experiential, systemic, Bowenian, ecological,* and *brief therapy* marked the different turfs. Some of this diversity came from theory and some from each clinician's own background, but therapists working with different populations also evolved very different theories and styles of working. My work with families in which the content of communication was sometimes sparse or even inarticulate, but the relationship messages were always powerful, shaped a style focused on relationship, distance and proximity, coalitions, and alliances.

Like everybody else, I was muddling through, trying, failing, and trying again, struggling to understand what worked when, and why. I was a clinician. I learned by doing and observing. Of course the observations that took center stage for me were those that made the most sense—in other words, those that fit in most easily with my own ways of being.

Working with families, and needing to make sense of their functioning, I began to see that family behavior was patterned—that family members responded in predictable ways. I had learned in my early training as a physician to focus on the physical structures underlying biological functions of organisms. So, as I was looking for heuristic metaphors that would convey the predictability and limitation of functions in a family, I began to think that a family, like a body, has an underlying structure. A body has bones, muscles, tendons, and nerves to direct and limit the movement of the arm. But the way it picks a flower is a function of the way the skeleton, muscles, tendons, and nerves are organized by an aesthetic inclination, the pleasure of holding a flower, or perhaps affection for the person to whom it is given. Similarly a family's structure does not dictate the ways people function. But it does set some limits, and it organizes the way they prefer to function.

I intended the concept of family structure to indicate functional constraints. It is unfortunate that the word "structure" lends itself to a different reading, implying a fixed state. I think today that a physiological metaphor, such as maintaining body temperature, would have been better, because it would indicate flexibility in the face of change. Family structures are conservative, but changeable. So the goal of therapy is to increase the flexibility of these underlying structures.

Another concept about families that fit well with my own background was the idea of family development. To a clinician trained in child psychiatry, it was obvious that families could be seen as organisms evolving through developmental stages. Each stage brings fresh demands, forcing family members to accommodate to new needs as family members grow up or age, and circumstances change. As families are conservative, their natural response to developmental shifts is to insist on continuing the familiar. So quite often the task of therapy is to help the family readjust to changing circumstances.

By the time I was working in Philadelphia a new element had been added to my learning: I had become a teacher. At the Philadelphia Child Guidance Clinic we worked very hard on deriving and operationalizing specific techniques in family therapy. This was criticized in a field still psychoanalytically oriented, but in fact it sprang from a deliberate theoretical contrast to psychoanalytic training, in which there was great emphasis on understanding, and very little on techniques.

My early teaching, like my therapeutic style at the time, tended toward confrontation. The intensity of these confrontations grew out of an almost evangelical fervor to jolt families toward change, growth, and improved functioning. The highly visible and dramatic confrontations turned out to be possible because I established a close bond with families. This connection, which I later called "joining," is a prerequisite to the challenge of restructuring. Families resist efforts to change them by people they feel don't understand and accept them.

In those years I didn't pay much attention to joining techniques. To me, joining seemed automatic—something you simply did. I also thought the ways of joining were idiosyncratic—a matter of a given therapist with a given family, not usefully generalizable. But in the seventies Braulio Montalvo and I began to look at the process of joining—that is, becoming part of a family system—by analyzing videotapes of sessions. We soon realized that the process of joining occurred on many different levels.

Language, for instance. I tend to adopt the language of families I work with. I become polysyllabic with intellectuals, romantic with Hispanics, idealistic with adolescents, concrete with the obsessive, spiritual with the religious. Conversely, I know a family is changing when some of its members begin to use my language. After I have challenged interruptions, I hear a mother tell her children not to interrupt. Family members become attentive to a scapegoated member after I have found her communications significant.

Or in behavior—I observe myself mimicking. I can be ethnic—Hispanic, Jewish, or Italian. I become a rabbi or a minister when the family needs it. I may slow my tempo and be distant with people who respect distance, or proximal and affectionate when this is the family's style.

Joining has nothing to do with pretending to be what you are not. It means tuning in to people and responding to the way they move you. As I began to study it, joining became a technique, something I could consciously do and teach.

During the seventies we developed "structural family therapy." I drew maps to clarify these concepts of a family organism as a structure. For instance, I might draw a strong affiliation between a mother and son as a double line, showing that that affiliation of mother and son excludes the father, like this:

$$M \equiv S$$
$$\overline{}$$
$$F$$

A coalition of father and son against mother appeared as:

$$F \equiv S$$
$$M$$

These geometric maps were easily readable and very valuable in the training of beginning therapists, giving them a sense of understanding family organizations.

What made these maps so useful was helping us see how one person's behavior is related to the structure of the relationships in the whole family. It may, for example, be relatively easy to discover that a little boy who misbehaves in school has a mother who doesn't make him behave at home. On closer examination we might see that she doesn't discipline the boy because she's overly involved with him. They're constantly together and interact more like playmates than parent and child. But why is the mother so close to the boy? Why does she need a playmate? Is it because she is emotionally distant from her husband? That's not uncommon. Perhaps she is deliberately lenient with the boy to counterbalance her husband's overly harsh control. The reason so many family dilemmas (even as simple as a boy who misbehaves at school) defeat us is that we fail to recognize that every family member's behavior is influencing and influenced by the behavior of the rest. Of course these easy explanations did not convey the complexity of the individual family members, but they did have the virtues of their simplicity.*

Later on, without abandoning the concepts of family structure and family development, I began to focus on the particular story that a family constructs to make sense of their life. People have the habit of becoming the stories they tell. When memory speaks it tells a "narrative truth," which comes to have more influence than "historical truth." The "facts" presented to a therapist are partly historical truth and partly a construction. The constructs that become the shared reality of a family represent mutual understandings and shared prejudices, some of which are hopeful and helpful, some of which are not.

When six-year-old Cassie's parents complain about her behavior, they say she's "hyper," "sensitive," "a difficult child." Such labels convey how parents experience and respond to their children, and have a tremendous power to control the parents' behavior. Is a child's behavior "misbehavior" or a symptom of being "sensitive"? Is it "naughty" or a "cry for help"? Is the child mad or bad; and who is in charge? What's in a name? Plenty.

I began to think about the way family organization relates to the family's view of itself, and about the fact that, as time goes by, the construction of family myth reinforces the structure that guides habitual movement, and vice versa. So we can listen to stories and deduce a family's systems of coalitions and balances, or we can look at behavior and infer the stories that support these behaviors. And more and more I moved from the teaching of technique to be applied in family therapy to the teaching of how to think about the family and its interactions.

When families come to me for help, I assume they have problems not because there is something inherently wrong with them but because they've gotten stuck—stuck with a structure whose time has passed, and stuck with a story that doesn't work. To discover what's bogging them down, I look for patterns that connect.

When a family enters my office, I see movements and re-

* S. Minuchin, *Families and Family Therapy* (Cambridge, MA: Harvard University Press, 1974).

sponses, counterresponses, and more movements. My gaze rarely stops on one person. When somebody is talking I hear what he or she says as he or she says it to the others. Each of us is constantly stimulus and response. Often I am acutely aware of the patterns of interaction between people before I have a clear idea of the content of what they are saying to one another.

As I began to see the process of interaction as well as hear the content of communication, the ways of the interaction frequently became more important than the content of the communication. I love to play with metaphors. I have always been a storyteller. I am sensitive to language. So it seems extraordinary that through my years of working with families I have come to look at the shape of the interaction as foreground, while the importance of content has receded.

When I see families I see strange shapes—conglomerates of people shifting forms but always connected. It reminds me of Castaneda's Don Juan, who could see the emotional links between himself and other people as a connective tissue leading from his navel to theirs. I imagine that there are families whose members seem so disengaged, so unrelated to each other, that one could imagine that the connections are not there. But probably that only means we have not looked closely enough.

Families come to me with a narrow definition of themselves. They are depleted after having struggled with problems, sometimes for years, and they define themselves by those problems:

"We have a problem with discipline."
"Johnny has an attention deficit disorder."
"Mary is anorectic."
"We don't communicate."
"My spouse is not affectionate."
"My mother is too critical."

These definitions dump the blame on one member. He or she is the problem—the stimulus. The other family members are responders, suffering and/or controlling. Even when a couple comes in conflict, it is always "she this" and "he that." Each labels the other. This process rigidifies the responses of family members, and as a result, attempts at solution often reinforce the problem. If professionals enter the situation and provide an official label for the pain, the rigidity of perceptions and responses is further reinforced by an expert's diagnosis.

The basic quest of family therapy is to release unused possibilities. That is the basis of its optimism. Families organize their members into certain patterns and, to an extent, it could not be otherwise. In order to feel secure, people must be part of predictable interactions. Unfortunately, predictability may congeal into limiting molds, so that the patterns become inflexible and family members use only a small range of the behaviors available to them. In some families there must not be anger. In others tenderness must not be expressed. Invisible rules prescribe certain behavior, and the family perceives the options they have chosen as inevitable and unchangeable. As a result, the family constructs people who function below their capacity in the family setting. Therapy may be a search for novelty, but all we really discover is what is already there.

When I meet a family I am on the alert—a hound dog on the track, a crossword puzzle addict with a new Sunday *Times* magazine. The whole picture will evolve while I join and begin to probe, but the information will come in tiny chips, like the pieces of a mosaic.

I do not take a "family history." Anything in the family's history that is relevant will show up in their interactions. Nor do I question a family's composition. I am as aware as any family practitioner has to be of the ideal American family (breadwinning husband, homemaking wife, and two and a half children) that is still somehow so dear to some politicians and self-appointed moralists, but I have never found it relevant to the family in my office. It is true that family composition can give clues where to look for problems. If I am seeing a single mother with an only child, I may look for overinvolvement, precocity in the child, and so on. But what I am always looking for is flexibility, complementarity, competition, empathy, hierarchy, chaos. Who starts talking? Is this the authority delegated to function in relation to outsiders? Who agrees with whom? Is there more support or more argument?

I know there is a pattern to what seems so spontaneous,

even unorganized. Families don't walk in and hand you the underlying structural patterns that are keeping them stuck. What they bring is the noise—their own confusion and pain. So I test for possibilities of order and interrelationship. If the family experiences my questions as fitting and expanding their possibilities, their response will tell me so and I continue in that direction. If the response is confusion or rejection, I try something else.

Eventually a dialogue evolves in which I offer possible explanations for their behavior. They respond by rejecting, accepting, or pondering the possibilities of my assumptions and feeding information back to me. Their idiosyncratic experiences reshape my generic structures. The dance that ensues is a dance of possibilities.

As therapy progresses we begin to develop a system of which I am a part. In this system I begin to experience the pushes and pulls of the family's preferred ways of being, and this experience modifies my ideas about the family. This is akin to what psychoanalysts call countertransference. I experience the pulls of the family, and that gives me some idea about the ways in which family members, too, experience the family's imperatives.

As I meet the family I listen, I watch, I make connections. I pay attention to positive statements, to signs of competence, to areas of distress. I affirm family members by commenting on their way of seeing themselves and the other members. This is the stage of therapy I used to call "joining," to highlight the active participation of the therapist in becoming part of the therapeutic system. But something more always happens to me in this stage. While I am joining them, the family members are also joining me. I am pulled by their demands, and they modify my behavior. Unwittingly I adopt the family's style.

This process can never really be a technique, for it is beyond awareness. Today I call it Zelig, for the chameleon character in Woody Allen's eponymous movie. Zelig has the strange quality of changing with his context. He darkens in a meeting with Afro-Americans and grows paler in a group of Hasidic Jews. He is not in command of these changes. They just happen to him. And they happen to me in the context of each family.

Therapy for me is challenge. The family comes to therapy with a way of doing things, depleted of resources because they have worn out their flexibility by repeating solutions that do not work. To the fixed perspectives that families present, my answer is uncertainty.

"Are you sure that no alternatives are available?"
"You are more complex than you realize."
"There is hope, there are resources that you have not yet explored."

Families do change. But the process of change usually involves some level of crisis. The therapist has to join, gain acceptance, elicit trust, and then motivate the family to jump into uncertainty.

I try a variety of techniques that do not rely only on analysis and interpretation. I may encourage closeness. I may remind a couple that without time and attention, the intimate bond between them will gradually erode. I may encourage distance. Some parents doubt that their children can get along without them, and that doubt robs the children of the space they need to explore. I may enter at the wordless level of communication, as when I wave my hand to silence a family member whose incessant talk silences the others. I may introduce a higher intensity of affect than the family is accustomed to. I may force conflict to appear in a family used to avoiding it. All these maneuvers are predicated on the optimistic assumption that family members have untapped resources. The one constant is that I ask people to try something new. The one axiom is: "You are richer than you know."

Readers probably have a familiar image of a therapist—kindly, benevolent, and relatively silent, interested in the past and in discovering meaning in a thoughtful, leisurely process. I want to prepare you for a very different kind of therapy, with active joining and an active struggle for change.

In the stories that follow you will meet families I have seen over the decades of my professional life. Whenever possible I will tell you about my life circumstances when I met them. I want you to know that the therapist, like the families, is enriched and constrained by life circumstances. So I will start first with a couple I know very well: my wife and myself.

4

The Formation
of a Couple

The *Rio Jachal* is the latest addition to the Argentinean fleet.
Built in Naples for pleasure cruises, it features the latest
technological advances of shipbuilding, ornamented with Italian elegance. It has only one class. Pat and I, married one
month, have said good-bye to her parents, who are sure that
our leavetaking in New York Harbor is the last they will ever
see of their daughter.

I met Pat while we were both working at the Council Child
Development Center. I was a psychiatric resident, Pat a psychologist with a brand-new doctorate from Yale. I felt very
attracted to her, but she saw herself as a serious professional
and me as a skinny dilettante. I took her to an Israeli night-

club, where I spent a month's stipend on dinner. That convinced both of us that I was serious, and soon after we were married. We agreed that we would live in Israel.

She introduced me to her parents. Her mother and I felt an immediate affinity. Her father was more reserved, concerned about this stranger with a murky past—this man who had lived in three countries. Still, they were impressed by my connection to Israel. And in any event they had no choice but to accept me.

Our next hurdle will be to introduce Pat to my parents. They couldn't come to our wedding. Their knowledge of the United States derives solely from Hollywood; they're having nightmares.

We are taking seventeen luxurious days to sail to Argentina. Every morning we have a choice for breakfast—filet mignon with or without eggs, while a three-musician combo plays Argentinean and Brazilian music. Our game at breakfast is to guess what's going on at the other tables. We invent romances: the handsome young Argentinean man (he has a well-trimmed mustache) who sits alone and the sexy woman who sits with her mother and sister. The young couple who dance the samba—the husband seems jealous. Our inventions go unchecked; therefore we are always right. We live in our own bubble, postponing reality. The sea is infinite, the future serene and cloudless. We explore our bodies. We read books and talk, sharing ideas and assumptions. I teach Pat some Spanish words to greet my family: "*Hola Mama, Hola Papa, Hola pobrecitos.*" With my childish, perverse sense of humor (or maybe some deep, unconscious deviltry), I am teaching her to insult my parents. But I will tell her the day before we arrive, and we will laugh as if it was a clever thing to do.

We hide from each other our uncertainty about the future (what will it be like?) and about each other. Our internal monologues are full of question marks that surface only in modified form, wrapped in small, meaningless arguments.

We arrive at Santos, a major Brazilian port where the *Rio Jachal* will stay two days. It is raining, but the black stevedores are indifferent to the water wetting their clothes, making rivers on their skin. In ten minutes the rain will stop, the sun will dry them. Soon we too are just as casual.

The people are different. We are conspicuous, clearly for-

eign. Pat says she needs to buy Kleenex, and I answer that I
don't know how to find a pharmacy. Pat insists, and I am
irritated by her inability to accommodate to new circumstances. She could use a handkerchief as I do. She could use
my handkerchief. She says handkerchiefs are unsanitary. You
put a mess in your pocket. I say that Kleenex is part of American conspicuous consumption. I extol the virtues of my handkerchief culture; she insists on the virtues of Kleenex. We
have a major blowup: We are beginning to see aspects of each
other that make us uneasy.

Pat left her world in New York. She expects me to be an
expert in these other worlds that will become ours. I am afraid
of her reliance on me. When she is anxious she insists, and I
call that nagging. When I am anxious I become loud and bel-
ligerent, which she calls bullying. We plan to stay in Argentina for three months before taking the *Conte Grande* to
Genoa. Then it will be twelve more days to Haifa. These
months will be full of obligations to the unknown.

My family is enormous. My father has eight brothers and
sisters, my mother seven. The cousins are reckoned in the
hundreds. All of them are obliged to visit us. Pat smiles as
long as she can. She is marvelously patient at their impatience with her Spanish. Some of my aunts pinch her cheeks
the way people do with a cute but not very bright young child.
This disturbs her self-image as an educated, sophisticated
New Yorker.

Soon we begin to build barriers against the intruders. But
the intruders are my family. My parents haven't seen me for
a year. They make demands on my time that Pat finds exces-
sive. I feel torn, but of course I recognize Pat's isolation and
her resentment of relatives who tell my parents, in Spanish,
what they think of my wife. I feel protective. My relationship
with my parents changes. I have always been the loyal, responsible son. Now I feel detached and annoyed at their insistence that things not change. I feel primarily a husband,
while they try to keep me a son. Pat and I search for islands
of escape. We go to the movies to disengage and be alone.

She talks to me about my family, and suddenly my perspective changes. I begin seeing my family through Pat's eyes.
My father, who has always been a prophet to me—a man who
grew with adversity, a just Jew whose wrath was always jus-

tified by his fine sense of honor and justice—begins to seem middle-aged, shy, uncertain, uneasy after his move to Buenos Aires from Concepción del Uruguay, financially insecure in a semiretirement that has left him without a real center of activity. What I used to see as my mother's controlling obsessiveness, her sense of order, now seems strength, protection. Through Pat, I see that my mother supports my father. She is always ready to complement his needs, to make him feel strong and right. Pat likes my mother, who is easy to relate to, engaging and sensitive to her needs, while my father, who is shy, tends to rely on his wife in all social situations.

My parents' maid works six days a week. She lives in a room at the top of the house. Pat is surprised that she doesn't have her own key, that she is on call with no set hours, that after years of working for my family, she is suspected if anything is misplaced. I never saw what abject servitude we inflict on the *criollas* who, all my life, have worked for us for meager wages with no rights, often serving as passive sexual partners for the young men of the house.

I begin to construct a new past, a past that includes Pat's way of seeing, even though she wasn't part of it. Whenever I think about my childhood now, it will include Pat's perspective. I don't think I can recover memories from before my marriage that have not been edited and reedited by forty years of marriage.

If creating a new past requires a shift in perspective, creating a future is simply done by living long enough in the present. Israel gives us the opportunity to invent a shared history. It is 1952, the time of *tzena* (rationing, belt-tightening). We have brought from bountiful Argentina, among other things, a sack of rice, meat extract, and two hams. We eat better than most. The Jewish Agency gives us a one-bedroom apartment in a settlement in Kfar Saba. We have the electric stove, refrigerator, the wonderful record player we brought with us—and we have neither electricity nor gas. The refrigerator becomes simply a box, and we buy a *ptilia*, a Primus kerosene burner, on which Pat cooks.

We begin to experience life as a couple. A driver comes every morning to drive me to work, and Pat goes to the *ulpan* to study Hebrew. We often go to the grocery store together, but my presence is vital at the fish and meat store because the shopkeeper is Sephardic, and because of my Spanish we get special treatment for the "Sephardic doctor" and his wife. We meet some people from a nearby town, the Davisons, and since we have no telephone and there is no transportation on the Sabbath, we walk the ten miles, hoping they will be at home. We know we will be welcome. The words *haver* (comrade) and *shelanu* (it's ours) are emblematic of the sense of building together that is in the air. With the food rationing and all the other difficulties comes an absurd faith in the future. Instead of saying good-bye, you say *"H'yetov"*—"it will be all right." Improvisation and downright lack of planning are okay— *H'yetov.* A road to run from Haifa to Tel Aviv is begun in both cities. Everyone knows there is neither money nor materials to finish it. *H'yetov.*

Memory romanticizes and glosses over rough spots. Life was hard, we were immigrants, we didn't know the ropes, and my salary as the medical director of Youth Aliyah was not much higher than that of the drivers who came to take me to work. Life was primitive and a little dangerous. The Jordanian border was only twenty miles away, and we were continuously aware of Arab marauders, crossing invisible boundaries called frontiers. One of our neighbors, an old woman, a concentration camp survivor, panicked and cried every time she heard shots in the distance.

Pat was a housewife here, adapting to difficult conditions. I had a job that took me every day to Tel Aviv, to one of the five residential institutions that I supervised, while she was essentially alone in the middle of nowhere, without friends, coping with a new language. She walked the two or three miles to the grocery store and fish market, sometimes more than once, to get a bar of soap or our allotment of eggs. I was preoccupied with my own difficulties in this new country, making my way in the face of *vatikim* (old-timers) who questioned my American psychological bag of tricks, and I didn't realize how difficult Pat's situation was. I marvel today how she survived these first months.

Many years later, when we were in London, Pat and I studied the families of American corporate executives and found the wives as a group stressed by the conditions of exile.

But that was years later, and the wives were other people's wives. At the time, in Kfar Saba, I don't think I fully understood her plight. I certainly would not have understood the feminist claim that it was gender related. When we talk about it now, she approves of my belated recognition, but she also pushes me toward a more complex understanding, including the fact that she had intellectual resources of her own and that she was sustained by her own fascination with a new culture.

In the first few months in Kfar Saba, Pat and I negotiated rules without noticing them. Some differences we could accept easily: Pat preferred to read at night and wake up late. I preferred to go to sleep and wake up early. We could sort out some of the chores that form the elements of a couple's contract of collaboration—who washes the dishes, takes out the garbage, pays the bills. But we had heated arguments about other details, like whether or not to keep the window open at night. The ability to resolve small, visible issues depends on goodwill and flexibility, invisible but nonetheless essential. The way each spouse feels the need of the other and is ready to give up his or her claim to the truth, the capacity of the couple to sense the absurdity in their struggle and laugh together, their willingness to put loyalty to each other above competing demands, the pleasure of small moments and the interest in dialogues around issues that are neutral and belong to the world of others.

After six months in Israel, Pat found a part-time job at the Lasker Clinic in Jerusalem. That meant two hours of traveling, so she would sleep over and return the next day. I felt it was only fair to have dinner waiting when she got home, but my Argentinean background had not prepared me to enter the kitchen. Fortunately we had a Polish neighbor who had studied hotel management in Switzerland and now worked for the tourist office. He became my instructor. We decided that my first foray into this area would be a delicious spaghetti dinner. The "meat" sauce would have onion, peppers, *hatsilim* (eggplant), and some of our blessed supply of Argentinean meat extract. Pat was delighted, and I felt I had made another escape from my past. My father had been allowed in the kitchen only to heat water.

Daily we nurtured out interdependence. We shared gossip

and friends, anxieties and joys, aesthetic pleasures, moral dilemmas, and intellectual puzzles. My job was difficult. My
training in the United States made universal assumptions
about people that my experiences in Israel challenged. I felt
my ignorance and sometimes reacted with unwitting intran-
sigence. Pat listened to my stories and my complaints. She
was supportive, but she also helped pull me back from my
distortions. I learned to rely on her expanded perspective just
as I had on her re-vision of my view of my family. There were
times I would have liked uncritical support, but I came to
value her different perspective.

She would tell me about her job, and we would share gossip about her colleagues and criticize the agency's psychoanalytic bias. Slowly, as we explored new territories and new
friends, we began to build a present but also a past that did
not belong to either of us alone; it was ours.

Six months after our arrival in Israel, my parents came for
a visit. We decided on a banquet and opened the sack of rice,
only to find it crawling with insects. It was mottled—white
rice and dark beasts—and repulsive. In our previous life we
would have thrown it away. Not in Israel. My mother took
charge. A tactician, she directed us to spread out the camp
bed. We spread the rice out on it, and waited for the sun to
help. Soon thousands of bugs were fleeing the sun-heated rice.
The battle was won, but not the war. The rice was still alive.
Mother put the rice for the meal in water. The insects rose to
the surface while the rice sank to the bottom, and the simple
physical process of separation left us with more or less clean
rice. There may have been some insects left, but we needed all
the protein we could get.

Forty years later the whole event remains vivid in our
shared memory. It forms part of our heroic period, a comic
interlude mixed with boring, stressful, angry, difficult, and
loving moments.

Episodes like this one marked a turning point in our relationship with my parents. Now they were visiting in our
home and experiencing with us the difficulties of our existence. But they also saw our resourcefulness and began to
respect our rights and prerogatives. We guided and protected
them during their stay with us. I became for the first time an
adult child in their eyes. They made their first contact with

Pat as a separate person. In this new relationship it was easy for us to accept their helpful intrusion.

In these first years of marriage, this trek of transformation from me to me-and-you occurred like the formation of self in childhood—a slow accretion of small moments. My view of my colleagues and the world around me was now enhanced by the stereoscopic image of our two perspectives. My coming home held the pleasure of someone waiting for me. My body image incorporated the extension of another body. I could pass the salt when I was closer to it, and use her arms as an extension of mine when she was closer. My hearing of music became clearer and more discriminating because she was musical. My internal monologues built on vague images and diffuse moods took on more precise shape, absorbing words as they became dialogues with her.

As I was moving from me to us, I did not lose myself. I expanded. A couple is a resonance box. Each one's experience reverberates and is returned amplified. In our forty years together we have expanded our individual styles of being, thinking, and feeling, but they are still quite distinct and different. I am self-centered. I don't pay attention to details. I look for connections. My memories are global. I express myself in metaphors or poetic images, since I lack details. I am goal oriented, frequently looking at the outcome without paying attention to the steps necessary to get there. Therefore I am frequently disappointed and feel betrayed when I don't find the supportive environment to reach the goal. When frustrated I get angry fast. I am in the anger and controlled by it. But it subsides rapidly, and I am full of guilt.

Pat sees many things at once. Like many professional women, she moves about among the tasks implied in multiple roles: wife, mother, psychologist, business and family manager. To know a subject she examines it from different perspectives, then comes to a new whole. I recognize the steps she has taken but would never arrive at conclusions in that way. She connects with people and remains connected. She has a keen sense of humor, usually subtle and intellectual, but she can be Harpo Marx to the life in mimicry that brings belly laughter.

I lose keys, leave windows open, and depend on her to read directions on trips and in life. She trusts my vision. We share political views. We are both liberals. We see the unfairness of an economic system that keeps people hungry, and in our own small way we work to change it.

I am different today because she changed me. And she is different because of me. Both are parts of a larger whole: a complex psychological entity, a beehive, an anthill of two.

When it works well we complement each other. We predict correctly, anticipate each other, when things are going smoothly. The pas de deux is generally efficient. When we find ourselves in new situations, or when something goes amiss in our private orbits and we need more support than usual, the dance changes in response. But when things get sticky, our competitive selves may flex their respective ancestries. I become Salvador Minuchin again, and she is Patricia Pittluck. I am right; you are wrong. No, you are. The beat of our individual drums gets louder. I grow deaf to the beat of hers. Use handkerchiefs, I say. Handkerchiefs are primitive, she says; use tissues.

I carry within me two models of what it means to be a couple: my parents' model, which I assimilated without question as a child, and the one I have been working at for four decades. This limits my knowledge. I have no personal experience of divorce and remarriage, serial monogamy, or the more esoteric ways of being a couple. When I work with other forms of being a couple, I am frank in describing my limitations and asking the couple I am seeing for help.

My parents' couplehood reflected the values of their time. As parts of a couple they knew their places. My father was the breadwinner and the center of power in the family. My mother accommodated to his leadership. Their relationship was complementary, but there was no doubt about *quien lleva los pantalones* (who "wore the pants"). In the turn-of-the-century Argentinean rural culture, a woman head of the family would have been a family disgrace.

This clear hierarchical organization represented the face of the family to the outside world, and in a modified way also to the interior of the family. My mother continuously monitored my father's moods and needs and translated to us children, reflecting the family response to the cultural values of male supremacy.

Inside the family, relationships were more complex. Father wouldn't question my mother's right as a decision maker in child-rearing and household issues or as an equal partner in significant issues of family life, as for instance when they decided to move from my hometown to a larger city, when my sister needed to continue her studies in high school, and later to Buenos Aires. Their relationship was a checkerboard of differentiated areas of responsibility. This arrangement was economical, but limiting. When my father died my mother didn't know how to handle her money—she didn't know how to write a check. My father's social skills had always been mediated by my mother. Their repertory as individuals was narrow; their flexibility lay in the complex richness of their complementarity.

Pat and I are clearly different. We are examples of some of the advantages and difficulties of a more symmetrical marriage. We saw ourselves as successful professionals, each of whom had areas of autonomy and success outside the family and shared in the family the more reduced world of family life. I brought to the marriage not only my belief in the culture of handkerchiefs but a model of assertiveness that came from my hierarchical family. Pat, although the second daughter of her family, was nonetheless the more assertive of the siblings. We believed in our capacity to reason out problems, but we frequently reasoned from different perspectives. Therefore our conversations often lead to an expanded point of view—and equally often to arguments. In this symmetrical model of couplehood, in which each partner insists on the complexity and breadth of his or her world, the couple is richer but more often in conflict.

Although I would say that the symmetrical model of the marital relationship is a product of a culture that insists on the primacy of the self, I cannot say it is better than the complementary model. It just is. It is different, and probably it both expands and stresses the individual in its own way. But I hasten to add that neither the symmetrical nor the complementary relationship exists anywhere in pure form. The fifty-fifty marriage is a mythical product of the late twentieth century, just as "He for God only, she for God in him" was a myth of the nineteenth. Every couple has some mixture of individual autonomy, specialization, and complementarity. But perhaps today we are more alert to gender inequalities and to the way family roles curtail individual growth. Probably we could use more recognition of the family's functions of nurturing and support.

As for Pat and me, we have experienced the tension between the couple and the self for forty years. We struggle, cooperate, and grow. Over the years our complementarity has grown more complex. Being alone does not mean betrayal. Giving in does not mean defeat. Dependency does not equal weakness. Initiative does not mean control. All these words carry an aura that comes from the value our culture places on the rugged individual. But complementarity can be mutual enrichment. It defangs aggression, so that individuals who dance together don't hurt each other.

After two years of marriage Pat and I added to the complexity of our lives and our couplehood by becoming parents. Our first child, Daniel, was born in Israel. I remember the hospital in Kfar Saba where he was born. I see myself as a figure in a Chagall painting, flying over the orange groves, my son in my arms, while Pat smiled in a gynecological world surrounded by the multiethnicity that was Israel, united in motherhood. Jean was born four years later at Columbia Presbyterian Hospital in New York. We were living on West Eighty-sixth Street, we had a large apartment, and I had a psychotherapeutic practice and was in psychoanalytic training. Pat worked as a research psychologist at the Bank Street College of Education. It should have been easy. It wasn't.

Each child brought pleasures and difficulties to our family. We discovered very soon that all our professional knowledge, all the books we had read, didn't teach us much about our own idiosyncratic children and how we were to fit with them.

The responsibility of parenting brought disagreements. We were both loving and nurturing, but as a developmental psychologist Pat—seeing children from the perspective of progressive education—was prone to encourage their exploration, paid attention to their perceived needs, and (I felt) was overfocused on them at the expense of our adult lives. I had incorporated from my family a model of parenting that centered on discipline and respect for adults. In my professional life I had learned respect for children's experimentation and growth, but Pat felt my parental responses as controlling. I saw her as too permissive. Simple issues triggered overblown arguments. The influence of my childhood as a correct model for parenting conflicted with Pat's feeling that she would not repeat her parents' overcontrolling mistakes.

Today I think that we fought our battles on the children's domain. Perhaps we could have profited from family therapy, but thirty-five years ago nobody thought of so bizarre an idea as seeing children and parents together. In time we learned to be more tolerant of each other's weaknesses and to respect each other's strengths. My experiences as a father radically altered my thinking about families and my practice as an individual therapist and later a family therapist. I lost the arrogance of believing that there was a correct way, and accepted parental fumbling, weakness, and uncertainty. At the same time my children taught me about child development in an experiential way I had not acquired in all my years of study. Daniel and Jean, four years apart in age, of different genders, but also of different reactivities and ways of apprehending life, expanded my experience every day. Through them I also learned about schools and teachers, about the social life of children, and about pleasure without words, apprehensions, love, guilt, selflessness: the whole gamut of being human.

Today Daniel is a psychologist and a family therapist, actively involved in issues of social justice. Jean, a sculptor and performer, teaches theater in an art school for adults. I owe them much. They have enriched my ability to understand challenge, to cherish growth and change. When I meet with families today, Pat, Dan, and Jean are part of me.

PART TWO

COUPLES

In the heart's business we like to think that personal qualities such as courage and generosity are what it takes to make relationships work. And yet, whether we recognize it or not, families take on structural patterns that govern our lives, not unlike the way anatomy governs our movements.

The first thing to understand about how families are structured is that some measure of complementarity is the defining principle of every relationship. In any couple one person's behavior is yoked to the other's. This simple statement has profound implications: It means that a couple's actions are not independent but codetermined, subject to reciprocal forces that support or polarize—and it challenges the cherished belief in one's own Self, that good old, free-willed, autonomous, island of a Self we like to think of ourselves as.

But there's an important distinction to be made here. Most of us know (or find out) that marriage doesn't complete us, in the sense of making up for what's missing—that a husband's self-assurance will make up for a wife's insecurity or that a wife's outgoing nature will resolve a husband's reticence turns out to be a fantasy. Two halves don't magically become whole by saying "I do."

However, two people who join together do make one relationship. In that sense two halves do make a whole. Whether or not it turns out to be the whole you want is another matter.

Couples therapy seems to go against logic. What members of a couple want is not help but vindication. They want to demonstrate to the therapist and the world how unfair the spouse is, how insensitive, and how difficult it is to live with such a person. At other times they want absolution. "It's my drinking, my affair, my depression, my temper." In either case, complaints are presented in individual terms: the accusatory "She this," "He that," or the penitent "It's me." They come to therapy to settle accounts. But, to the family therapist, they're both wrong. It's not him; it's not her—it's the chemistry between them.

If they come because she drinks, they may be startled, even offended, to hear the therapist ask him: "How do you make her drink?" If one gambles or is phobic, it will go against the grain and against logic for the therapist to dig into the complicity of the other. After all, individuals are responsible for their own behavior, aren't they? Not entirely. That is the absurdity and the power of couples therapy. It turns reality on its head and introduces perspective, novelty, and hope.

But first, of course, they have to accept the notion of interdependence as a truth at least equal to their belief in self. The family therapist comes armed with a set of beliefs about how systems operate that needs to be translated from the level of theory to that of the couple's idiosyncrasies.

The family dramas that follow take place in a therapist's office. The family members present their individual reality in their own terms. I, the therapist, try to uncover hidden connections, correspondences that are invisible, by challenging and provoking family members. The process combines monologues, dialogues, and polemics. They respond more frequently with "but" than with "aha!" I keep listening and keep pushing, always guided by the notion that we are simultaneously initiators and responders. What keeps people stuck is overlooking their own participation in the problems that plague them. What sets them free is seeing their role in the patterns that bind them together.

5

The Wife Beater

In the summer of 1991 at a national meeting of family therapists in San Diego, three experts spoke about family violence. Although the dirty secret of domestic violence had been out of the closet for some time, the assembled therapists were stunned into silence by the raw statistics: There are more victims of domestic violence in Canada and the United States than all victims of car accidents, rape, and muggings combined. During the Vietnam War, when 39,000 American soldiers were killed in battle, 17,500 women and children died in incidents of domestic violence in the United States. Domestic violence—let's call it what it is, wife battering and child beating—is a major public health problem, right up there with alcoholism and depression.

Along with this ugly evidence of the extent of family violence, the audience of therapists was told that they themselves might be part of the problem: that a systemic view of family violence, which treats family members as mutually involved in the problems that plague them, tends to excuse and perhaps even perpetuate wife beating. Domestic violence, many experts believe, is not a "family problem"; it is an evil done to women by men.

Violent men, from this perspective, don't lose control—they use brutal means to *take* control. Any attempt to treat violent couples together is, to this way of thinking, insensitive to women's safety and tends to excuse male violence by implicitly blaming the victim for her victimization.

Certainly those who commit violent acts are responsible and accountable for their behavior, and certainly there are cases of brutal violence where steps must be taken to punish the perpetrator and protect the victim. Yet of course family violence is not limited to these extreme cases; it is, rather, extremely common on a more restrained scale, most often involving the slapping or shoving of one spouse by the other, usually the husband. Often it is an escalation, albeit unacceptable, of the emotionally destructive behavior that characterizes many marriages.

When family therapists begin to analyze such destructive patterns of interaction, part of what we do is to disentangle individuals from their automatic yoked reactions. We help them discover their individuality, their power, and their responsibility. It's paradoxical. By helping people understand their connections, we empower them to take responsibility for their choices and change.

"Marital problems." That's what he said. He was Philip Lockwood, a neuropsychologist on the staff of a prominent hospital. A mutual friend had given him my number. He apologized profusely for calling me at home, saying he knew how busy I must be, but he wanted very badly to see me as soon as possible. As a matter of fact, I'd been expecting his call. The friend who recommended me had called and said that he was afraid the Lockwoods were on the verge of divorce. I told Dr. Lockwood I'd been expecting to hear from him and offered him an appointment that he accepted immediately.

The Lockwoods were waiting in my reception room when I arrived just before nine. Philip Lockwood was a tall, handsome man, elegantly groomed and carefully dressed. His short curly hair was still black, but his meticulously trimmed beard was flecked with white. He introduced himself and shook hands. Then he introduced his wife, Lauren. She took my hand but didn't shake it. She spoke with a refined Southern accent. Lauren Lockwood had the natural ease of a woman who knows she's beautiful but is no longer self-conscious about it.

I invited them into my office, and Philip sat down on the couch, crossed his legs, and clasped his hands around his knee. Lauren started toward the couch but then moved to the chair next to it.

I asked who wanted to begin, looking automatically at Lauren. She turned to her husband and said, "Why don't you start?" That surprised me. Usually when couples come for therapy, wives start in with their list of grievances, while their husbands sit back in the dock and wait to defend themselves.

"Well, we've been married twenty years," he began. "I'm fifty, Lauren is forty-two, and we have one child. We met in Zambia, when I was in the Peace Corps—we both were. I thought what we were doing was important. That we could make a difference. Lauren seemed to feel the same way. She seemed to believe in the same things I did—back then." He paused. "Well, anyway, at the end of our tour we got married by the village headman. Then we had a large formal wedding in the States, for the families."

I glanced at Lauren. She seemed prepared to sit and listen patiently, so I listened too, nodding occasionally, waiting for him to get to the "marital problems." He spoke at great length, making sure I got all the facts, and that I got them right. He talked about going to graduate school. He'd gotten Lauren a job in the personnel department of the university, and they'd lived on her salary until he'd gotten an internship that paid forty-five hundred dollars, "which back then was pretty good." He talked on about his career and eventually about their son, Jeffrey, now twelve. He talked about how they'd waited so long because they didn't want to bring a child into the world until they were secure enough to support him. I glanced at Lauren, and she nodded, accepting this statement of the facts.

Philip went on talking, still not getting to those marital

problems. He'd been talking nearly fifteen minutes, giving me facts. I was struck by the orderly march of his narrative, his emphasis on himself, his love of complicated phrases. Absent from his arid account was any sense of the affection and desire that keep two people together for twenty years, or of the frustration and bitterness that make it a trial.

I looked again at Lauren, wondering when, if ever, she would challenge his version of events. But she seemed content to sit and listen, silent, lovely, composed.

Finally, as Philip approached the present, he touched on what brought them to see me. "Over the years we've had some basic differences of opinion—which . . . we aren't always able to communicate in a civilized manner."

"*Communicate*?!" Suddenly Lauren was blazing. "Why don't you tell him how you communicate!" She turned to me. "He hit me and knocked me down! He broke my collarbone! And it wasn't the first time, either."

I waited to hear more, but she fell silent. The anger she'd been holding back suddenly erupted, and then, just as suddenly as it began, it was over.

"I didn't mean to hurt her," Philip muttered. He was sullen, clearly embarrassed but not quite contrite. "She keeps harping and harping at me. I never get a break. Sometimes she makes me so mad I don't know what I'm doing, and that's the truth."

I've heard that complaint many times. It's what some psychologists call "pleading violence": "Please stop making me hurt you."

I turned back to Lauren, giving her the floor. Now I heard a very different story of the marriage. Lauren's account was more about the relationship and feelings.

"When we were in Africa, I looked up to him." Calmer now, she spoke quietly. "He seemed so mature, so sure of himself. Of course he was eight years older. Then again, it was a special time. I'll be honest. I joined the Peace Corps mainly because I wanted to live abroad for a few years; I wasn't all that idealistic. Philip really believed in what we were doing. I really admired that. He made me feel important, too.

"But from the day we were married, everything revolved around him. It was *his* Ph.D., *his* career. Things were fine as long as everything went his way. As long as I was the good little wife, he was happy. I put him through graduate school. I typed his papers, I did all the housework, and when he wanted to throw parties for the department, I did that too. All he ever thought about was himself. He'd come home whining about how hard everything was or how someone hurt his feelings, and I was supposed to hold his hand."

Philip shot her a look of pure hate.

"Then we had Jeffrey. And I did everything for him, too. If Philip condescended to change a diaper or take the baby for a walk, he expected to be showered with praise. It used to kill me when my parents would visit and he'd hold the baby for one minute. They'd gush all over him. 'Oh, what a wonderful father!' It used to make me sick."

I listened, as I usually do in a first interview, trying to hear beneath the content of what they were saying to the desires and fears that kept them from hearing each other. Lauren's presentation puzzled me. Her anger seemed to switch on and off. When she listened to Philip, she seemed totally receptive. When she did finally speak, she showed only her anger and none of the hurt and longing behind it. And Philip listened about as well as most people do when they feel attacked.

Their story was common enough. A perfectly decent, somewhat insecure, somewhat self-centered man had married a beautiful and intelligent woman. She had many attractive traits, none more attractive than how good she made him feel about himself. A perfectly decent, somewhat insecure, twenty-two-year-old woman, with little sense of herself other than someone who was attractive to men, had married a serious man who adored her. What could be more natural?

Like most couples, they'd learned to cope with conflict by using a combination of distance and compromise. Only Lauren had done most of the accommodating. This seemed natural to both of them. Philip had his career; his struggle was to make it in the larger world. Lauren had the relationship; her struggle was to make it work.

The first crack in the structure of their relationship came when Philip started putting more into his doctoral studies and less into the relationship. In marrying Philip, Lauren forsook any prior existence of her own and stepped into her husband's life. She moved from Charleston to New York to be with

Philip, giving up friends and familiar surroundings. But as Philip began spending long hours at school, his interests increasingly excluded her. When she complained or asked for more attention, he'd react as though she'd broken the rules: "Why have you become so demanding? What's the matter with you?" As far as he was concerned, she'd changed.

He'd come home tired. (He'd come home late.) He wanted to rest. (She wanted to talk.) He'd turn on the television. She'd make some crack, "You're so selfish," and he'd respond, "You're such a baby." They traded insults, but neither could bear the heat of the other's anger and so they'd back off, smoking and sputtering until they cooled down. After a day or two they'd resume as before, with the unresolved issues between them forgotten for the moment.

Then something happened that upset the whole balance of the relationship. When Jeffrey was old enough for day care, Lauren went back to school and got an MBA—"with Philip's full support," she emphasized.

Lauren was amazed at how well she did in graduate school. She'd never thought of herself as particularly intelligent, and so it came as a real surprise to discover that she was able to grasp economics with so little trouble and that she had a real flair for analysis. After completing her degree, she landed a job in a management consulting firm. There, her unused energy, charm, and ability to analyze complex management structures propelled her to a full partnership in less than five years.

If the first crack in the harmonious structure of the marriage occurred when Philip started putting his career first and Lauren second, the real rupture came when her success made her no longer dependent on him. Now, she said, she was making more than Philip. She shot him a look.

After Lauren started working and the balance of the relationship shifted, their arguments took on a different quality. Philip felt the threat of her independence much more powerfully than her previous complaints of neglect. And now when Philip started in on her, instead of backing off, Lauren snapped back at him. That's when the hitting started.

As Lauren told her side of the story, her face hardened in rage and pain. She was, understandably, furious. When she first mentioned the hitting, Philip looked away, ashamed. But as she went on and on, I could see him getting angrier and angrier. Lauren said that she was afraid: "I don't know if I can stay in this marriage." She glanced at Philip, then dropped her eyes.

I said to them, "I'm sorry, but I don't work with primitive people." Philip looked down. Lauren looked hurt.

I let that sink in for a minute. "Therapy is a privilege. People who hit people are too primitive to take advantage of it. They don't have enough self-control."

My words were hard. In this volatile situation I didn't want to be understanding; I wanted to be in control.

Lauren looked at her husband. She looked at a stone wall.

"I will, however, offer you a consultation on one condition. I'll see you for six sessions. At the end of that time, I'll give you my recommendation as to whether you should separate or seek therapy to stay together. But I must have your absolute assurance that there will be no hitting during this period."

Grateful for this chance to prove himself, Philip said, "Don't worry, it will be all right."

"It's not *it* I'm worried about," I said bluntly. "It's you. If you even start to lose your temper, leave the room. Go for a walk, go in the kitchen and break a dish. But cool down. And Lauren, if there is any hitting, if you even think there might be, I want you to call me at once. Promise."

"I will," she said.

I ended the session with a question. I told them that they seemed to have become inflexible with each other. Their success in other areas of their lives indicated that there had to be more to them. Why had they become so intolerant and unforgiving with each other? "Maybe you can begin to think about what you two do to trigger this reactive emotionality in each other."

They left, and I sat alone in my office. In agreeing to see Lauren and Philip together, I knew I was taking a risk, and I was aware of the alternatives. I was taking the chance of seeing them together because I believe that this is the best way to get at the sequence of events that triggers violence. But I also knew that I had to structure the sessions carefully and take a directive stance. With violent couples I remain distant, controlling the nature of the communication even while we explore patterns of interaction.

I knew that I would have to stop the spiraling escalation of emotions. With most families I encourage dialogue between family members right from the beginning, as a way of explor-ing how people talk together and of exposing the structure of their relationships. In violent families, however, I discourage interaction. I tell couples that until they can have a dialogue with more light than heat, they should take turns, each talk-ing to me without interruption. I do everything I can to slow them down and make them think. I encourage them to be specific, using concrete details as an antidote to emotionality.

This isn't my natural way of working. It's something I learned from Murray Bowen twenty years ago. "Don't tell me how you feel," he said to a violent couple. "Tell me what you think."

To my considerable surprise, Philip and Lauren were very late for the second session. He walked in alone twenty-five minutes late. While we waited for Lauren, I asked Philip to explain why they weren't together.

"We were waiting for the subway, and she suddenly an-nounced that she wasn't going to ride on the subway with me. She was going to take a cab. She's always doing things like that. Maybe she decided not to come, or maybe she had trouble finding a cab."

Three minutes later Lauren arrived, red faced and out of breath. She gave Philip a withering look, and he glared back. Before their anger erupted in the usual barrage of recrimina-tions, I said, "Please tell me exactly what happened this morn-ing, from the time you got up. I want a very detailed account, from each of you, one at a time." This couple operated at two speeds: idle and out of control.

Philip spoke first. "I got up at five, as I always do, so that I could do my exercises and my meditation. I knew Lauren wouldn't get up until about six-thirty, as usual, and that I'd have plenty of time to dress and get ready, so I thought I had time to finish the book I was reading—Henri Bergson's *Intro-duction to Metaphysics*. Do you know it? It's the one where he talks about two different ways of knowing, the symbolic way of science and—"

"Oh, Christ, Philip, get on with it," Lauren cut in. "No-body's interested in your—"

"Can't you keep your mouth shut for two minutes?" Philip was livid.

I stood up and said, "Please, slow down." I asked Philip to move his chair away from Lauren, closer to me, so that I could hear each of their versions without interruption.

After Philip had done his exercises and meditation, while he was reading his Bergson, Lauren got up and made breakfast for Jeffrey. She got him out of bed, dressed, and into the kitchen, where she ate with him and got him off to school. She showered and dressed, but when she was ready to go she found that Philip was still reading "his stupid book."

She said "I'm ready, let's go," and he said, "I just need to put my jacket on." But when he was dressed, she discovered that he still had to pack his briefcase. Lauren said "Why don't you pack everything the night before instead of always making us late? If you would just think ahead five minutes, instead of leaving everything to the last minute—" "Oh, just shut up," he told her. "Go hail a cab; I'll be right there." She went, but by this time she was seething. Down on the street Lauren couldn't find a cab. When Philip arrived they waited a few more minutes, but still no cabs. Then he said, "It's getting late, let's take the subway." They walked to the train, but as they entered the station, Lauren said, "I can't ride that thing. My shoulder aches. I'm going to find a cab." And she left.

These people lacked both the capacity to see the other's perspective and the sympathy that allows tolerance of differences, so that every issue became a struggle for the survival of self. Every conflict became a conflagration, while they remained ignorant of the ways they provoked each other.

Philip held Lauren entirely responsible for their being late. Even though he had gotten up an hour and a half before his wife, he still expected her to take charge of getting Jeffrey off to school and making sure that they got to their appointment on time. They were like the couples Catherine Bateson describes, in which the wife is expected to respond to and manage multiple events in the family, while the husband remains focused on what for him was the "main event." I knew I would be challenging this structure.

One reason people react with alarm to applying a systems point of view to a case where a man beats his wife is that such a viewpoint may be seen as denying the awful wrongness of physical violence and overlooking the need for strong steps to stop it. Cases in which a man batters a woman to bend her to his will generally do require restraint by separation and, often, intervention by the police and judiciary; the priority is to protect the victim. But there are couples, like Philip and Lauren, who want to stay together and who are locked in a cycle of mutual provocation that leads to violence.

In this case my first priority would be to control Philip's attacks. But I would also challenge Lauren's sense of helplessness with him. For some reason she seemed to think of herself as dependent and incapable. I would focus on her competence, supporting her ability to stand up for herself until she accepted it.

By the third session I felt comfortable with Lauren and Philip, and I sensed that they trusted me. By staying with them in the face of their snarling and snapping in the two previous sessions, and remaining respectful of them, I'd given them hope. But I decided that they still weren't ready to talk together without slipping into attack and defense. Somehow the rational maturity they demonstrated as individuals got lost when they interacted as a couple.

I decided therefore to continue with the same format, asking each one consecutively to talk with me. When I do that, I always accept each person's perception of what the other does as correct, but I explain that I want them to learn to see their own behavior. "You're so focused on responding that you're blind to yourself," I explain. "I want you to look at your contribution."

I started with Lauren because something seemed to be happening with her. She was more involved, interested in the process, and she seemed more ready to look at her role in the couple's troubles. Besides, I wanted to keep Philip uncertain of my affiliation with him, as a way of keeping him alert and in control of himself.

"Lauren, I'm really interested in what you do to diminish each other. The way you make each other less than what you are. But I want to talk to you one at a time, until you can talk to each other without attacking." I kept my tone formal, almost pedagogical, as part of my message that there were rational solutions to their emotional quandaries.

"Well, I think he doesn't like what I do—"

"No, no," I said. "That's for him to say. Let him make his own complaints. What does he do that bothers you?"

"Oh, you want me to tell you what *he* does to me?"

"Yes."

"Well, he makes me just furious sometimes, the way he treats me."

"What does he do?"

"Everything centers on him. He expects me to listen to every little thing that goes on at the hospital, but he never asks me about my work. If I try to tell him something, he may listen for a minute, but that's all I get. I think he's jealous of the people I spend time with. He just can't stand it that I might have a life of my own."

"What do you want me to do?" Philip began.

"Philip, please," I said.

Lauren glared at him.

"Go on, Lauren," I said. "How does this jealousy make you feel? How do you two so quickly end in a rage?"

"I don't know. I just know he makes me crazy," Lauren said, packing into that one sentence a whole complex set of emotions that were unavailable to her because she condensed her hurt and longing and frustration into explosive outbursts. Philip never heard the hurt or the longing; all he knew was her anger.

I tried to explore with her what she did when Philip was unfair—when he was mean, when he was annoying, when he was cold, when he was jealous—in order to move her away from quixotic eruptions of anger and avoidance. Lauren needed a clearer idea of the sequence of events that took place between her and Philip—and a clearer idea of her own power.

When I asked her how she reacted when she felt attacked, she said, "I try to avoid him. I answer abruptly. I go into my shell." All these responses were the response of a frightened person, someone avoiding attack. Lauren couldn't see the alternatives available to her.

"Do you ever daydream about killing him?" I asked.

"Certainly not!" She was shocked.

"Haven't you ever thought of pushing him out the window or poisoning his coffee?"

Lauren flushed and shook her head and said, "Oh, no, nothing like that."

She didn't say anything, and I didn't say anything. And then, looking embarrassed, she said, "Sometimes I have these dreams. He's been killed—run over by a car, or a sudden heart attack—and I wake up terrified. But it's never anything *I've* done. It just happens."

I laughed and asked her who she thought dreamed up her dreams. She looked thoughtful, and I turned to Philip.

"Tell me about some small incident that illustrates the conflicts between the two of you. A very small incident."

"Well, one thing comes to mind, but it was kind of silly."

"Okay. Let's talk about that."

"Well, as I said, it was kind of stupid. I asked the cleaning lady to throw out some flowers that were starting to wilt. Lauren hit the ceiling. She said I was talking down to the woman. I just asked her to throw out some flowers, for Pete's sake! I can't do anything!" He seemed on the verge of tears. Here was the other side of Lauren's helplessness and fear: Philip's self-pity.

"Regardless of what hoops I jump through to please her, nothing I ever do is right."

"Was your mother a queen?" I asked.

Philip looked startled. Then he said evenly, "A queen? She was Catherine the Great. Everybody did what she wanted. Us kids, even my father. Especially my father."

"That's fascinating," I said.

"Lauren," I said, "would you mind taking off your shoes and standing up on that chair?"

She gave me a funny look, but no argument. Then she bent down and slipped off her stylish pumps and stepped up gracefully.

"Tell me about your mother, Philip." He looked up at his wife, standing on the chair, and then he looked at me. He got the point.

Catherine Lockwood was a tall, formidable woman. An elementary school principal. "She looked it, too. Absolute type casting. Heavyset, long hair braided and coiled, unsmiling. She kept everything in order, in school and at home."

"Sounds grim," I said.

"Well, she was a good mother. She was always concerned, always ready to help. I owe her a lot." Philip glanced up at Lauren, smiling a little uncomfortably. Perched on a throne she didn't know she'd inherited, Lauren smiled back, a little awkwardly, but she made no attempt to get down.

When I said that it was time to stop, Philip looked up and said, "I'm sorry," as though in talking about himself and his memories he'd been guilty of a forbidden act of self-indulgence.

I knew he could talk a long time about his past. But the past was something I wanted to dip into only long enough to help him realize that—brought up as he was to see requests as royal commands—he was overreacting to his wife's needs.

"You know, I'm absolutely fascinated by the pair of you!" I said, rising to help Lauren down. "For a couple of intelligent people, you're playing the damndest absurd drama I ever saw."

At this point I felt a sense of understanding with Lauren. She seemed able to examine her own motives and reactions and ready to see new possibilities for relating to Philip. I didn't have the same sense of connection with Philip, but I felt that he and I were working toward it.

I helped them gather their coats and briefcases, and Lauren thanked me with a smile. "What would we do without you?"

I smiled back, accepting her reliance on me as a step in the direction of coming to rely on herself. Perhaps her confidence in me would make her feel safe enough to explore new possibilities.

Five minutes after the next session was due to start, the phone rang. It was Lauren. "Can you tell me your exact address?" she asked sheepishly. I was surprised but I told her, and she said she was one block away and would be here in two minutes. But it was Philip who arrived first, apparently unconcerned about being late. "Where's Lauren?" he asked.

"She just called. She'll be here any minute."

Quite a few minutes later I heard Lauren open the outer door, but it was a few minutes more before she walked into the office, still a little out of breath, but her makeup perfect and every hair in place.

"I'm sorry I'm late," she said. "I was only a block away when I called, but then somehow I walked west instead of east. It's so hard to find the numbers on these buildings. Before that I took the wrong subway. It wasn't until I got to Fifty-ninth Street that I realized it was going uptown instead of downtown. I'm sorry."

Was Lauren late because she didn't really want to come? Was getting lost just an ordinary human mistake or was it a sign that she wasn't used to relying on herself? All these things might be true, but I decided to focus on that part of the truth that related to Lauren's underutilized competence.

"Lauren, you amaze me," I said. "Clearly you are a bright and capable woman. No one gets to be a partner in a consulting firm without talent and ability. Yet in many ways you present yourself as helpless. You get lost coming to the office. You put up with your husband's hitting you. Don't misunderstand me. I'm not excusing him. But Lauren, how can you be so competent and see yourself as so helpless?"

"Well, I suppose I grew up that way." She sat down, apparently not minding my calling her helpless. As she went on, her vowels traveled south. "Where I grew up, in Charleston, girls weren't expected to be independent. My Daddy always told me how pretty I was. I didn't do real well in school, but I was popular, and I guess he thought that was enough. When I got to be homecoming queen that seemed like all the success anyone could want. It was the same at Clemson. I kind of majored in parties." She smiled, as though not doing well in school was something to be proud of, a feminine accomplishment.

I don't take histories at the beginning of therapy because the historical facts change, depending on context and on trust of the therapist. I let the facts emerge later, organically related to what's happening in therapy. Lauren's historical exploration at this point was related to how she learned to be helpless.

Lauren had grown up petted and pampered by a doting father who loved her but didn't take her seriously. Later she learned to depend on the status that great beauty confers. Now, although she was still beautiful, she had ceased to rely on her looks or on her role as Dr. Lockwood's wife. She'd become an independent woman. But old habits die hard, and in many ways she still thought of herself as defined by her femininity and good looks. Homecoming queens don't need to know which subway to take, or how to defend themselves against a man's fists.

As Lauren talked about her well-bred Southern upbringing, I couldn't help thinking about Blanche DuBois's: "I have always depended on the kindness of strangers." She seemed to take a strange, stubborn pride in being helpless. Like many women, Lauren paid a lot for this curious accomplishment.

Philip had been very silent. It occurred to me that I had just handed him some ammunition in his battle with Lauren, so I moved to involve him. Childhood may have set the stage for Lauren's dependency, but the roles in this marriage were mutually determined.

"Philip, do you like a woman who is a little bit helpless?" I asked. At that moment the radiator began to clank, and in jest I said, "Lauren, please make it stop doing that."

Lauren smiled, indulging my little joke. Just at that moment the noise stopped, and I said, "Thank you, Lauren," with a straight face.

"Why do you give me that power?" she asked in all seriousness.

We grow up, but in some ways we never do. Here, perhaps in response to the tension generated by their conflict, I had slipped back sixty years to childhood to make a silly joke. And then Lauren, perhaps in response to her own anxieties about the situation, had shed thirty years to become a credulous girl, willing to believe, or pretend to believe, that I was serious and that my remark must have some unfathomable meaning. Until she began to feel whole and worthwhile, she would continue to long for someone to look up to, someone to rely on.

"I don't mind when she asks me questions," Philip went on as if there had been no interruption. "At least then we're connected." His face darkened. "What I do mind is that when she doesn't want something, she ignores me. She pays more attention to her friends than she does to me."

I remembered Freud's famous remark that a patient was cured when the neurotic symptoms lifted and the person returned to the normal miseries of everyday life. Now Philip's

complaint sounded more like the normal miseries of an unhappy couple than the pathological extreme of violence.

"Talk with each other about that," I said. "I want to see
how you two talk together."

Now that Philip and Lauren had explained their relationship to me, I wanted to see them demonstrate it by how they
communicated. I'd waited this long because they were so volatile and reactive. Now, however, they seemed less defensive,
and perhaps they could begin to listen to each other.

Lauren's complaint was that Philip didn't take her seriously. His was that she didn't pay him enough attention. As
they talked I could see why.

"Well, let's see," Philip began. "You remember that article
in the *Times* magazine we were talking about the other day?"

"*You* were talking," she said. Lauren made this crack
without bitterness, and Philip, who either didn't notice or
chose to ignore it, went on. He talked about the article, and
how he'd tried to explain it to her, and how she never gets
involved in these discussions. As far as he was concerned, it
was her fault, some combination of reticence and deliberate
withholding. "There's an unwillingness on her part to enter
into dialogue," was his ponderous way of putting it.

Lauren answered in monosyllables. It was hard to tell
whether she disagreed with Philip or didn't fully understand
him or was simply bored. Her silence made him try harder to
get through to her, until their "conversation" took on a familiar form: He talked, she listened. The less she said, the more
pedantic and verbose he became. And the wordier he became,
the more silent and sullen she grew. In less than five minutes,
he'd become the kind of long-winded teacher who doesn't understand why his students don't participate in the discussion.

As Lauren sat there, trapped by Philip's verbosity and her
own silence, both of them grew increasingly impatient. I could
see the seeds of a scene to come. After a while she'd say something nasty. He'd retaliate, and pretty soon they'd end up in
the kind of spiteful finger-pointing that would escalate into a
fight. Not wanting them to get anywhere near that point, I
interrupted.

"Stop!" I said, and they both looked up, startled. "There's
no flexibility in this dialogue. You're both still too invested in
being right to listen to the other's perspective, or to change."

I told them that we weren't getting anywhere and ushered them brusquely out of the office.

I ended abruptly because I wanted to force them to recognize the signals of a loss of control. The possibility of further violence—even one more episode could destroy this marriage—made it imperative that each of them become alert to their intentions and aware of how they expressed them. Spontaneity, here, was dangerous. There are times in any relationship where distance and caution are necessary. For the Lockwoods, this was surely one of them.

The following week, when Lauren arrived on time but alone, I started with her alone. It gave me a chance to hear her individual perspective. But, because I didn't want my understanding to come at the expense of helping the couple learn to understand each other, I planned to repeat what was said when Philip arrived.

Lauren was in an upbeat and hopeful mood. As usual she was dressed for work the way some women would dress for dinner.

She said that things had been status quo, though communication had been better. Philip, she said, has been allowing her to talk—he's even listening. "It's been nice. In fact, we spent the whole weekend without any major blowups."

At that point Philip walked in, and I said that I was going to take a minute to tell him what Lauren had said. I told him that she said communication was better. He was allowing her to talk, and he was listening, and it was nice. Philip looked relieved, as if he'd just been told that he passed a test.

"But," Lauren put in, "I also said that things were status quo."

Philip looked wounded. He hadn't passed after all.

I jumped in before he could say anything. "Lauren, what happened just now?"

"Nothing. I just wanted Philip to know exactly what I said."

"Lauren, did you feel that I was siding with Philip? Or betraying your meaning? Are you afraid that if I rephrase what you say, Philip or I will use it against you? Why can't you trust me?"

This was a reach, but I felt that Lauren might be able to see her experiences with her husband from a different perspective if she could see herself also being anxious and mistrustful with me. "I won't hurt you, Lauren. I'm on your side. I respect you, and I support you. How is it that you can't trust me? Does the world seem that dangerous to you?"

She was silent for a moment. "Well, I suppose that I grew up—"

"Don't tell me about your childhood. Childhood ends." I didn't want to hear about the past, where she learned helplessness; I wanted to hear about her career, where she unlearned it. "Tell me about your work. Your colleagues. What if I asked your partners to describe you? What would they say?" Surely she must think of herself as competent and powerful at work.

"Well, I'm a people person. I don't really know that much about management. Most of my success comes from supporting other people. I know how to get along, to flatter people, how to come out of a deal with everybody feeling like he's gotten something. You get along by going alone, and—"

I stood up in mock despair. "Lauren! Lauren, Lauren. How can I wake you up?" I went over and knocked on her forehead. "Lauren, please wake up! You don't have to deny your competence."

She looked at me, dismayed. Minimizing herself was something Lauren did so automatically that she had ceased to be aware of it.

Philip laughed out loud. I turned to him. "What about you, Philip? How was the week from your point of view?"

"Well, I believe the matrix of our communication is changing. I've been trying to accept Lauren's unavailability, her disengagement, as having to do with her, not necessarily as a negative response to my input." While I was still trying to digest that, Philip went on, saying, with his characteristic cloud of words, that he was learning to live with Lauren's silence. Lauren leaned forward, listening intently.

On and on he went, making an important point—that he was beginning to feel that the only way for them to live together was if he became resigned to Lauren's disinterest and distance—but spinning it out in so many words, circling around his feelings, that the point, and any real chance for

Lauren to respond, was drowned in words. She sat, meanwhile, listening with apparent interest, until I broke in.

"Lauren, at what point did you stop listening to Philip?"

Taken aback, she said, "What do you mean? I was listening."

"I don't think so. I didn't see the exact moment, but at
some point you stopped listening. And so instead of a dialogue
there was a monologue. But this isn't just something he does.
It's something that you—both of you—do together."

Philip stiffened slightly. Hearing himself accused of being
pedantic was unpleasant but not, after all, unfamiliar. Lauren
said, "Well, I guess I do tune him out sometimes. I know he
needs to say what's on his mind. And I feel I owe it to him to
listen. But I get so tired of his never offering to listen to me.
Damn it!" Suddenly there were tears in her eyes. "It's always
your lousy day. What about my day? Why can't you give me
even a fraction of the attention—" And suddenly she stopped
herself, as though by complaining she had somehow broken
the rules.

Philip was astounded. Lauren's anger, stored up from long
hours of one-sided conversation, seemed so extreme, so unfair
to him. If she had something to say, why didn't she say it?
Philip didn't lecture Lauren into silence, boredom, and finally
fury because he sought to dominate. He'd been brought up to
achieve and be interesting. She'd been brought up to attend
and be interested. The two of them brought these roles into
the marriage so naturally that neither had ever given it a
thought. Hard as it was for either of them to change, it was
twice as hard in the relationship—where mutual habits were
reinforced by mutual expectations.

"You both want something you're not getting," I pointed
out. "Attention. Genuine attention. That's not too much to ask
of a marriage.

"Now I'm going to give you some homework," I said. "I
would like each of you to find some other way of getting what
you want from each other. Philip, your attempt to reach Lauren with words is pushing her away. Maybe words aren't the
answer."

Philip made a helpless gesture. "What do you suggest?"

"I don't know," I said. "This is one of those things everybody has to do in his own way. But I do know that you—both
of you—are more complex than you know."

"And Lauren, you need to find words to express your point of view—and to interrupt Philip when he's giving one of his monologues." Lauren glanced at Philip.

"I've suggested to Philip that he make an effort to stop dominating conversation between the two of you, but I doubt that he can change without your help."

Lauren smiled. "You don't think we can learn to do that in one week, do you?"

"I'm not asking you to *learn* anything. I'm only asking you to start doing something you're perfectly capable of doing."

"Well," Lauren said, "maybe it would be a good idea not to meet for a couple of weeks. That would give us a chance to practice."

I took this as a good sign. Most people think that therapy is something that happens in a therapist's office. Maybe therapy does, but change takes place at home. I agreed to see them again in two weeks.

Lauren arrived on time, without Philip. I gave her a questioning look, and she said calmly that Philip should be there in a few minutes. "He's never ready on time. But I decided that I didn't want to argue with him, and I didn't want to be late. So I told him I was leaving, and he should come when he was ready."

Lauren said this without any of the usual antagonism. She'd left on time, before Philip, not to provoke or antagonize him, but simply because it was time to go. It was a small declaration of independence.

"Well," she began as she sat down, "I've been working on your suggestion. I've been trying to be more honest with myself, accepting my competence, and my right to make demands."

Actually, that wasn't what I'd said. The task I'd given them was simple and concrete. But Lauren had gone beyond the specifics of my suggestion to work on the essential imbalance in the relationship. I nodded. It sounded good.

"I'm trying not to put up with his brutality. I'll give you an example. Last Sunday I was sitting in the living room, relaxing for a minute with the *Times* in my lap. Philip came in and grabbed "The Week in Review." I said, 'Hey, I was just about to read that. You can have it when I'm done.' He looked surprised, but he gave it right back. I felt I'd done the right thing."

"Of course you did the right thing," I said. "But I'm surprised to hear you use the word *brutality* to describe Philip's taking the paper away from you."

"It all feels the same to me. Grabbing the newspaper, or going on and on forever, or slapping me—it's all part of the same thing. But I guess I don't have to put up with it. Any of it."

I thought that it wasn't the same thing—that in time she would have to make distinctions. But for the moment her progress seemed wonderful. So the thought remained silent.

"I've been working on the second task you gave me, too. You said I should start participating more in conversations with Philip. You said he needs me to be involved, and I have been. He's always reading highbrow stuff. I never used to know what he was talking about. But lately I've been reading what he reads, so I have some idea what he's talking about. Some of it's actually interesting."

At that moment Philip walked in. "Are you always late, Philip?" I asked. "Or is it only here?"

He looked offended. "Maybe the truth is I didn't feel like coming today. Last time we were here you suggested that Lauren start speaking up more. What about me? It seems to me that you always pay more attention to her. What am I supposed to do?"

If at that moment Philip sounded like a rivalrous sibling, perhaps it was understandable. In this couple, who got so little appreciation from each other, the partners were understandably jealous of any attention paid by anyone else. What Philip didn't seem to understand was that if Lauren started speaking up more, saying what was on her mind rather than just sitting there in bored silence when he talked, he'd gain a partner.

And then Philip got to what was really weighing on his mind. "Besides, I was afraid to hear what you would say today about us staying together or not. Lauren hasn't said a word. I have no idea how she feels."

Lauren cast me an urgent look, but I said nothing. For fifteen minutes she'd talked with me about how hard she was working to make her relationship with Philip better. What was amazing was that she had conveyed none of this commitment to Philip, and that he could be in such doubt about what was so clear: that Lauren was fighting hard to preserve the marriage.

"I know she's been making efforts to become more informed. I appreciate that. And she's stood up to me a couple of times—showed me she thought I was being overbearing, when I didn't mean to be. And I think that's good. But the big question, our staying together . . . "

Characteristically, Philip began to repeat his points. Lauren frowned, shook her head, gave me a helpless look.

"Lauren, for heaven's sake," I interjected. "You clearly have something to say. Why don't you say it?"

"Well, yes, I do. I have a lot of feelings about what he's saying. But he keeps talking. He'd just get mad if I interrupted him."

"I've told you a million times," Philip said peevishly, "if you have something to say, say it!"

"You could try asking me what I think. Just once in a while. Give me a chance to speak without having to interrupt you. As though you were interested in what I have to say."

Philip started to retort, but he caught himself. "But I *am* interested."

"Excellent, Philip. You too, Lauren. Go on talking."

They did, for the rest of the session. He was very clear about the problems her silence caused. She was very clear about his talkativeness. There were complaints. But somehow they got past blaming and accusations and down to the place where the deep hurt resided. The complaints and the hurts were confined to words, and they were words that left room to listen to the other's point of view.

"This is really promising," I said. They turned to me. I think we all sensed it was time for the verdict.

"I promised you my opinion," I said. "I'm not going to try to tell you whether to stay married or not—that's up to you. What I can tell you is that the violence in your marriage is predictable, and if you want to, you can change that pattern. As a matter of fact, you've already begun to change. You both want the same thing from each other—a little understanding and a little respect. You haven't been getting it, and that's sad. But Philip, hitting your wife is not sad. It's unconscionable."

He looked down. Lauren looked away. "It must not continue. But I don't think it will. You know it's wrong, and you know you can control yourself. What's more, and maybe more important, I don't think Lauren will tolerate it any more." Lauren's eyes filled with tears. So did Philip's.

"You're not dangerous people. You're destructive. I don't think there will be any danger if you decide you want to stay together. But I do think you may continue to be unhappy. That, I don't know."

"Well, I think we both want to change that," said Philip. "Don't we, Lauren?"

"Won't you help us?" she asked.

That was two years ago. There have been no further incidents of violence. I continued to see them for several months, and, off and on, their son Jeffrey as well. Philip and Lauren's marriage is never going to be the match made in heaven they once hoped for in the unreason of love. But they did return to the "normal miseries of everyday life." To say that they still clashed in many ways, and in many ways disappointed each other, is to say no more than that they were married, and for a long time.

When Philip and Lauren first came to therapy they both felt controlled and helpless, victims of each other's stubborn refusal to cooperate. As far as they were concerned, they had no choice in their ritual battles but were only submitting to a fate that the other forced on them. It was their acceptance of themselves not simply as victims but as two people who had survived and had the power to make choices that finally liberated them. The explosive quarrels that once ended in violence have changed to occasional arguments that they both know how to start and stop.

6

The Unspoken Contract

Complementarity enables spouses to divide functions, to support and enrich each other. When one has the flu and feels lousy, the other takes over. One's leniency is balanced by the other's strictness. Complementary patterns, such as pursuer-distancer, active-passive, dominant-submissive, exist in most couples. They begin to cause problems when they are exaggerated or fail to shift to accommodate to changing circumstances.

When two people in love decide to share their days and nights and futures, they must go through a long period of adjustment before they complete the transition from courtship to a functional marriage. Marriage isn't something you enter, like the state of Arizona; it's something you create. And, sometimes, it's something you re-create.

———◆———

Sarah and Sam fell sentimentally in love in their twenties; and they were still in love when I met them fifty years later. It was an old-fashioned arrangement: Sam was the bread-winner; Sarah was the dependent housewife. Her vulnerability enabled him to feel protective. Their roles fit together like two interlocking pieces of a puzzle that held each other in place.

For fifty years Sam and Sarah had made the large and small compromises that cement a couple into a unit. What begins as mutual support ends with two partial selves holding each other together. Such fixed complementarity is fine in an unchanging world, but as we all know, circumstances change and so must we.

When Sam retired and his energy began to falter, the balance of his relationship with Sarah was upset. Like many people who work all their lives, he had let his job structure his time. Without the imperative of work, his days became shapeless and vacant, and lacking friends and hobbies, Sam looked to Sarah to fill the void. Sarah worked part-time and had her customary routine, so she found Sam's need for more of her space intrusive. For the first time their smooth fit was disrupted. Sam experienced these changes in the rhythm of life as an erosion of strength. He slowed down and gradually became depressed. Both Sarah and Sam were troubled by these developments, and so they sought help from Monica, a family therapist who had helped Sam's sister cope with widowhood.

Monica was a psychologist in her early thirties who juggled an active professional life with a husband and two small children. She saw Sarah and Sam's relationship as flawed because there was no independence, no autonomy, no fun. To Monica, the resignation of the old was defeatist. Sam and Sarah responded to Monica's challenge of their ways as old people often do to the well-meaning young. They didn't argue; they just walked more slowly.

Monica brought tapes of her sessions with Sarah and Sam to me for advice on how to get the couple moving. As I viewed the tapes, I was intrigued by the threesome—Monica, Sarah, and Sam—and their response to a well-known dilemma: retirement and its associated depression. There was Sam, the fish out of water, filled with worry and regret. There was Sarah, the classic retiree's wife, whose motto might be: "I married him for better or worse, but not for lunch." There was the pair of them, dealing with their experience of aging and decay, the daily small encounters with death. And there was Monica, an excellent therapist, but one whose own image of what a marriage should be tempted her to try to reconstruct a relationship that only needed a little readjustment. All very familiar. But this couple was unusual. Their clothes were up-to-date, but they seemed to be of another era. Something about what they said and how they said it conveyed an unquestioned acceptance of the roles on which their relationship had been founded fifty years ago. Monica, equally a product of her time, was working with people who could have been her grandparents.

Monica suggested that I see the couple for a consultation, and I agreed.

As the session opened I sat behind the one-way mirror and watched while Monica greeted the couple and asked them about their week. It's instructive to observe a therapist at work. The consulting therapist isn't like a consulting physician who can have a direct impact on a case by changing the medicine. In family therapy, the therapist, in this case Monica, is the medicine.

Through the mirror I could see Sam and Sarah sitting next to each other on a small sofa facing Monica. It was our agreement that I would watch for a few minutes and then enter with my observations. After all, it wasn't just the couple who were stuck, it was Monica-working-with-the-couple.

Sarah had forgotten the homework assignment. "So I said to Sam on the way over, we're two old fogies who forgot their homework." She had a nice laugh.

"Well, whatever it was—I'm being fair to you, Monica—it was a nice week." Sam's voice was a husky whisper. He smiled at Monica, and then he smiled at his wife. Sarah didn't look seventy. Her hair was skillfully dyed, and she hadn't lost her figure. She could have been fifty-five.

"You were going to find out what Sam likes to do," Monica reminded Sarah.

Monica was addressing Sam's depression by challenging Sarah's passive response to it. Though logical enough, this challenge would turn out to be an attack on a contract of fifty years' standing.

"How would he like to spend time together, now that he's retired?"

Retired was not Sam's favorite word. "I worked all my life," he said. "Then all of a sudden I was retired. I don't really know what retirement means. I didn't want any part of it. I don't really enjoy too many things." He dragged his words out the way a sick man gets out of bed. "Things that I do enjoy, she, Sarah, my wife, doesn't enjoy with me. This morning I put the radio on. I *love* QXR. I love semiclassical music. To her it's just noise. It bothers her." When Sam complained there was more energy in his voice.

"I wonder why it bothers me so much," Sarah said, as though her preferences were some special mystery. Sarah complained cheerfully and spoke with lively gestures.

Monica reminded them again that the task was for Sarah to find out what Sam likes to do. She was eager for change and a little impatient with the foibles of these two old people.

"I like to go for walks," Sam offered, "listen to music, or go to certain museums of interest." He hesitated, then gave up. "I guess I don't like too much. I am, internally, a quiet person."

"He wouldn't care if we never did anything." Sarah said this without malice, and Sam took it without anger.

"Is there something so terribly wrong with not wanting so much?" Sam asked Monica. "With only wanting for her to be well, to enjoy whatever she can? As long as we can't both enjoy the same things, then let her enjoy herself." Sam's voice was thick with tenderness, the romantic husband serenading yesterday's bride.

Monica was skeptical. "I guess there's nothing wrong—as long as that's what you really want."

Is there really something wrong with wanting my wife to enjoy herself? says the man to the expert. It was touching. But we live in a world in which a person who says "I am a giver" is suspect. Monica was just doing her job, probing Sam's professed unselfishness for signs of resentment.

Behind the mirror, I was chafing. An old fogy myself, I saw

Sam and Sarah as a normal couple whose minor differences were being turned into major problems. I thought of my in-laws and their trips to Florida. They spent three months every year in that alien climate, she because *he liked it so much,* he because *she loved it.* I thought of Pat and me and all the stress we felt when we retired. We weren't used to being together all day, and for a while we were anxious for some individual space.

In their seventies Sam and Sarah were discovering their differences. Now that he was retired and the cushion of separate routines was gone, minor differences began to grate on them. Sympathy, they were finding out, is a little easier to sustain at a distance.

Sarah complained about Sam not wanting to go places and do things. He worried too much about money. "With him, it's always 'how much is it going to cost?'" Monica nodded encouragement. "We go to a restaurant, I have to be aware of how much it's going to cost."

"But we go," Sam protested.

"I'm not saying that. But I'm always—like, *This is going to cost money.* It takes away from the pleasure of enjoying it."

"All those years I worked so hard," Sam said with feeling, "and the money came in so slow. Now it's going out so fast."

Sam's anxiety wasn't hard to understand. When you get old you worry about diminishing resources. Money, energy, enthusiasm—even possibility itself begins to run out. Driving Sam through all those years of hard work was a fear of privation. Now, having exhausted himself trying to make life good for his family, he wanted to feel secure. Sarah, too, had worked hard. Now she wanted to enjoy life.

Most of us have a certain amount of inner conflict about choosing between Now and Later. Sarah and Sam played out this conflict between them. The more she opted for Now, the more he felt pushed to protect Later.

Watching from behind the mirror, I thought that Sam and Sarah were simply in the throes of transition. I was concerned that Monica, defined as the expert in this situation, would see maladjustment where I saw a process of readjustment.

So, ten minutes into the session, I went into the consulting room. Up close Sarah and Sam seemed more vivid, and more vulnerable. Her large, tinted glasses made her face seem small, and I could see the girl she had been. His skin was smooth and dark. The deep wrinkles of his years must all be inside.

I felt a tenderness for them, as I would for an aunt and an uncle. We shared both culture and old age, so I felt free to greet them with a challenge.

"You are a lovely couple. It's obvious that you care for each other. You have been complaining for fifty years, and you'll probably keep complaining for another twenty years. So why do you need a therapist? What do you want from her? What do you want from life? You seem like perfectly nice people. You could be my neighbors. Why should you change?"

I meant no irony. I felt only tenderness for these two, and I hoped they could learn to accept each other a little more.

Sarah was quick to answer. "Life can always be improved upon."

"Means you want to change him?"

"Oh, I know I can't change him, and he can't change me. I'm trying to accept things that bother me about my husband. I try."

"It's difficult to accept him?" I said. "Who would you prefer to be married to, Gregory Peck?"

"Gregory Peck!" She laughed, a little confused. Which end of the deck was this strange mean dealing from?

I wondered myself. Why had I said that? These people touched something in me, but they also had a certain stilted quality that triggered me to tease them, to be provocative. She was trying to change him while denying that she was doing so. He was an uneducated man who felt the need to use big words, like a bullfrog swallowing air to make himself formidable. I wanted to help him stop puffing himself up—but not by deflating him.

"What would you like to change?" I asked Sarah.

"Some of his habits."

"Sam, come sit in front of her so she can look at you and see what she needs to change." He got up and sat down patiently, a man used to cooperating.

"A lot of things he does were not annoying to me when I met him. Maybe it wasn't there, or maybe I didn't see it when we were younger."

I handed Sarah a silver ballpoint pen. "This is a magic wand. I just want you to have it." She took it without blinking

an eye. Sam was okay, but she was ready to make "a few
slight improvements."

"I would like him to speak well."

"To speak well—how do you mean? Poetically? Metaphor-
ically? Do you want him to speak Hebrew? Yiddish?"

"English!" she laughed again, not minding my irony. She
was enjoying this. "I would like him to be more articulate,
because I myself am not articulate."

Sarah said openly what most people only hint at or keep to
themselves. That's what was so special about this couple: They
made no pretense about their feelings.

Then Sarah went deep into her past and drew out the
memory of a young girl's total, trusting love. "When we were
first going together I thought he was the smartest, nicest,
most wonderful person in the world—that I could lean upon
and he would make all the decisions."

"And it worked like that?"

"More or less, yes. When we were younger. I depended on
him like I depended on my mother."

"That much?"

"Oh, yes. He was like a rock, a tree that I could lean on and
depend on. A very wonderful person, very concerned about
me, loved me very much, and was there when I needed him.
And I still feel that way."

"That's lovely." I thought for a moment of Jorge Luis Bor-
ges's story "Circular Ruins," which tells of a magician who
dreams a son into being, then sends him off to a life of his own
to spare him from realizing that he is his father's invention.
No one wants to discover that he is only a projection of another's dreams. Except maybe Sam.

Sarah reached out to return the pen. "No, no, keep it," I
said. "Because maybe we can make him go back to being
wonderful. How is it, Sam, that you became such a strong,
sturdy person to her?"

"Well, it was a question of either forcing myself to become
strong, or perhaps she having to go off the wall, or to a psychologist, or a psychiatrist. She is, hypothetically, a very nervous person."

"What Sarah is saying is that for her you became a very
strong rock. Someone she could lean on. And you're saying it
was her needs that made you strong."

"I think so."

"That's interesting. So that's how you developed a relationship. You made him your protector, and he protected you. That's nice."

You probably know couples like Sarah and Sam. He's strong, she's weak; she's a giver, he's a taker; he's ambitious, she's content; she's practical, he's a dreamer. It's not simply that opposites attract. These polarized pairings are as much a product of relationship as of personality.

One partner may learn to accommodate to the other's strange desire to go camping or eat out two nights a week, but his reluctance to pick up a tool may turn her into the official handyman; her carelessness may result in his becoming the bill payer. That such contracts often don't get spelled out doesn't make them any less powerful. Marriage is a balancing act.

Sarah and Sam's rather extreme version of reciprocity had served them well up to now, but old arrangements don't always work in new circumstances.

I turned to Sam and asked, "When you felt weak, when you felt doubtful, could you lean on Sarah? Or was that not part of the contract?"

Sam looked up. "That's a marvelous, marvelous question that probably comes out now for the first time in a lifetime. I almost—almost—looked forward to being sick for a day. Because when I was sick, she took care of me. It was almost even better than sex." Sarah made a face, but Sam went on. "She was there. And she was only there when I was sick or something."

With anxious love she tended him, releasing him and her from their rigid construction of couplehood, but only when he was sick.

"So she was there when you needed her?" Was it my imagination or did his eyes glisten?

Surprisingly, it was Sarah who answered. "When he wasn't well, I was concerned about myself. I was afraid that I'd be left alone. That I'd fall apart."

Sarah admitted the selfish side of her behavior with simple guilelessness. She was always resourceful, a doer, but it suited both of them not to see her as such. Marriage limits, or shapes, our definition of self. But shapes should not—need not—be carved in stone.

"It's very important for you, Sarah, to keep that wonderful tree alive and strong. At the same time you, Sam, were longing for the possibility of being taken care of sometimes. I understand that she is a kind of nurturing person. You're a Florence Nightingale?"

"No, not at all," Sarah said. "I am a very weak person." She spoke simply and without apology.

"I want to congratulate you," I said and reached out to shake her hand. "You trained him so well."

This is sleight of hand, turning "weakness" into an active force. I wanted them to see that the roles they played were mutually determined. In a marriage weakness is a powerful demand for support, and the role of the strong one exists only by consent.

Sarah laughed, pleased and a little embarrassed. "Are you serious?"

"Absolutely. He has organized his life to look after your needs. That's very good training."

"What do you mean, *training*?" Even this implication of competence had to be resisted. "I didn't train him. He was like that."

"No, no. He wasn't like that. Because every once in a while he wanted to be weak, and you told him it wasn't in the contract. So he knows he cannot really be sick, because you would nurture him, apparently, only for a day or so. So—how old are you, Sam?"

"I'll be seventy-three in July."

"So you see he has a problem now. Because he knows he cannot be sick. Because you need him strong. Maybe that's a wonderful thing, to have such a strong drive to remain strong because she needs you strong."

I wanted to challenge Sarah's incomplete definition of herself, but gently. I didn't want to suggest that she was selfish and must change or that she was weak and must change. I wanted to help her see her "dependence" on Sam as her contribution to the vitality of the marriage. She was not in fact either weak or dependent; she was affiliative, committed to connection, and this is a powerful strength. But now that the balance of the relationship was shifting, both partners had to learn new roles.

Sarah leaned forward, resting her chin on her hand. Sam sat remarkably still and said, "My brother-in-law passed away just seven months ago." He spoke slowly, giving emphasis to his words. "My sister used to say if anything happened to him she couldn't go on. He passed away, and she was put into a home for the aged. That really scares me."

The death he feared was the death of Them. How would Sarah, who leaned on him for fifty years, be able to manage without him? I wondered too.

"Sarah, you're seventy? Do you work?"

"I have a little knitting shop. It's a small place, not many customers, but it's a place for me to go."

"Are you a good businesswoman?"

"Not really, no. As an empret—empretta—"

"Entrepreneur," Sam supplied.

"I'm more or less—I'm not that good. I'm better at showing somebody else what to do."

"She's had that shop for eighteen years," Sam said. "One girl comes in Tuesday and Thursday. That's her business. It grosses eleven thousand a year. *Gross.* That means between the rent and the girl there's very little money of any kind left over. But it is imperative, I felt, that she have this shop. Something for herself."

"So this is part of your protection?"

"Yes."

"That's wonderful. So you managed to have a relationship in which you are weak so that he can be strong, and you are strong so that she can be weak. It's wonderful."

By now I knew it wasn't so wonderful. Sarah's role was too narrow, and Sam's was too demanding. It robbed them both of flexibility.

Sarah leaned forward. "One thing is, I think he's so good to me because—this is my opinion—he feels that he had not been successful in life, and he can give me of himself more than he can give me worldly possessions." Sam listened to his wife's judgment with no sign of resentment. These two were remarkably resigned to each other.

"Do you think you need the magic wand?" I asked Sarah. "Because it seems to me you created him in the image that you needed. You know, you created him as a protector, and he became your protector. You are the only thing that he cares about. It's marvelous."

I praised their arrangement as "wonderful" and "marvelous" to call attention to the rigid roles they had created for each other, without making them feel scolded. It was also out of respect. What may sound patronizing was, in fact, very much in keeping with Sam and Sarah's sentimental way of speaking.

"Except, then, that if he's not going to be there, I have to stand alone," Sarah said, picking up my concern. "Will I be able to do it?"

"Oh, you will probably be depressed for a while, and then you will do very well." Sarah was so wedded to Sam that she could not imagine life without him. I remembered my mother. I understood Sarah's fear, but I wanted her to know that widows eventually grow new limbs. "When do you plan to bury him?"

Again I teased, and again they didn't mind.

"Well, look," Sarah replied, "realistically, how long have either of us got?"

Sam was healthy but death wouldn't wait forever.

"Can you strengthen yourself in the next few years?"

Sarah pursed her lips and blew out some air. "I'll try. I think I'm stronger now than I was when we first got married."

"Maybe you can begin to train her, Sam."

"He's doing that, and I don't like it," Sarah said, and she sounded as if she meant it.

"I have been trying," Sam said with a smile. "I try to make her cognizant of it. If I am not here, she might need a few dollars." Then he turned to face Sarah. "So it would be a good point that we know where we're spending it, so if I passed away you'd have some money, because the world out there is a misery, and you'll be standing on your own." He wasn't smiling now. "*Nobody,* not even your daughter, is going to be there. She'll be there to console you, but that's not going to pay the rent."

"And is she learning that?" I asked.

"She resents me, sort of. She says that I'm instilling in her 'money, money, money.' Actually, I'm not. We still go to a restaurant. We still spend a few bucks. We still give our daughter a few dollars from whatever we have. But I try to make her cognizant of these things, so that if something happens to me," he looked at Sarah, "you'll have a few bucks. Sure, go on spending, but minimize. Know what a dollar is."

Sam the protector was also Sam the controller, as stubbornly dominant as Sarah was persistently submissive.

"So," I said to him, "you are trying to act as if you will pass away tomorrow."

"Oh, yes," he said, nodding vigorously.

"Could you make it, Sarah?" She rubbed her chin and looked thoughtful. "Or should he stay alive a couple more years? He's training you; it's nice. He will not die until you are ready."

"Somehow people think—my family, my son-in-law—they think I'm a competent person, that I'm able to do things," Sarah said. "See, they feel that way, but I don't."

Clearly I was going to have to do better. Childhood training, reinforced daily for decades, won't be laughed off with jokes. But I couldn't find a handle to challenge while still confirming them. So I carried on with my absurdities.

"Please, do not let them think that way. If Sam begins to think that you can manage life without him, he might die. He's an extraordinary man, kind of staying alive for you."

I turned to Monica. "She has done a marvelous thing for him. Instead of thinking about his own body changing, he worries about what he can do for Sarah. If you want to continue working with these people, what you need to do is help Sam become incompetent. That's the only way he can train Sarah, because she is very afraid that if Sam thinks she is competent, then he could die."

"What a marvelous thought," Sam said.

We were approaching the end of the session, and I realized that Sam and Sarah, for all their sweet, old-fashioned charm, were not so different from any other couple. They were simply going through one of those periods of readjustment required from time to time in any durable and lasting relationship.

Every relationship that works must have a formula for stability and a formula for change. Sam and Sarah had achieved stability with an exaggerated form of complementarity—at the expense of autonomy and flexibility. He had subordinated his nature to her, and she had subordinated hers to him. It was the traditional marriage carried to an almost absurd extreme. Their touching mutual dependence was functional when Sam was working, but not anymore.

A successful relationship also requires the ability to adjust to change. Whatever type of balance a couple works out, their relationship will need to be rebalanced at transitional points in the life cycle. Healthy couples need flexibility as well as stability.

Could I give Sarah and Sam a small push in the direction of flexibility? What followed was a playful, friendly struggle. But a struggle nonetheless.

"Maybe you need to become incompetent, Sam. Maybe you will be sick for two days a week. In a month, what is it, eight days of illness? So that during these two days—maybe Tuesday and Thursday—you will be so weak that she needs to take care of you. What do you think, wouldn't that be lovely?"

Sarah interrupted. "You know, it bothers me a lot. I feel now that he is down—on a wane, on a down wane. If he doesn't remember things that I think he should remember, and I remember them, then I feel he is not as strong as he used to be. He isn't as competent."

"And that worries you?"

"Yes."

Challenging her directly only pushed her to resist. Why shouldn't she? She was fighting to protect the defensive order of things. So instead I turned to Monica. "The question is, can these two people change the contract? I don't think either of them wants to. But it would be very nice if Sam could be incompetent two, three days a week."

"Over my dead body!" Sarah laughed and her earrings shook. It was funny, but it was also her life. "I won't let him."

"Oh, it's for your training. He would probably discover that he wanted that for a long time, but he couldn't because you needed him strong. But now that he knows you really need to be trained for his death—" I turned to Sam. "Maybe you can train her by becoming incompetent, two, three days a week."

"She won't let me," Sam said, and he wasn't laughing. "She's got something for me to do every second."

"Sam, that's *good*. She will have these things, but you will not be able to do them. You will begin to do them and you will fail."

"Then *I'll* have to do them," Sarah said. "Is *that* what you're saying?"

"I don't know." Sometimes the best answer is no answer. "Sam," I persisted, "it will be for her. You will have a cold one day, so she can make you chicken soup. You will be depressed another day, so she can cheer you up—maybe take you to the movies. If you need to buy things at the supermarket, you will forget the milk, or the bread, and then she will need to think— slowly, in a month, she will begin to know what will happen when she's alone. In the process maybe you will have a good time because you like her to take care of you. Who knows? But you will do it to help Sarah."

My final comment was to Monica. "This is a fascinating couple. She's competent, but she keeps it secret. He feels weak sometimes, and he keeps that secret. They're really quite remarkable."

As I was about to leave, Sam stood up and said, "May I take a picture of you, sir?"

Surprised and pleased, I said, "Yes, of course, but it should be with Monica." And so I stood side by side with Monica while Sam took our picture. The moment was fittingly anachronistic, like a formal daguerreotype of the nineteenth century.

Sam and Sarah were just two ordinary people who loved each other. The extent of their mutual dependence was perhaps extreme, but some degree of complementarity is a feature of every marriage that works.

In the closed system of their marriage, with only each other to play off, Sarah and Sam were cast as types in a long-running performance. Sarah played the dependent wife so Sam could play the man of the house.

Sam worried that Sarah would not survive without him because they were so bound together. That, as much as the aimless days of retirement, made him depressed. Had I made too little of Sam's depression? I don't think so. Sam and Sarah both were feeling the inevitable anxiety and uncertainty we all feel at transition points in life, as we search for new ways of being.

Recalling the consultation, I wondered if I was a little better able than Monica to join with this couple because of my age. Does a therapist need to have life experience that parallels the patient's? I think it helps. But a more important point to remember is that every family is unique, and to that extent every therapist is a little bit ignorant. Therapists must be alert to their ignorance and willing to allow families to educate them.

I heard from Monica that Sam and Sarah continued as before. Bound together by habit and need, they played out the roles they had assigned each other. Sam did not get sick two days a week. He continued to worry about money and continued to needle Sarah about it. Sarah continued to work at her shop and continued to needle Sam about going places and doing things.

Apparently there was little need for them to change the habits of a lifetime. What did change was that they became a little more tolerant of each other. They continued to complain, but no longer with any illusion about changing each other. I helped them see the reciprocity that governed their lives, hoping they would be able both to accept themselves and begin to explore the possibility of change. They settled for acceptance.

I saw Sarah and Sam again four and a half years later. Writing up my notes on them for this book rekindled my affection and curiosity. I wondered: Did she still lean on him? Was he still her Rock of Gibraltar? So I called Monica and asked her to arrange a follow-up visit. Our reunion—for that's what it was—turned out to be relaxed and friendly, and somewhat surprising.

Sam complained cheerfully about the weather. He resented the rain, the traffic, the city. "They don't know what they're doing. Trucks everywhere—parking is impossible."

His hair had receded farther back from his forehead, and his smooth skin was beginning to wrinkle. He was seventy-seven.

Sarah still worked at her shop two days a week. She described it as something to keep busy, and Sam, right on cue, made a point of saying she still didn't make any money: "Doesn't make a penny."

Sarah hadn't aged. Her hair was still dark and handsomely styled. She was seventy-four, but she looked much more than three years younger than Sam.

They had recently celebrated a wedding anniversary and were both very conscious of their age and very aware of their mortality.

Sarah said, "Now, at our age, we're on a precipice of being—what's going to happen tomorrow? It's just like we're not going to be here."

Sam, too, worried about the day when the old man with the scythe would come to the door. "More and more it is a remarkable feeling to lie in bed with her and have this feeling that she may not be there. I don't know whether it's sheer love or sheer fear. I think, God, if anything happens to her, who's going to take care of me?"

After seven years Sam still found retirement difficult.

"Being retired, it's a very difficult thing?" I asked.

Sarah said, "Oh yes," and Sam said, "There is a forgetfulness. I'm starting to forget and it makes me mad as all hell."

"He's frightened," Sarah said.

This loss, this treason of his own mind, shook him. There was nothing he could do, his mind was aging. All of him was aging, without his consent. Of course, he had always known this; he was not such a fool as to think he would not grow old, but knowing it and living it were two different things.

"What do you do with your time?" I asked him.

He puttered. He drove Sarah to work, washed the floor, helped her out in small ways. He did a few chores for his friend who owned a drugstore, and he put his old knowledge of electric appliances to work by repairing discarded radios and vacuum cleaners: "People throw out things that are absolutely unbelievable."

Sam was aging faster than Sarah, and the balance of their relationship was shifting—had shifted. More and more, she was the one who took care of him. That was new, for both of them.

"It never was like that when we were young," Sarah said. "When we were young he would do anything. He was the sweetest person in the world. It was unbelievable how kind and wonderful he was. And now he's unhappy, he's frustrated."

Looking back over a life well lived produces an inner peace and a conviction of personal worth. Sam, like a lot of men of his generation who worked just to make a living, did not have that sense of satisfaction. What embittered Sam, though, was not that he hadn't gone further in school, or taken up a profession, or in some other way developed himself, but that he hadn't been more successful. Perhaps if he had accumulated more money, now in old age he could still feel like Sarah's protector.

A shifting of roles between two people often takes some getting used to. Perhaps the most familiar example of role reversal is the shifting relationship between parents and children as children move through adolescence. This mutual readjustment often produces the kind of clanking and grinding that railroad cars make when they are uncoupled and switched.

Sarah and Sam were so closely coupled that every shift on his part was matched by a reciprocal shift on hers. If there was an argument, she now was the one to make up. Where once she was the complainer and he the reassuring one, now the parts were reversed. As Sarah said, with characteristic candor, "I was always the depressed and unhappy one, complaining about things. He took that over."

Sam's cantankerousness was particularly evident in his response to the grandchildren. Their only daughter had three boys, aged five and three years, and six months. To Sarah and Sam, who had few friends, this daughter and her family were their world. Mondays, Wednesdays, and every other Friday, Sarah and Sam would watch the grandchildren while their daughter went to work. Sarah enjoyed being with the boys; Sam didn't. The children made him cranky and impatient.

Sarah said, "He can't handle the activities of a five- and a three-year-old. He gets mad and yells at them. I am at this point more tolerant. I don't care what they do. Let them play. Let them do what they want."

This woman, once so fragile and concerned with herself, had changed a lot. I pointed out that she had become more flexible and unselfish, and I asked her how that had happened. She had, she said, become more reconciled to where she was in life. "Maybe in my younger life I was always dissatisfied. I wanted more. But maybe now, at this time of my life, I said, This is it. And there's no place to go. This is what I have."

Sarah was aging more gracefully than Sam. His life had been his work and taking care of his family. Now that was gone. Sarah, on the other hand, was growing into a very mature individual.

"And what about you, Sam?" I asked. "What happened to you?"

"Well, I've met with a lot of people and gone to a lot of meetings. I *can't stand* the stupidity of the city."

Sam rambled on about the government and big corporations, and I could see how old he'd become. The flesh around his jaw had grown slack, and his chin dipped down and disappeared in the folds of his neck.

Sam lost the trail of his argument and got sidetracked onto another of memory's grooves that had to do with meetings: "I remember, I took a course with Albert Einstein some forty years ago. It only lasted two days. And this man"—he searched for the words—"was a brilliant genius."

Forty years earlier Sam's company had sent him and another man to take a course in mathematics at Princeton. When the professor got sick, Einstein filled in for two days. Somehow, to Sam, the great man's eccentricities gave them some kind of kinship as men outside the Establishment. "I don't think he ever took a bath. I don't think he ever combed his hair. He was a vegetarian, and he never wore shoes."

But the thing that was burned into Sam's brain was a demonstration Einstein did with a fishbowl filled with sand and a matchbox full of ants. He poured the ants into the fishbowl, then took one and crushed it. "Gentlemen, come around," Sam remembered him saying. "And a very strange thing happened. An ant being what it is, they buried the dead ant. And Einstein looked at us and said, 'Who told the ants to bury their dead?' The point I'm making is that the few who are controlling the masses . . ." Sam shrugged, unable to make his point.

But maybe he *had* made his point. Sam, who feared death, found it comforting to remember Einstein's demonstration of how all creatures care for and bury their dead.

As Sam rambled on, Sarah seemed embarrassed, but she didn't interrupt or criticize him. She didn't enjoy hearing the same stories over and over any more than anyone else does, but she was patient. Sam had become more impatient and cranky. Sarah had become more accepting and tolerant.

I pointed out that they still complemented each other's needs, only now their roles had reversed.

Sam agreed; she had become the stronger of the two. "Oh yes, absolutely!"

Sarah agreed, too, but she said, "I don't like it." Sam now was the one who complained about all his aches and pains. "That's my shtick!" Sarah said.

Some things never change. Sam was still Sam, and Sarah was still Sarah. But they, Sarah-and-Sam, had changed. The strength of their couplehood was proving itself in its flexibility.

Sarah complained good-naturedly about Sam's usurping her role as the weaker member of the pair, but the thing that really bothered her was his impatience with the grandchildren. She, on the other hand, took great delight in the children.

"With my own daughter, I was too uptight to enjoy her when she was little. But now I am positively in awe of how my grandchildren grow and change every day." They were teaching her something about taking pleasure from life that she hadn't known before.

Sam couldn't wait until the grandchildren got to be ten or so, when he could carry on a conversation with them.

"But we won't be there!" Sarah said. She was crocheting a yarmulke for the oldest boy's bar mitzvah, "In case I won't be there."

Sarah, who was still attractive and still concerned about her appearance, had also developed an inner beauty, something that might be defined as the ability to care about other people, just for them, rather than for the possibility of their appreciation.

I asked Sam how it felt to be more in need of Sarah now, and he said it wasn't easy. "Maybe it's a man-woman thing. I would like to still be that strong one for her."

"He used to be your Rock of Gibraltar," I said to Sarah.

"He still is. I'm strong right now because he's here with me."

Sarah still felt dependent on Sam and didn't fully realize

that it was his need, not his strength, that made her strong. She had become more complex, more mature, and more unselfish; but she didn't see it. They were what they'd always been: a team, an intimate team.

Once again we said good-bye, and once again I marveled at the power of love that held these two people together.

PART THREE

PARENTS AND CHILDREN

Nobody taught me how to parent. Pat didn't have lessons either. We're supposed to know, instinctively, as a bird knows the right time to encourage its young to fly, or a bear knows how to teach its young to fish. Nobody teaches them—at least we don't think so.

I have seen films about chimpanzees and admired the patience of the mother with her young. They cling to her belly, then scamper off, detaching themselves a few steps but remaining close to her, ready to take refuge again. There are forays of independence, playing with older siblings, tentative jumps into space. Then they return to cling to Mother.

If it's instinctive to them, it should be so with us. There is a natural affinity between mothers and babies; milk flows in the mother's breast when it's needed by her young. Parent and child teach each other how to communicate. Baby talk—those repetitive, nonsensical sounds that parents universally make—seems to come instinctively as part of the natural system of signals exchanged by parents and children. But as time goes on, things become more complex. The world makes many demands on us, and we don't have time to accommodate with ease to each other's needs. If we had only to fish or fly or look for food, if we could concentrate on learning to be proficient at survival, our lives would be simpler. But the demands of socialization become more and more difficult. Parenting turns into a lifelong endeavor, and a variety of people and institutions become involved in doing the job, with varying degrees of success.

All in all parenting is an almost impossible task, and all parents fall short in some ways. I suppose, though, that for many parents this knowledge will not be sufficiently reassuring, and they will still look at friends or relatives whose children seem perfect. Let me tell you, it is an illusion.

What is useful to know, however, is that if conflicts and problems are unavoidable, solutions are usually available. Parents often find ways of getting out of difficult situations with their children, but sometimes they get stuck and repeat the same useless solutions again and again, with the same useless results, until everybody is exhausted. It is in these situations that a family therapist can be helpful.

Experts usually agree on certain basic premises—the behavior of a child is maintained by the combined effort of all family members. While this may not seem like a revelation, it is nonetheless an important perspective when looking at a child's behavior. Most parents, in their efforts to help their child, focus so much of their attention on decoding the child's behavior that they become experts on the child but blind to their own contribution. I don't mean that the child is nothing but a product of parental treatment—which would ignore the complex reality of the child and contribute to the legion of parent bashers. It means simply acknowledging that children are actors and reactors and often more adaptable than we realize.

Let me give an example: A couple in their mid-forties comes to consult with me about their three-and-a-half-year-old youngster. He clings to them and cries whenever they try to leave him. The boy, who has been in nursery school since he was two, plays in my office with toys the parents brought, while I talk with them. He seems well coordinated, bright, and quite independent in his play. I notice the disparity between the parents' report and the child's behavior, and I gently ask the mother to leave the room. She smiles and leaves. The child continues playing. I then ask the father to leave. He does so, and the child continues making a hangar for his plane, quite absorbed and seemingly unconcerned. When I ask him if he wants his parents to return, he shakes his head and says no. I nonetheless ask him to bring his parents from the waiting room. They now tell me that he is sometimes, as on this occasion, quite independent.

I tell the parents that their observation of the child was correct. He is in effect a clinging child—something they have seen many times. What they don't see is their contribution to his behavior. Mother cries; Father fidgets uncomfortably. They acknowledge that as older parents of a young child they have made him the center of their pleasure, concern, and control. We chat; we consider alternatives. I suggest some tasks. Three sessions later we finish our encounters. Treatment is usually more complicated, but in cases that work like this, there is a great sense of clarity and pleasure. I feel wise, the parents feel grateful, and the child does not know that he has been "in therapy."

I will talk later about more complicated cases, but in every case, success comes with a change in perspective—when family members, parents and siblings, begin to see and change their way of connecting to the child; when one spouse doesn't recruit the child in a coalition against the other; when children stop protecting parents from each other or from grandparents.

In treatment the focus frequently shifts from a child's symptoms to conflict between the parents. When this happens I continue to concentrate on the child's problems but expand the focus to include the marital problems—that is, I ask the spouses to look at how their conflict is being played out in the child's symptoms. Once again, we have a kaleidoscopic shift. I don't deny the child's symptoms; I don't minimize the spouses' conflict. I simply suggest that they are both part of a family grappling with difficulties and getting stuck with narrow "solutions."

This systemic way of looking is not the way people feel things themselves. Pain is always an individual experience. But when family members learn to look at problems in an interrelated way, they see anew. Novel and more sensitive ways of being emerge. For example, spouses in conflict may be more willing to postpone their game of "You did"—"No, you did" once they begin to understand that when marital conflict becomes parental conflict, the ones who pay are the children.

7

A Crutch to Move Away

I was leafing through the mail in my office at the Philadelphia Child Guidance Clinic when my secretary buzzed. Joseph Pasquariello, a retired high school teacher from North Philadelphia, wanted to talk to me about his eleven-year-old granddaughter, who lived in Venezuela because her father's work had taken the family there. Jill suffered from hysterical paralysis. Her father's company had agreed to send the family to Philadelphia and pay their expenses for one month so she could seek treatment. Would I take the case?

I dislike measuring therapy in terms of time. I much prefer to work until we've done what needs to be done, rather than constrain the process of change to some arbitrary number of sessions. Who's to say how long it will take to change the life of a family? If I took this case, I would have one month to treat a family I had never met, with a symptom I had never seen. Finally I decided to see them; I never could say no to a challenge.

Nevertheless, after accepting the case, my reaction was mostly excitement. Hysterical paralysis. Very few people still select this nineteenth-century European way of expressing conflict, and very few living therapists have seen it.

The last time hysterical paralysis was anything but anomalous was during World War I, when hundreds of soldiers, caught between the terror of suicidal assaults and the fear of cowardice and disgrace, found an unconscious solution in the form of somnambulistic trances, catalepsy, and hysterical paralyses. Few things show the power of the mind more vividly than a patient struck blind, or suddenly unable to walk, for no organic reason. These strange and puzzling disorders have baffled healers since ancient times.

The Greeks believed that hysteria was due to a wandering uterus. Ancient physicians attempted to coax these migratory uteruses back to where they belonged by applying foul-smelling substances to the afflicted body parts and aromatic herbs to the area of the womb. That these remedies sometimes worked proved, to the satisfaction of those who employed them, that the wandering uterus theory was correct.

In the dark days of the Middle Ages, hysteria was believed to be brought about by witchcraft and sorcery. This theory, too, produced many cures. The fact that few sufferers survived the cure only proved the gravity of the disorder and the inadvisability of alliance with unholy powers. Freud too believed that hysterics were possessed, but by unconscious longings rather than supernatural forces.

Invariably Freud found hidden sexual fantasies at the root of the problem. Fräulein Rosalia H. was a gifted pianist whose hands became palsied because, Freud discovered, she had been forced to massage her brutish uncle's back when she was a girl. And of course there was Dora, the girl Freud tried to bully into believing that her disgust at the advances of a middle-aged neighbor was evidence of repressed desire. According to Freud, she protested so much because she was only defending against her real feelings. But what if Dora didn't

protest too much? Was it possible that her parents didn't protest enough?

Already I was thinking like a family therapist. Hysterical
paralysis? The very term seemed an anachronism in a time of
sexual revolution. The nineteenth-century hysteric had been
an isolated creature, a specimen plucked from her surroundings and treated as though she had a past but no present.
What would hysterical paralysis look like in the twentieth
century, in a young girl seen in the context of her family?

———•—•———

The family I met in the waiting room two weeks later seemed
out of place in the clinic. Most of our clients were poor, many
of them black or Hispanic. These people were not only white
and well dressed, but all of them, even the six-year-old, were
reading. As I approached the mother consulted her watch.

I introduced myself, and an intellectual-looking bald man
with snow-white, shaggy eyebrows stood up and said he was
Joseph Pasquariello. He introduced me to his wife, Rose; his
daughter, Janet Slater; his granddaughter, Jill; and her
brother, Davey. Jill's father was detained on business and
would arrive in a few days.

As the family entered the office, Jill clutched her mother's
arm. One leg dragged, and her arm on that side was rigid
against her body. She sat down heavily and sank into a slouch.
Were her hunched shoulders an attempt to hide her budding
adolescence? I thought of Freud again. Was the symptom in
any way related to the fear of becoming an adolescent, to the
clear signs that a little girl was becoming a young woman?

Mr. and Mrs. Pasquariello appeared to be in their late
seventies. He wore a tweed suit, which—with his bushy, white
eyebrows poking over dark-rimmed glasses—gave him a ven-
erable appearance. They were glad to come, he said: "Anything we can do to help." She was short and round, with no
neck, like one of those Russian dolls that nest one inside the
other. She was colorfully dressed in white slacks and a bright
paisley blouse. She looked at Jill and her eyes glistened. I
recognized the anxious love of protective grandparents.

Mrs. Slater, a handsome woman with thick, auburn hair,
settled Jill and sat down next to her. She told me about the
accident that had paralyzed her daughter.

They were at the country club by the pool. It was a hot, cloudless day, and Mrs. Slater was stretched out on a chaise longue next to her husband when suddenly she heard a scream. Jill was thrashing in the water, screaming for her father. "Very funny," he said, assuming it was a game. Then he realized it was serious, and he jumped in to get her. When he carried Jill out of the pool, she could not stand.

Apparently Jill had been playing with some boys who had pushed her into the pool. Rushed to the emergency room, she was admitted to the hospital for observation. Test after test turned up normal results, yet she could not move her left leg or arm.' Then Jill spent a couple of months working with a physiotherapist in the rehabilitation department. After that she had six months of psychotherapy. There was still no improvement.

Jill listened intently to this story she'd heard a dozen times, her brown eyes shuttling anxiously between her mother and her grandparents. Nothing about the incident or subsequent tests gave any clue as to why a healthy eleven-year-old had suddenly become unable to move her leg and arm.

I asked how long they had been in Caracas. Mrs. Slater explained that her husband was a geological engineer for an international oil company. Because of his job they had always lived abroad, assigned for two or three years at a time to oil-producing countries in the Middle East and Central and South America. His previous assignment had been to Houston, where they'd had a beautiful house, and she'd found a wonderful teaching job at a private school. But it was only a two-year tour, and a transfer to Caracas had ended it. It had been hard to leave that job and all her friends. And the first few months in Venezuela had been especially trying. Their furniture hadn't arrived for weeks, and workmen were still finishing the interior of their house.

I wondered if Mrs. Slater had dragged her feet on the move from Houston to Caracas, and if Jill was dragging half her body as a symbolic expression of that reluctance. A few minutes into the session, I had a working hypothesis: Perhaps the child's paralysis was an expression of her mother's resentment at moving. First hypotheses will change many times as an exploration continues, but they are useful—in fact, necessary—in organizing the gathering of information. I kept watching as well as listening as the family talked.

Chatty and unrestrained, Rose, the grandmother, laughed easily, spoke rapidly and boldly, and analyzed with restless force. "Well, if you want my opinion, doctor, I don't think all this traipsing all over the world is a healthy environment for the children."

Mrs. Slater complained of the burden of having to do everything for Jill. "Richard's never home. He's always working."

Rose Pasquariello said what her daughter implied: "Richard should think more about his family and less about his precious career." Mrs. Slater accepted her mother's support. Meanwhile Mrs. Pasquariello babied her granddaughter— "*poor* Jilly"—and interrupted her daughter freely. Janet seemed used to it. Once in a while she looked a little impatient, but she didn't say anything.

Sitting there, slumped in her chair, wearing an old summer-camp T-shirt, Jill seemed very young. But then, without hesitation, she'd push her way into the conversation, participating with the grownups like an equal. This, too, her mother seemed to take for granted.

At first her little brother seemed pleased to be witness to these adult transactions, but he soon lost interest. Once in a while he heard something that caught his attention, but most of the time he sat there dazed by boredom. Could this be anybody's idea of something worth doing?

I felt connected to this family very quickly. They were good people, perhaps a trifle too close-knit, but warm and familiar. Later I would have to challenge them, pushing them into unexplored areas. But now I concentrated on building connections.

Jill, the invalid, was a bright young girl with beautiful dark eyes. She had pale, luminous skin and shiny black hair pulled taut into a thick braid. Like many first children she was remarkably articulate. When I asked her what she enjoyed doing, she said, "I like catching lizards and watching birds and picking tropical flowers." She didn't like going to school because most of the kids were older than she was. I liked her, and she could tell that I did.

I told Mrs. Slater that I would arrange for a complete medical workup at the Children's Hospital. She protested that all that had already been done, but I said it was best to make sure. I didn't want to be one of those psychiatrists who invent clever psychological explanations for what turn out to be medical problems.

As I arranged to see them three times a week, my satisfaction with the first meeting left me somewhat—only twelve sessions, and one was already gone.

The second session took place three days later. Mr. Slater had arrived, and so this session included father, mother, Jill, and Davey. Mr. Slater had suggested that his in-laws stay home. He didn't think their presence was necessary.

Richard Slater was a tall, handsome man with wavy, dark hair and a deep tan. He had a rich voice and a precise way of speaking that gave weight and authority to what he said.

Jill shuffled into the interview room, clinging to her mother. Richard walked behind and stood by while his wife helped Jill into a chair.

As we sat down I noticed that Richard seemed a little less self-assured sitting with his family than when he greeted me in the waiting room. I asked him about his work, and he described it with an enthusiasm no other subject seemed to elicit. Otherwise he seemed detached. He was not really involved, not implicated.

I was beginning to develop a preliminary map of this family's structure. Jill's illness had riveted the family's attention on her symptom. This was natural enough, given its drama. Jill the person had given way to Jill the cripple. Not walking had become her identity card, the doorway and barrier to any approach to her.

This seemed wrong to me, and so did the family's pattern of proximity. Jill clutched her mother, visibly demonstrating the weight of the mother's responsibility for this family. Richard was distant, but it was not a comfortable distance. He entered the room as if he had been brought by his wife, the mother-in-charge.

Of course this was only a map, and like all maps it showed only the outlines, not the details of the territory. Something human is lost when a family is reduced to a diagram of proximity and distance. But something is also gained—clarity.

It was beginning to look as though this very unusual case wasn't so unusual after all. The symptom, hysterical paralysis, was certainly different, but the family dynamics that supported the symptom were sadly familiar. It was, in fact, the signature arrangement of the troubled middle-class family: a mother's closeness to her children substituting for closeness in the marriage that had never developed or been lost. So common was this pattern that it could not explain such an unusual symptom; that remained a mystery. But Jill was now embedded in the pattern, and it was hardening around her like concrete.

At the time Jay Haley had developed a three-step strategy to pry apart what he called "cross-generational coalitions." The goal was to guide the child(ren) to autonomy. Step one was to hook up the disengaged parent with the dependent child, in order to separate the enmeshed parent and child. In this family, step one was clear. I would move Richard closer to Jill.

So, in the third session, I proposed the following plan to the Slaters. Since Janet was tired of being used as a crutch, for the next week Richard should look after Jill. Whenever she needed to walk someplace, she was to call her father, not her mother, to become her crutch. I wondered if Richard would turn out to be like most fathers, an amateur when it comes to mothering.

The second step would be to move Richard and Janet closer together. Only if the couple could create a boundary between themselves and the children could they begin to address whatever conflicts stood between them and intimacy.

The third step of my strategy would concern Jill directly, exploring the meaning of her symptom and challenging its paralyzing effect.

The diagnosis was easy. Doing something about it was another matter. If strategy was the science of therapy, spotting the land mines along the way was the art. And there were only nine sessions left.

Treatment strategies are generic; the results are idiosyncratic. Three days later the strategy of increasing proximity between father and daughter was working the only way it could in this family. When Richard took over, he did it the way disengaged fathers often do: He became controlling.

He helped Jill when she needed it, and he helped her when she didn't. He not only lent Jill his arm but took it upon himself to cheer her up whenever she was quiet, as though her moods were not her own and her silences were an accusation. He didn't want the part her helplessness pushed him into, but he couldn't help himself. So she was incompetent, and he was a nag.

Since Richard wasn't used to accommodating to his daughter's rhythms, he insisted that she accommodate to his. When she didn't, he got angry. She got cranky. But Jill did what dependent children do, even when their parents annoy them. She increased her demands and her helplessness, reinforcing her father's impatience with her. Now Janet was anxious, and Richard was a tired and irritable father who insisted on making his daughter unhappy, pathetic, and childish.

That wasn't what I wanted. My goal was to increase the child's autonomy. The first step was in place, and the father was involved, but Jill, walking with him, was a pitiful cripple. Each step was an effort. She leaned heavily on her father's arm and dragged her leg behind her. It was hard not to feel sorry for her. Sitting down, she looked like a sulky adolescent. She sat between her parents with her chin on her fist and a look of sullen defiance aimed somewhere off into the corner.

I decided to ignore Jill for the moment; her family already hovered over her as if she were some rare orchid. Maybe Jill needed something other than hothouse attention. So I asked her parents to tell me about Caracas.

Richard loved it. His Caracas was a wonderful place of warm sun and cool breezes, charming plazas, fountains, restaurants, nightclubs, and friendly people. Janet hated it. She missed their beautiful old Spanish house in Houston, her job, her friends, her parents. Caracas was "a hick town plastered over with concrete and glass. It has no soul." I said kiddingly that it sounded as if they lived in two different places. Richard smiled, amused. Janet was less amused.

I asked the children what they thought, not so much because it was important as to see who sided with which parent. Davey mumbled, "I don't know." A noncombatant. Jill said, "I hate it. There's nothing to do there." No doubt about whose side she was on.

"I was joking when I said it sounds like you two live in different places, but maybe it isn't funny. Janet, can you explain to Richard why you miss Houston? Try to make him understand how you feel."

Their dialogue was stiff, tense, and formal. Janet was unhappy with the children's school. She felt isolated from the local community. The only people they ever socialized with were Richard's friends from the oil company. "You get pretty tired of hearing about oil reserves after a while."

"What makes you so down on everything?" Richard's voice was thin and bitter now. "Maybe if you'd find a job or make some friends you wouldn't have so much to complain about."

"But you're always working," Jill interrupted, as if on cue. "Why don't you come home once in a while and take us places?"

Jill was sitting between her parents. I got up and walked over to her. "Jill, trade places with your mom," I said, helping her to the other chair. "Now, Janet, talk with your husband."

The result wasn't much different: a desultory conversation and a dramatically sullen child. Jill, not used to being excluded, leaned on her elbow, put on a sour face, and sighed audibly. Children have so few defenses, but they certainly perform wonders with those they have.

"Is this really necessary?" Richard said. "Jill looks miserable."

I agreed, but not the way he meant it. "Jill is acting like a five-year-old who isn't getting her way. Ignore her. Keep talking with Janet."

I was working now on step two, supporting the couple's autonomy in the presence of the children. Attacking Jill's behavior as age-inappropriate created a separation. The child, rightly insulted, is challenged to be more mature. The parents feel attacked. Their discomfort is a useful disrupter to a pattern of intrusion and overresponsiveness.

To a psychoanalyst this might be a variation of a Greek tragedy—the Oedipus complex—a mother-father-child triangle that becomes internalized inside the child's head. But in real life, which is at once less dramatic and more open to change, children fall in and out of love with each of their parents many times, creating a series of shifting triangles. These triangles usually resolve into some kind of balance, but they can harden into lasting coalitions.

By the fifth session I wanted to see the spouses alone, so I asked Richard to take the children to the waiting room and come back. I wanted to explore their difficulties as a couple.

When Janet met Richard, he was twenty-four; handsome, sure of himself, and serious-minded. He had grown up in Connecticut, the oldest of three boys, attended private schools, and then graduated from the University of Pennsylvania with a master's degree in geological engineering. He was a nonobservant Episcopalian and a faithful Republican, who worked for an oil company in their international development division. She thought he was going places—figuratively. Unlike other boys she knew, he wasn't always hanging all over her. But as the years went by, the independence she took for strength turned into distance and avoidance.

Janet had grown up an only child in a rambling old stone house on a street arched with ancient oak trees in North Philadelphia. Her father started out in the insurance business but decided he didn't like it, so, at thirty-seven, he became a high school history teacher. Her mother took care of the house. After she graduated from the University of Pennsylvania, Janet planned to go into journalism. But when she met Richard and they fell in love, she traded her ambitions for domesticity. Here was this extraordinary man, and he needed her. That, she thought, was enough.

Richard was immediately drawn to Janet's openly affectionate ways. Her humor and warmth were a welcome relief from his family's restraint. Like Janet, he married a dream, a dream that didn't quite come true.

It's hard when the dovetailing of desires comes apart, when someone you thought you loved turns out to be so hard to live with. Gradually they drifted apart. They'd hoped for love but settled for stability.

It was sad listening to them talk, two bruised and bitter people. But they spoke with more sorrow than recrimination, and I hoped that this talk would remind them of what they once had together, and raise the possibility that they might recover it. Their coming together would give Jill the space to move away.

It was time now to bring the grandparents back. I had seen enough in the first session to realize that Janet's disengagement from Richard was supported by enmeshment with her parents.

All families are extended families. Even in the United States, where young families are often cut off from their kin, the larger family is still there, a dormant resource. But keeping this resource from becoming a liability requires a negotiation of boundaries in the early years. Wise parents respect this boundary. When they don't, the larger family is not a resource but a source of unfinished business.

When the Slaters arrived for the sixth session without Janet's parents, I was a little worried. But the Pasquariellos were only late.

Rose, red-faced and breathless, came in with a long story about taking the wrong bus from the train. She was generous with details.

Janet interrupted, impatiently, "You wouldn't take a taxi, Mother."

Her mother smiled and said nothing. Her father said, Never mind, what did it matter? The main thing was they were there. He didn't challenge his wife, he dismissed her. While her husband was speaking, Janet's mother sighed audibly and wiped her curly white hair away from her forehead.

Richard had a pained look on his face.

The triangle in the Slater family, in which Janet and Jill were close and Richard distant, was supported by a triangle in the larger family, in which the unresolved distance between Janet and Richard was frozen in place by her unresolved attachment with her parents. It often works that way.

Janet's father considered his wife frivolous and so, although they stuck together, a Couple, he had long since ceased to take her seriously. Janet's mother responded to the emotional disengagement in her marriage by becoming overly attached to Janet, and it was this attachment that helped make it difficult for Janet to connect with Richard. Thus the pattern of enmeshment and disengagement in this family was a three-generational affair:

Rose —⊣ ⊢— Joseph
Janet —⊣ ⊢— Richard
Jill

The advent of children and her overly close attachment to

Jill hardened the boundary between Janet and Richard, doing little to separate her any further from her parents. Janet wanted to be treated like an adult, but her mother had nothing to replace the protective role of being a mother. If Janet and Richard had been closer, or if Janet had been more self-reliant, an adult in charge of her life, she could simply have resisted her mother's intrusion and control—*if*.

Part of the boundary-making strategy was to have Janet and Richard negotiate a respectful distance from the Pasquariellos that included an acceptance of Richard as an integral part of the family. Janet and Richard began talking about whether or not her parents accepted him. She was saying how hard it was for her that Richard didn't respect her loyalty to her parents. He was trying to say that he had changed in recent years—"I think I have been doing that"—but she wasn't hearing him.

The Slaters were caught up with who was right and who was wrong. As with the arguments of the Lockwoods, the content was only a vehicle; the engine was a struggle for dominance and control.

"At this point, Janet, you are more interested in winning this argument than you are in accepting Richard. You are hearing him with your old ears. Can you give him a smile?" Janet smiled and laughed. "That's nice," I said. "He needs smiles from you more frequently."

"And vice versa," Janet's mother said in a loud stage whisper.

"The footnotes are beautiful," Richard said, not very successfully trying to mask his annoyance.

"No," I said bluntly. "She has done something that she knows she should not do. Janet, what makes your mother think you still need her to protect you from your husband?"

"I don't."

"Oh?"

"She's just trying to help."

"But she knows that this moment was between you and your husband, and yet she still allows herself to interrupt. She really interferes between you two. It's something that mothers do early in the marriage of their children. She is really insisting that you should still be her little daughter—still, after seventeen years of marriage."

"She just interjects herself," Janet said. "It never fails."

"You need to help your mother not to interfere between you and your husband. It would be nice if you could help your parents. Then they could have a son-in-law, instead of you feeling pulled in two directions."

Buoyed by my support, Richard opened an old sore. "I come to your parents with respect. However, when things happen like that crack of your mother's, I have all I can do to control my anger. When they come to visit, I'm always happy to have them—and I enjoy coming to visit you," he said, looking at his father-in-law.

Mr. Pasquariello met his look and said, "You may feel that way, but you don't project it to us."

"No," his wife interjected, but he put his hand on her shoulder and said, "Let me finish." And then he turned back to face his son-in-law. "For example, the last time we were at your place I felt very much an outsider—"

"Neglected," Mrs. Pasquariello added.

"Please, I don't need your help." His voice was hard now, with an edge to it. "Because the feeling I got was, you were cold and distant. You never really communicated. That's the feeling I get. So, think in terms of how you look, and the voice you use, and the manner—it's distant and cold. Think in terms of a longtime attitude—a sourness and a surliness—that we feel from you." He'd been holding this in for a long time. "You may respect us, that's one thing. But a feeling of ease with each other, relaxing with each other, that's something different."

The old man's indictment hung in the air, and it stopped all of us for a minute. Richard didn't answer. He sat frozen in one position, stony with resentment.

Then Janet, the one least able to tolerate an outbreak of hostility, spoke: "I know there's animosity on both sides."

"Too strong a word," her mother said, trying to smooth things over. "Resentment, on occasion."

"What are *you* resenting?" Janet wanted to know.

"Behavior toward you. Behavior toward us."

"The first thing you said was behavior toward me. What did you mean by that? Have you ever said that to Richard?"

"Hold it," I said. "Janet, you need to help your mom. One

of the ways of helping her is telling her that Richard's behavior toward you, it's not her business. If you could help her, it would be so nice for her to stay out of your marriage. Can you do that?"

"I don't tell it to her in so many words," Mrs. Pasquariello said. No one likes to be called meddlesome.

"Oh, Mother!" Janet said.

"I see little things. I see your burdens."

"Mother, I don't feel they are burdens, and that's the only thing that counts. If I felt they were burdens, I would discuss it with you."

"Janet," I said. "How old do you think your mother thinks you are?"

She laughed. "Younger than Jill."

"So why do you let her do that?"

"Well, she's a difficult woman to resist."

"No, I think you're wrong. She's intrusive, but you let her be. One of the ways you can help Jill is by establishing what are acceptable boundaries. If you help your mother not to intrude in your marriage, you will also have a model not to let your daughter intrude in your marriage. Because she is also very intrusive. Your mother is intrusive and helpful. Your daughter is intrusive and demanding."

Jill isn't sick, she's intrusive. She is playing her grandmother's role. It is an honorable tradition.

Now Richard spoke up: "I'd like to ask a question. Your father made some comments about how cold I am. I'd like to know if you share that feeling."

I broke in. "Before you answer, I want you to understand what Richard is asking you. He's asking: 'Are you with me, or with Daddy?'"

Again there was silence. And then Janet said, "I'm with you." And she said it as if she meant it.

A few minutes later, when her mother interrupted with a question, Janet said, "Mother, please, we're having a private conversation."

It was easy to see the grandmother's intrusiveness as the problem. But a lack of boundaries is maintained by both parties. For one person to intrude, another must tolerate it. I was pleased to see Janet adopting my language, the language of boundaries and autonomy.

Jill was an issue, but not the only one. Janet's unsettled conflict with Richard, which led her parents to think she needed help, had become another issue.

Ten days earlier, the family reality had been clearly defined: They were a normal family with a symptomatic child. This directed all effort toward the child, amplifying helpfulness and narrowing alternatives. Now there was a challenge to this certainty. Things were not so clear, and confusion might spark alternatives.

Therapy moves along at several levels. While I had been emphasizing the couple and the extended family, Jill and her symptom were never out of my awareness or the family's. Using her father as a crutch, she had become more mobile, but it was time to move further. As we neared the end of the session, I asked Jill about the disruptions in her life since the drowning incident. She talked about all the inconveniences and all the doctors, but she didn't seem overly upset about limping through life. I told her and her parents that the next step in her recovery would be learning to walk without the literal support of her parents. I would consult with experts in the orthopedic department of Children's Hospital, and we would create a special crutch just for her. In the meantime, I told Richard to bring a sturdy umbrella to the next session so that he could begin to teach Jill how to walk.

Before the next session I received the neurological report. After studying the history and performing all the necessary tests, the neurologist concluded that there was no organic or structural reason why Jill shouldn't walk normally. In the language of the report, "Her symptom complex was entirely functional." Jill's infirmity was in her mind.

Next we sent Jill to the orthopedic unit to be fitted for a crutch. The technicians asked Jill if she had a favorite color. Purple. So she was to have a purple crutch.

The Slaters showed up for the eighth session without Davey. Richard didn't see any need for him to come. I decided not to make an issue of it. Siblings who aren't the center of family attention have their own agenda, but we had limited time and a serious symptom.

As the family entered, I was glad to see Richard carrying a newly purchased, sturdy-looking umbrella. Unlike therapists who see individuals and must rely on patients' reports of what goes on in their lives, family therapists can bring life itself into the treatment room. In this session I would be reinforcing step one, bringing Richard closer to his daughter by teaching her to walk with a cane.

And so we began. Richard was a bit tentative when he helped Jill to her feet and then handed her the umbrella and asked her if she could lean on it. As he tried to play the unaccustomed role of nurse to his daughter, she cast imploring glances at her mother.

"Good," I said. "Janet and I will stand at the other side of the room to give you two more room to operate."

Richard was more decisive now, and he succeeded in getting Jill to stand alone with the support of the umbrella. At his urging, she took a few halting steps and then, sobbing, collapsed onto a chair. "I'm scared!" Both parents looked upset. Jill was pitiful. She was helpless. She was dramatic.

This was a difficult moment, for all three of them. It was hard for the mother to stand back, to be only an observer. Jill, afraid of falling, paid so much attention to her legs that she could not use them. Her paralysis came from real fear. The father wanted badly to help but didn't know how. Apprehension and frustration made him a little harsh. His daughter's tears softened him, but he felt more defeat than compassion.

"You are doing beautifully! Richard, you need to help your daughter to overcome fear, and you are doing very well. You—both of you—have made a tremendous beginning."

For them the issue was Jill's learning to walk, and they were both afraid. For me the issue was prolonging the interaction between father and daughter and helping him to feel competent and successful.

When I was a child psychiatrist I used to play with the unhappy children whose parents brought them in for treatment. As a family therapist I wonder why parents don't play more with their own children.

"Jill, it's hard for anyone to understand how difficult this is for you. So, to make your father understand, it will be necessary to teach him to walk like you do."

"I want you to observe and imitate, Richard. Did you observe how she shifts her weight?"

I asked him to roll up his trouser cuffs so that Jill could see if he was moving his legs properly. He rolled the cuffs midway up his calves and said, slightly embarrassed, "Is this okay?"

"No, no," I said. "Much higher. We have to see how your muscles move."

The corporate vice president gamely limped across the room with his pants rolled up to his thighs. Janet tried to keep a straight face but couldn't and finally burst out laughing. Jill, watching her father's stilted, ungainly walk, started laughing too. Richard was embarrassed, and then he wasn't. He was on to me.

I, too, was enjoying this. I felt like the director of a Keystone Kops movie, getting people to do outlandish things in precise ways. It felt right to prolong this scene.

So I told Jill that her father was not quite getting it, and could she take his arm and show him. Let her be the competent one, expert in the ways of limping.

I told him, "It's extraordinary what a mind can do. You see, her mind is saying to her 'walk crookedly' and she walks crookedly. So your mind can also tell you—Richard, I want you to say to your mind 'walk crookedly,' like she says to her mind. Then walk together and see if you can both walk crookedly."

"Crookedly." I began to play with the word, giving the "r" a Spanish roll, creating a tempo, a beat. The two of them limped across the room, a strange couple engaged in a ritual dance.

"You need to have a crooked mind to learn how to do it, Richard. Your mind is too straight." We all laughed this time. We were all part of this absurd scene with serious implications.

Like every symptom this paralysis served many purposes in the family's psychic economy. For that reason no simple attack on it would succeed. Thinking structurally, I had worked with the extended family on the appropriate boundaries between the generations. Thinking behaviorally, I had attacked the symptom, telling Jill to walk first with Daddy and then with a crutch. Now I was moving from the concrete to meta-phor, telling Jill that she walks with her mind. A symptom that is in the mind can be overcome with mind games.

A mood of play had replaced the earlier one of threat and fear, and I risked a more pointed comment. "Jill, your leg is straight but your mind is crooked. You see, Richard, when she is not telling her mind to walk crookedly then she is not crooked. So the issue is not that her body is crooked; her mind is crooked. You, Richard, have a straight mind, so you will need to help your daughter."

And then I told them that the special crutch would be ready soon. "Jill, did they remember to ask you what is your favorite color?"

"Yes. And I told them purple."

"Lovely. You will begin replacing your father, first with this special crutch, then with thinking straight, then with walking straight—but don't hurry. Take your time."

I wanted her to be in control—but of course I *did* want her to hurry.

Realizing that Jill needed more experience in sensing her body alignment, I sent her to a trainer in Alexander tech-niques. (Although our sessions seemed to be going well, I am never so certain of the magic of therapy. It seems wise to look for many ways of trying to solve a problem.) I had learned to respect the Alexander techniques when I was treated for lower-back problems. The therapist herself was a bit of a ma-gician. I called her and said whatever unblocking of energy she could achieve with Jill would be appreciated. (In giving these instructions, I was aware that now I would never know whether Jill's improvement would be due to my magic or hers.)

Jill's crutch—in fact, a fairly elaborate cane—was a hand-some piece of work. It was purple tubular steel, with a curved handle and a telescoping end. When extended it made a noise like a rifle shot. It was an interesting object, fascinating to a child.

I admired the cane and handed it back to Jill. "My good-ness, what a beautiful cane. Show me how you use it to stand up."

"I can't!" she whined.

"Yes, you can," I said just as firmly. "It's difficult but you can." Then I turned away. Tantrums don't last long without an audience. Besides, I didn't want to get into a power struggle with this stubborn, frightened child. If she won, we'd both lose. If I won, I might appear to succeed where her parents had failed.

"Richard, I cannot do it. Please ask Jill to stand up with the purple crutch."

Partly to please me, I suspect, he was uncharacteristically firm. "Come on now, Jill, *I want you to stand up*." And, partly to please him, she did. Scowling, she heaved herself up with a mighty show of effort. She was very dramatic, but I also sensed she was very scared.

Janet allowed Richard to take charge. She had been turned into an overly helpful mother by the long, grinding process of always being at someone else's beck and call. She was learning that being too helpful allows others to be helpless. And she was learning to let go.

Later in the session Janet talked about how Jill used to cling to her when she was little. Even in play group, instead of joining the other children in their games, she stayed close by. I told Janet that things didn't seem to have changed much. Then I went over to Jill and asked her for the crutch. Holding it up for Janet to see, I said, "I just want you to look at this. This is a substitute parent. From now on, Jill, you will substitute this for your parents. And I hope, Janet, that you will become a little bit distant. Jill will be very angry because she will need to use herself, so it's a very difficult thing I am asking. Janet, you will need to help Richard become a little more involved. And, Richard, you will need to help Janet be strong enough to resist being Jill's crutch."

Now that Jill was walking, I spoke of the problem as clinging rather than not walking. Not walking is an individual problem; clinging is an interactional problem, related to independence and autonomy. When Richard was imitating Jill's limping gait, I had played with the word *crookedly*, drawing it out into three syllables. Jill walked *croo-kèd-ly* because she had a *croo-kèd* mind. It was an incantation. Now I used a number of labels to refer to the cane. It wasn't just a cane, it was a parent substitute. When meaning becomes less fixed, certainty disappears and alternatives emerge.

Richard wanted to know what they should do if instead of using her crutch Jill leaned on the wall or the furniture to support herself, and I said, "She needs to learn to use her legs. So you need to give her space and distance. Then she will do whatever she wants."

It wasn't just Jill who was limping and clinging; it was the whole family. And they all had to learn to walk differently. Richard's question was a hard one for parents not to ask. What should they do to help their children grow up? Sometimes the answer is nothing: Let go.

When it was time to leave, Richard and Janet stood up and started for the door. Bravely they pretended not to worry about Jill. I held my breath. And then, with no one to help, Jill hauled herself up with the purple cane and limped after them.

The next session began with a continuation of a scene that started out in the hall. Jill was peevish over some slight, and her father tried to cheer her up by pinching her cheeks. She was annoyed, he was frustrated, and they were focused on each other.

"Why does he always look at Jill?" I said to Janet. "Why doesn't he look at you? Maybe your face has become too familiar."

"I guess I don't turn him on," she said with a sad smile.

At that point I asked him if they wanted to talk alone. They said yes, and so I took the children out to the waiting room and asked the receptionist to keep an eye on them.

Back inside Janet spoke of the deadness between them. They shared so little—except for the children. They never did anything alone together anymore.

"You never had a vacation without the kids?" I said, not trying to hide my disapproval.

"I never noticed," Richard said, a little offended.

Janet still remembered the long six-week trip they took to Europe the year after their honeymoon. "It was horrible. He was so remote. We never talked. He would never tell me what he was thinking."

He thought she talked too much, just like her mother.

Proximity tests any relationship, and six weeks is a long time. But it isn't just events that make two people drift apart. It is events plus the stories they tell themselves about them. Janet told herself that Richard was cold because he was uncaring. He told himself that her dependence on him was childish. It's always other people's behavior that causes trouble.

After that came the children, distracting Janet and Richard from each other and pushing the possibility of divorce out of their minds. I took it as a good sign that they were now able to talk about these old hurts without becoming defensive and attacking each other.

After this session, Janet and Richard went on a three-day trip to Vermont, leaving Jill and Davey with Janet's parents. They stayed at an old inn, in a room with a fireplace and a brass bed. They were alone together, and they liked it.

Janet's parents had a wonderful time with the children. On Saturday Grandma took them both to get haircuts, and then they went shopping and had lunch at the Food Court, with its wonderful array of all the junk food kids love. On Sunday Grandpa was going to play ball with them but it was too hot, so they went to the park to feed the pigeons. It was one of those parks that still offer a haven for lovers and mothers and children and old people sitting on benches. The only beggars were squirrels and pigeons. They laughed and enjoyed the small pleasures of playing together.

Their grandparents treated the children with benign tolerance. It was easy. They didn't need anything from the children, and they didn't feel the need to mix guidance with play. So they were free to enjoy them.

Jill was now walking easily with the crutch, and I sensed that she would soon be ready to give it up. But I also knew that sudden improvement carries with it the possibility of relapse. Psychoanalysts who first noticed this phenomenon spoke of "symptom substitution," as though symptoms were nothing but signals of underlying conflicts, and until the conflicts were resolved the person *needed* a symptom—if not one, then another. This makes sense as long as you look only at one member of the family.

Sometimes people backslide not because they need symptoms but because improvement does not occur simultaneously in all family members. Though I felt that Jill's progress toward independence was matched by a growing closeness between her parents, I didn't want to take chances, so I prescribed a return to the symptom.

I said we would need to try a little experiment, and that it was important that everyone do their part: "I will keep this lovely crutch for one week, and during this week, Jill, you will need to rely on your parents to help you walk. Richard and Janet, you will take turns helping Jill on alternate days. Today is Tuesday. Richard, can you begin to be your daughter's substitute crutch? And tomorrow, Janet, it will be your turn, and so on. Jill, this experiment is especially for you. During the week you will make some important discoveries."

There was time for only two more sessions before our month was up and the Slaters had to return to Caracas. That time was needed to reinforce changes in the family organization and give Jill the last little push she needed to begin walking on her own. I knew now that she would make it.

The following session was a short one. Janet and the children had accompanied Richard to New York, and the train bringing them to Philadelphia had arrived late.

They seemed happy. Janet was more relaxed; Richard was more animated. Davey, walking at his father's side, still looked as if he'd rather be out playing, but he too seemed more comfortable. Jill walked in, holding on to her mother. The warm smile she gave me crossed the distance between us. She was no longer a depressed, willful child.

We talked about the task of the parents supporting the daughter. Richard discovered that he preferred Jill to use her cane and retain her independence. "Every time I turned around I felt constrained—I mean it was nice having her around—but I felt constrained."

Jill knew what her father meant: "I felt like I was in the way."

By now Davey had decided that none of this concerned him. All this talk went over his head, and so he leaned back, his feet dangling in midair, trying to memorize the back of his hand, like a child sentenced to an hour in church.

Janet also said that it was a burden to have Jill leaning on her. "In fact," she said, "maybe the cane isn't so bad after all." Jill looked away.

Janet and Richard had found it trying, as I expected, to have Jill hang on their arms. But Jill was so excessively concerned with her parents' doings that she said nothing about feeling constrained herself, only about sensing that her parents felt that way.

"She's so involved in watching you two, and worrying about how *you* feel, that she doesn't know how *she* feels. She's a parents watcher. She knows what you think," I said, looking at Janet, "and what you think," looking at Richard. "But she doesn't know what *she* thinks. Isn't that extraordinary?"

Jill smiled sheepishly.

Janet spoke with feeling about the burden of Jill's constant preoccupation with her. "She's like a jailer—or a straitjacket." If this hurt Jill's feelings, she didn't show it. She didn't do much more than press her lips together and narrow her eyes.

And then Janet spoke directly to Jill. "You know I love you, but a person likes to feel that she has some breathing room. That there's some space around you. That someone's not choking you." She reached across and pretended to choke Jill. Jill fiddled with the top button on her shirt.

Richard began to talk about a wedding reception they'd attended over the weekend. At one point he noticed that Jill was all alone, leaning up against the wall, and so he had to go over and find something for her to do.

"Beautiful!" I said. "Jill, now I will tell you something that is very interesting. Not only are you a straitjacket for your parents, but sometimes they are a straitjacket for you."

Then I got up and went over to the wall and leaned against it while I held on to the purple cane. "Okay, so you were there, minding your own business. And probably feeling—what?—a little bored? Or maybe a little unhappy? And you were there for perhaps fifteen minutes? Those fifteen minutes are very important. Because you will learn to cope *only* when your parents will not look at you so much. They love you so much that they smother you."

Then, lowering my voice, I talked directly to Jill, projecting her into the future. "One day very soon you will be able to do something that you know how to do. You'll walk on your own—without a cane, without a mother, and without a father. This is something you know will happen. And you're already ready. But it needs to happen in your own time. You will decide—*you*—that you don't need the cane. But it will not happen according to your father's timetable, and it will not happen according to your mother's timetable."

And then Janet said to me, "There's something I don't understand. She swam for the first time this weekend. How did she do that?"

Richard started to answer, but I cut him off and said that Jill should speak for herself.

Jill's answer to her mother's question was startling. "I kept thinking what a pleasure it would be if you and Daddy could see me swimming."

I went over to Jill and shook her hand. "Beautiful! Did you drown?"

"No," she said, laughing.

"Good, that means you must have used both arms and legs. Beautiful. Very, very nice. First you thought of your parents, and then you discovered that you enjoyed it. You are discovering your body. If your parents will let you, you will grow up."

At this Jill smiled shyly. But then she said, "You said that in the very near future I will probably leave the cane, right? But knowing me it probably will be that I *want* to leave the cane—I'm just too afraid to."

She was feeling pushed, and she responded by asking for instructions. I said, "You will discover that you can overcome your fear." *You will discover.* It was becoming a code word. I was trying to push her not to walk but to decide. As I watched them leave, I knew she would be walking soon.

When Jill showed up with her family for the last session still using the cane, I was more than disappointed. But there had been a change in the family organization. The grandparents were giving Janet and Richard more space, and the Slaters had become more involved with each other and more respectful of Jill's autonomy. Theory said Jill would abandon the cane in the near future. For the moment I had to be content with that.

Six months went by before I heard from them. This time it was Richard who called. Jill was doing well in school and was very popular, but she still walked with the crutch. They were worried. The pediatrician said that if she continued to favor her right leg the muscles would never develop properly. Could they come for a week to see me?

A week isn't much time. But I felt very connected to this family; we had fought demons together. And there was no reason for Jill to use a crutch. I thought that by now the symptom might be more of a label than a psychological force. If that was true, perhaps this time I could find the right healing ritual.

Our first meeting was more like a reunion than a therapy session. They were glad to see me. Time collapsed as if the intervening months had been hours. There was no discontinuity; we were still connected. I had ceased to be a doctor and had become an uncle.

Janet talked about how well Jill was doing, getting good grades, making friends. Hearing herself praised, Jill could not suppress a little smile of pride. In the last six months she had turned the corner from childhood to adolescence. Already she was a beauty. She talked enthusiastically about school and new friends, with no trace of her former depressed sullenness. The wide world outside her family began to fill with things that had been there all along: pretty clothes, chummy friendships, popular music.

As we started the second session, two days later, I asked Jill to pass me her cane. It was an old friend, something that united me to them and also to our time together six months earlier. My holding the cane was a way of saying hello. "What is the meaning of this purple animal?"

"What do you mean?" she asked softly.

"What does it mean in your life?"

"A help?"

"Yes, and such a lovely creature."

"It could be a weapon," Davey said. "Like with a sword inside."

"Yes." I pointed it toward the ceiling and extended it to its full length. "It makes a sound like a machine gun." And then I shortened it and waved it like a conductor. "It could be a conductor's—*batuta*?"

"Baton," Jill said.

The longer we talked the more we invested this simple object with mystery. It was no longer an uncomplicated, inanimate thing. It had meaning and significance.

They were coming to therapy because Jill was continuing to walk with the cane. But the cane was more than a cane. It was part of the family. I played with the cane and its meaning the way a primitive healer throws magic powder into the fire, to call up spirits of change. I was using mystification—not to mask the truth but to introduce uncertainty.

When I asked Richard what he thought, he said, "Well, little kids might carry a blanket. So maybe carrying a pretty little cane is a substitute for carrying a blanket." That answer was too narrow. It said simply that Jill was dependent. Unless I could broaden the focus, the short time we had would be wasted.

"But why would a kid as bright as Jill need a blanket?"

"I just don't feel right without it," she said, a trace of the former whining creeping back into her voice.

"Well, I think this is you two," I said holding the cane up for Janet and Richard to see. "Of course, it's thinner." Janet laughed. "But why should Jill need you—in this form? The question is, Do you still need your parents?"

"Yes."

"Of course. But in this form?"

Jill was puzzled, Davey was no less bored than usual, Janet listened politely, and Richard yawned. Still playing and without thinking, I reached out and hooked Richard's leg with the cane. I pulled. They all laughed. Suddenly I had found a new use for the cane. What began as a spontaneous playful gesture gave me an idea. I hooked Janet's ankle. I pulled in Richard's direction. Again they laughed. "It's a parent-catcher!"

The magic of metaphor lies in ambiguity. As the parent-substitute became a parent-catcher, it carried new meaning. I addressed Jill: "Do you think you need to hook them together? Are you sometimes afraid they will separate?"

"Yes," she answered, very softly.

No one spoke, and in that instant of hesitation everything suddenly shifted. I said to her, "That's a very important thing you said. Talk with them about that."

"Well, it could happen. It happened with your friends, and it happens all the time in books and on TV. And you're always arguing." She was only a child, and what she said was only the truth—part of the truth, really, but to her the whole truth.

Richard, ever reasonable, was explaining. "Sometimes it's better to get things out into the open. It's not good to keep things inside."

Janet felt accused, and she didn't like it. "Do *you* think we always argue, Richard? You said that before, that we're always arguing."

"I don't think we always argue but—"

Davey piped up: "No."

"See, Davey doesn't think we always argue."

And then Jill said, "No, but at least once a day there's always some kind of argument."

"Why shouldn't there be!" Janet said. "Why should we always agree on everything?"

"Well, you shouldn't. But you don't get along together, right?"

Janet didn't answer. Richard, who wasn't ready for what seemed to be happening, said, "We agree on most things, don't we? We agree on most of the important things."

Jill reminded them of a recent argument during which they called each other mean names. Janet said, "Well, yes, we were acting childishly that time. Maybe you could help us. Why couldn't you have told us we were acting like children?"

"Because you would have told us to stay out of it—'It's none of our business.'"

"Janet," I said. "Can you promise your daughter that you will continue fighting in your marriage, and you will resolve it without her help?"

She laughed. "I guess we will."

Richard laughed too. "We have been for seventeen years."

"Yes, but your daughter thinks that you need her to resolve it. Probably you've fought the same fight for the last ten years, no?" And then I turned to Jill. "Old people become very boring. Why are you so interested in them? Why do you keep watching them?"

And then I held up the crutch again. "This thing—it's a two-way street. It's a symbol of her need of you, but it's also a symbol of Jill's feeling that you need her."

"Jill, you don't need this anymore. But you *think* that you need it. See—" And then I went over to stand between Richard and Janet, leaning on the crutch. "—you are here, and you think that as long as you are here your parents will not separate. Neither from each other, nor from you. So it's nice; you sacrifice yourself for them."

Here was another twist. Parent-substitute, parent-catcher, parents' need. The cane could never be a simple cane again. Jill, Janet, and Richard would have to negotiate their needs directly.

"So one thing you will need to do is to reassure your daughter that you will continue arguing and resolving things in the best way that you can. And that you don't need her."

And then I said directly to Janet, "Are you certain that you don't need Jill to resolve things with Richard?"

"Yes. I'm certain," Janet said with feeling.

"What you're saying is very important. Can you tell Jill that she is fired?"

"Yes. And I mean it."

"Jill, do you understand that your mother fires you from being her mother? Richard, you will need to help Janet keep the promise to fire Jill, and you have to fire her too."

"I'd be delighted."

"Can you do it?"

"We don't need you, Jill," Richard said evenly. "Mother and I are firing you. Is that clear? You don't have to be in the ridiculous position of being your own grandmother."

As the session drew to a close I repeated the assignment I had given them six months earlier: Jill should put aside the crutch and lean on her parents. I felt that we had finally broken the back of this stubborn symptom in the session, but I didn't want to leave anything to chance.

"I gave you the crutch to help you move away from your mother. Now, for the next four days—but only for four days—I want you to experience again leaning on your parents. And I will keep the crutch."

Jill looked at me very seriously, took her lower lip between her teeth, and said nothing.

Once again Richard and Janet had found it annoying to have Jill hanging on to them for the four days of the experiment. They were all sick of this arrangement—and, I hoped, of the pattern it symbolized.

Something else happened too. They had finished what we had started—the airing out of old, unspoken grievances. They'd talked and listened, and raised their voices, and faced their ghosts, and cried. Trapped between two things they feared, anger and emptiness, they chose anger, and found it less lethal than they imagined. They took up much of the session talking about their time together. No matter what happened with Jill, they were grateful to be resurrecting their marriage. Jill seemed visibly relaxed, a hostage released.

The hour went by very fast, and then it was time to go. We all stood up. Then Jill asked me for the crutch.

I gave it back to her, but I asked her to stay with me a moment. I sat her down and asked her to give me the crutch. She handed it over but looked at me with very big eyes. "I don't think you need this any more, Jill. And I would love to have it."

She said no, she still needed it. If she was going to give it up, it would be easier after she got back to Caracas.

"It will happen soon. You are ready, but you will be the one to say when. It all depends on you."

We shook hands and Jill walked out. She was still using the purple crutch, but she wasn't really leaning on it.

———◆———

Two weeks later I received a letter from Caracas. It was from Jill.

August 30

Dear Mr. Minuchin,

You asked me to write to you the day I walked without the cane, and that is exactly what I am now doing. I sincerely thank you for what you have done this year to help my family and me; and I don't know if I could ever repay you entirely, but by being your friend.

I certainly hope that I shall see you again, and in Europe if possible, or even here in Venezuela, but one thing is sure, I would like to go on corresponding with you wherever we go and whatever we do. I shall miss you very much.

Love,
Jill

P.S. My family sends their regards (even Davey). And please:

DO WRITE BACK!!

I never answered that letter. Until now.

8

Parents as Prisoners
or Jailers?

"Where does it hurt?" asks the doctor, and we point to the sore thumb or aching ankle or whatever else happens to hurt. We're confident that pointing to the symptomatic spot will enable the doctor to find out what's wrong, and make it right.

Somewhere along the line, though, we discover the strange phenomenon of referred pain. A painful soreness in the heel can turn out to mean a strained Achilles' tendon, or, more ominously, an ache in the left shoulder can be a symptom of a heart attack. How can we feel pain in one place when the real trouble is somewhere else? The mystery of referred pain clears up once we understand something about the underground rivers of nerve pathways that channel sensations of pain to the brain.

When family sorrows get to the point of hurting enough to produce symptoms, we often point with equal confidence to where the problem is. It might be a depressed father, an agoraphobic wife, or a hyperactive child. When I meet with a family for the first time and ask what the problem is and I hear, "It's me, Doctor, I'm depressed," or "It's the children—they're completely unmanageable," I often think, "Don't be so sure."

Families, too, have mysterious pathways of pain.

———— •••• ————

From the day the Wardens brought Steven home from the hospital, he was a real handful. At most he slept two or three hours at a time; then he was up, screaming, demanding to be fed, cuddled, carried, tickled, and changed. His parents were exhausted. By his first birthday he'd become a motorized little talking machine, all over the house and into everything. "No" meant nothing to him.

The Wardens' second child, Ryan, was an easier baby. By two weeks he was sleeping through the night, and, unlike his brother, he was often content to play by himself. But as he grew older he became more and more willful, like Steven.

I learned all this from Dan Farragut, a former school psychologist who was now in private practice and working with the Warden family.

Dan Farragut's treatment focused on behavioral techniques for controlling behavior. The results were meager. The Wardens and their boys took enthusiastically to each new technique, some of which bore results, but all of which kept the parents and children glued together. After a year in which each new sign of progress turned out to be a mirage, Dan Farragut called and asked if I would agree to see the family for a consultation. "Perhaps," he said, "I'm missing something."

It was nine o'clock in the morning when I met the Wardens in my waiting room, but the parents had that haggard look people get at the end of a long, hard day. Honey Warden was only thirty but looked middle-aged and tired. An overall impression of pallor was heightened by her fine yellow hair, which

hung long and limp. For the last five years she'd been consumed with the joys and miseries of raising children. She
looked exhausted.

Tom Warden looked five or ten years older than his wife
and equally worn out. He had dark circles under his eyes and
a look of constant aggravation on his face.

The two little boys, on the other hand, looked well scrubbed
and happy. At five and four, they looked close enough in age to
be twins. Both were dressed in jeans and white turtlenecks.
Steven's hair was brown, though not as dark as his father's.
Ryan had the same fine yellow hair as his mother. Both children had those long hanks of uncut hair at the backs of their
necks that kids call "tails."

The boys seemed capable of amusing themselves for just a
few moments before they felt the need of grown-up attention.
First Ryan tugged at his father's sleeve and asked him to
come see what he was making. When his father refused, Ryan
went over to his mother and asked her for a pencil. He sat
down, and Steven got up. The two of them took turns buzzing
around the room, lighting here and there for a minute or two,
then circling about and worrying their parents. They were
like a couple of pesky gadflies that just won't settle and are
impossible to ignore.

Tom and Honey responded to their small boys' noisy antics
the way ineffectual parents often do, with a series of criticisms
and directives delivered in a tone the boys could tell didn't
mean business: "Steven, don't bang against the wall, okay?"
"Ryan, why don't you build a house with the blocks?" They
seemed neither to be able to control their kids nor to know
how to let them be.

Working with difficult children and ineffective parents, I
always need to restrain my impulse to take charge. It seems so
easy to say, "Johnny, don't do that," and he'll stop. But I know
that *my* ability to make other people's children respond tells
me nothing about *their* daily drama of helplessness and despair. It only tells me something about my skill with the children of strangers.

After two or three minutes of trying without much success
to converse with Tom and Honey, I asked them to tell the boys
to play in the corner so that we could talk. This simple re-
quest, which gives me a chance to observe how the parents go

about establishing control, usually re-creates some of the problems they have at home.

When they succeeded in getting the boys settled, I asked them, "Why did you come to see Dan Farragut? Maybe you can tell me a little bit, so that I can see if I can help him to help you."

Before they had a chance to answer, the boys started quarreling noisily over who was going to play with which toy.

"Steven, please!" his father said.

Then instead of resuming their play, the boys started swarming around their parents again.

"Ryan pulled my hair!"

"Steven is making faces!"

"Ryan—"

This made conversation a matter of trying to talk over the noise the boys were making. The parents, like volunteer firemen, moved from one brush fire to the next. Very soon conversation stopped, as both parents became preoccupied with trying to deal with the children.

"Can you two relax, ever? Is it ever possible to have a conversation without needing to watch them?"

"Not unless they're asleep—or watching TV," Honey said. She talked with her hands, punctuating her comments with rapid, nervous gestures.

I was trying to focus their attention on our conversation and make the children invisible.

"Do you have a very large house?" I asked.

"No," the father said. "It's a ranch."

"And how many bedrooms do you have?" This was not an idle question. I was interested in space and boundaries.

"Three," he said. When they were younger the boys shared a room, but now each had a room of his own.

"And when you come home from work, what happens?"

"I get home anywhere from six-thirty on. Sometimes I just wait until they're asleep."

I hadn't asked him what time he came home, and his telling me seemed like a confession.

"But usually they're still awake?"

"Unfortunately, sometimes, yes."

As the parents began to respond to my questions, the children settled in the corner and concentrated on their toys. Steven had one of those elaborate Japanese "transformers," a toy that changed shape from a giant alien to a futuristic naval ship, and Ryan had a modest American sports car.

The scene at the end of the day at the Warden house is one that's played out in households all over the country. Tom somehow expects to come home to a wife who will listen and understand. But just about the time he gets home the boys are winding down like little clocks. Honey has her hands full. So Tom goes into the other room and turns on the TV or picks up the newspaper.

In her words, "By the time I put them down he's already watching TV or reading. A lot of times he's already asleep by the time I finish."

"So, you cannot—" I began, but I could see that Honey was too distracted by the boys to hear what I was saying. She was facing me but anxiously watching them out of their corner of her eye. And so I said, "You're looking at me, but the boys have all your attention. Your life is mostly being a mother?"

"Yes, mostly." She sighed. "Trying to keep them happy, educated, and in line."

"Wow! 'Happy, educated, and in line.' That's quite an agenda."

Then, as if on cue, Steven took Ryan's toy, and Ryan poked him.

"Hey!" their father barked, jumping up to pry his two small sons apart. "Steven, did you take his car?"

The boys said what you'd expect. "No." "Yes, he did!" "No, I didn't!" It's an old song.

It becomes a song and dance when anxious parents step in to settle every dispute, as though the siblings were Cain and Abel, and fraternal jealousy might lead to murder. Clearly, Steven and Ryan didn't need their father to settle their squabble. Clearly, Tom and Honey needed some freedom from the yoke of parenting. Neither side respected the other's autonomy.

Whenever I see grown-up, heavyweight parents being defeated by lightweight preschoolers, I know without a doubt that conflicts between the spouses are being played out in the parenting battlefield—and that as they pull in different directions, the confused children become casualties.

The boys resumed yapping and nipping at each other, and

again their father leaped up and growled at them. Then he sat Ryan down roughly in a chair and said, "Sit there until you calm down."

"Do you have your breakables put away somewhere?" I said, trying to resume an adult conversation.

"They're all broken," Tom said.

He went on. "The walls have holes all through them. The doors have holes in them. I don't even bother trying to patch them anymore."

"I can't believe it," I said with unfeigned amazement. "Really?"

"Yeah, really," he said.

"How do you manage?"

Before he could answer, Tom was again distracted by something the boys were doing. As he was about to get up, I gestured with my hand to restrain him. "Look at your wife." He couldn't keep his eyes off the boys.

"I am concerned for you two—not for the kids, but for you. Your life is so impossible."

"Yeah," Tom agreed, and then looked at his shoes. Honey looked at him and then back to me.

"Do you have any time together? Do you like to dance?"

"I do. He doesn't," Honey said.

"Do you like to go to the movies?"

"I do . . ." she said.

"I do," Tom said without conviction. "We just . . . don't."

"Do you have *any* time when you can talk for fifteen minutes with your wife?" The answer was no.

"I am concerned for your marriage," I said. "How can your marriage endure?"

Honey looked at Tom. He didn't answer.

We talked for a few more minutes about how busy they were and what a handful the children were, but Honey couldn't stop looking over to see what the boys were up to.

I said, "It's very difficult for you to talk without looking at the kids."

She laughed and said, "You have to, with these two. They're quick."

There were no neutral moments between generations in this family. All the children's play involved parental control. The

greatest thing about the games children play is freedom—
freedom from adult constraint, freedom for the imagination to
raise its wings.

Steven and Ryan didn't have this freedom. By fixing so
many of their hopes and anxieties on the boys, Tom and Honey
had crossed the boundary between their world and the children's, and taken over their play. To play, children need benevolent neglect. They need play time to manipulate objects
and their imaginations, not their parents. If children are preoccupied with their parents, and vice versa, pure play disappears and becomes part of the struggle for control.

"Is it that they need continuous surveillance, or that you've
gotten so accustomed to looking at them that you can't stop?"

She laughed. "Probably I've got so accustomed to watching
them."

Tom said, "Well, they're always breaking things, and fighting."

Meanwhile, unattended for the last several minutes, the
boys had been playing quietly on the floor.

"Steven," I said, and gestured for him to come over. "I just
want to tell you, you were doing wonderful." I reached out and
shook his hand. He beamed. "It was very nice how you were
playing." He grinned again.

Then I looked at the toy ship he'd been playing with and
said, "What's that?"

"It's a secret Steven battleship," he announced proudly.

"And how does it work?"

Like most small children, Steven was eager for attention
and happy to show off his battleship. It was a futuristic gray
plastic model complete with realistic details, like movable
gun turrets and a dome-shaped pilothouse. When you moved
some of its parts, it could change shape.

"Wow!" I said in appreciation of what he showed me.

Ryan came over to join his brother and share the attention. In this family without boundaries, what one boy did was
automatically assumed to include the other.

I said to Ryan, "No, I am talking to Steven now. You can
go and play over there."

If Ryan felt excluded, he didn't show it. He just went back
to playing where he was. And I returned my attention to
Steven. "Show me how it works," I said. And then I sat down
on the floor with him to see the world from his level.

Many interventions are exploratory probes. When I asked Steven to join me, it was not to make him come but to see what he would do. Similarly, when I told Ryan that I wanted to talk with his big brother, I didn't know how he would respond. His willingness to leave us alone showed me that although these boys weren't used to having separate space and that they questioned control, they did obey when given calm and unambiguous directions. There was clearly a reservoir of good behavior here, if I could help the parents tap it.

I wanted to play with Steven to restore him to the little child he was instead of the monster his parents described. I wanted to explore his best potential. Could he concentrate? How bright was he? Did he calm down with attention? A child's play is an X-ray of his intellect and ingenuity.

Steven showed me how the gun turrets swiveled, how the men in the tower piloted the ship, and how his imagination worked. His play was complex and concentrated. He became a different child, calm, thoughtful, and fun to be with. But at the same time I was enjoying our play, I was concerned about displacing his parents. The more a therapist takes over and demonstrates his competence, the more likely he is to make the parents feel incompetent by comparison. I didn't want that. So I said to Steven, "Does your daddy know how this works?"

Steven, absorbed in play, didn't answer.

"Invite him," I said. "Steven, ask Daddy to come and sit here also, so you can show me and him at the same time."

Steven went over to his father and took his hand. "Want to come with me?"

Tom sighed loudly and came over to join us. Sitting on the floor with his son was apparently not a familiar place for him to be.

"Okay," I said. "Now show us how this machine works." He did.

Now instead of an exasperated father futilely remonstrating with an impossible child, we had a little boy playing happily with his daddy. Because his father had joined him on his level and on his terms, it was a chance for Steven to shine. When it came to his battleship, *he* was the expert.

As they played together for the next few minutes, I confined my remarks to trying to prolong the pleasurable transaction. The secret of doing so was to follow Steven's lead. I wanted both father and son to realize that struggling for control wasn't the only way for them to interact.

Once again Ryan crowded in, and I said, "Ryan, Steven is showing me and your dad something, so go and play over there."

This time he went over to his mother, who gave him a hug. He wasn't used to being excluded, and she understood how it felt to be left out.

"Steven," I said, "can you sometimes play with your toys alone, or does Ryan always play with you?"

Experts on the family usually underestimate the importance of siblings. Perhaps this is because the highly charged interactions between parents and children are so salient, and often so much in need of improvement, that the world of siblings is obscured. The only well-known term for sibling relationships in the professional literature is "sibling rivalry." Actually, children learn about life by learning to get along with their siblings and by following or turning away from the example of brothers and sisters.

After we had been playing for a few minutes, Steven looked up and noticed one of the built-in video cameras rotating around to track our activity. "What's that camera for?" he wanted to know.

"Come here," I said. "I'll show you." He moved toward me and became a small, trusting child. I put my arm around him, and he cuddled next to me, watching as I pointed up at the video camera.

"Tell the camera to move," I said.

"Move."

And, wonder of wonders, the camera moved! Steven was fascinated.

"Now tell the other one."

"Move!" he said in a big voice. And it moved.

"You see," I said. "It's magic."

Steven stared with wide-eyed wonder at the electronic contraption that obeyed his commands.

The language of children is the language of magic—and awe.

"Are there moments, Tom, when you can play with Ryan and have a relaxed time?"

He wasn't sure. "Maybe once in a while," he said grudgingly.

Steven, still enchanted by the magic camera, told it to move again. Still obedient to his command, it did.

"Now I will tell you a secret, Steven," I said to him. "Do you want me to tell you a secret?"

He nodded and brought his head near me. I whispered in his ear. "There is a guy in the other room controlling the camera. Open the door and go into the other room and you will see the guy who is moving the camera. His name is Jonathan. You can say hello."

I wanted to explore Steven's autonomy, to free this boy who was always controlled, and see if he could act capably on his own. By asking him to investigate the other room, I was giving him a rather complicated task: to leave his parents, open the door of the consulting room, turn to the left, find the observation room door, enter a dark room full of strangers, identify the one who was operating the camera, and introduce himself. I was also interested in how his parents would respond. Could they trust him? Therapy with young children is a therapy of action and movement, not talking.

Steven marched right out of the room and went next door and introduced himself to the cameraman. As soon as he left, Ryan moved in to take his big brother's place.

"Do you want to play with me?" I said.

He did. Ryan showed me his little car and firehouse. He played quietly and happily for a moment or two. Then Steven returned, and I suggested that he show Ryan the cameraman.

Again I was probing for flexibility. Would Ryan accept Steven's leadership? Would the parents allow Steven to take charge? How narrow was their view of the boys?

Honey watched anxiously as the two boys left the room. She laughed when I said, "I just wanted to give you some time to rest."

Both parents, but especially Honey, were tense and vigilant. They carried the weight of their worry about the boys into what might have been time to relax (and they brought back that unrelieved tension into their interactions with the children).

I asked Honey if she had any friends, and it turned out that she went out on Wednesdays to a club to dance and sometimes to watch a comedian. It was, Tom said, the girls' night out. Thinking it odd that she would go dancing without her husband, I asked when they had time together.

"Usually late at night," Honey answered.

Just then Steven, who had returned with his brother, turned out one of the lights.

"No!" Honey said sharply. "Turn that back on."

"It's okay," I said. I wanted to help break the cycle of control and defiance by turning the boy's behavior into a game.

So for the next few minutes I asked Steven to turn various light switches off and on. He complied happily. In the process, his misbehavior was transformed into exploratory behavior.

"Very good!" I said. "You were very good. Thank you very much."

Steven beamed and said, "I know how to work switches."

"Yes, you do. And how high can you count?" I asked him.

"I can count to one hundred!"

While Steven proudly began to count all the way to a hundred, his father, who had talked only about negatives, smiled and counted silently along with his son.

One of the problems for a therapist is that being successful at eliciting good behavior from children becomes, unwittingly, a challenge to the parents. The goal is to make the children's competence part of the parents' competence. But how would I be able to communicate to these two parents, locked in a losing struggle to control their two small boys, that they already knew what to do?

Finally, Steven said, "ninety-nine—*one hundred!*"

"That's very good," I said. I then asked him to spell his name, which he did. I asked him to spell a few more words, and when he got stuck he went over to his mother for help. She told him to sound it out. The next time he got stuck, I suggested that he ask his daddy.

"How do you two help each other?" I asked the parents. "One of the things I noticed is that when the kids are playing, Tom is very tense."

"Yes," Honey agreed. "So I even keep my eye on that. I, like, oversee it."

"That means even if your husband is on duty, you are keeping your eye on him?"

"Yes," she said, and laughed, a little embarrassed.

"Why?"

"Because he doesn't know the kids like I know them. Like for instance he doesn't know which clothes are which."

"My goodness, Honey, then you are stuck for life."

"Well, what I usually watch out for is when he's had enough of being on duty. And that's when I jump in. So, if it's a matter of trust, it's up to a certain point. He has done some weird things in the past when I've left him alone with the children. Like falling asleep when he was watching them."

"That was years ago," Tom protested.

"They could get hurt," Honey said.

"I fell asleep in the chair, which was only a couple of feet away."

They were giving evidence as though I were that court of appeal to which they might at last present their case. But the truth was that she was far more responsible for and burdened by the children than he was. He was the breadwinner; she was the nurturer. In this they were following scripts they were raised on.

There was also a second script, an ominous one, obscured by the drama of the difficult children. It was the tragedy of estranged spouses. Their conflict with the children seemed to offer a detour for their own conflict.

"So, Honey, you are a prisoner. Just now Tom was doing the necessary things to control the kids. Sometimes what's necessary to control the kids is *not* to pay attention to them."

Somehow my success with the children and my repeated digging into the couple's avoidance triggered an alarm. And so Tom challenged me.

"This one's always after knives," Tom said, indicating the older boy.

"Knives?"

"Yes, knives. We're always finding knife holes in the walls, on the ceiling. I don't trust him not to stab his brother with one."

"And how does he find the knives?"

"There's *nothing* he can't get into. Like you said, he's not stupid."

"No, he's bright." Five minutes ago, the boys were playing on the floor as friendly as puppies, and then showing off their ability to spell and count. Now Tom was reminding me that the real problem was the children.

"I can't live like a jailer," Tom said. He was agitated, angry, insistent. "You know, you go from room to room and you've got to lock up this and put that away."

"Is that how you live your life?"

"Yes!" he said with feeling.

Honey, who also felt victimized by her two small children, tried to explain further about the knives. "One of their games is throwing our paring knives up to the ceiling."

I asked the obvious question: "How is it that you have the knives in a place where they can get them?"

"Because there's noplace I can put the knives," she said. "I use them to cook with. Unless I put them under lock and key, and I don't have anything that's under lock and key."

After an hour of chipping away at their view of the children as monsters, we were back at point zero. She was saying what people who are stuck generally say: "What can I do?" "It's impossible."

I found myself at a crossroads. Any direction I chose could take me to a different but equally significant exploration of family issues. I could continue the focus on the marital conflict and the way it played itself out as parental conflict, or concentrate on the children and issues of control. Given the resistance I felt from Tom and Honey whenever I approached their relationship directly, I chose to focus on the children, hoping I could come to the couple's problems by a different route.

I have a number of concrete maneuvers and metaphors to tame child monsters—and I think I used them all.

"Steven," I said, "come here for a moment. I just want to see how tall you are."

Steven came over, and I asked him to stand up tall. Then I called Ryan over and asked him to stand next to Steven. Standing, they were no taller than I was sitting down. Steven had become larger than life in his parents' eyes. This was a way of shrinking him down to his own size.

Next I asked Steven to make a fist and punch my hand as hard as he could. At first he was a little hesitant, as though he too subscribed to the theory that he was a heavyweight. But with a little prompting—"No, harder! With all your might." —he wound up and gave me a good sock.

I was trying to demonstrate how small the children actually were, and to disabuse all four of them of the myth that the little boys were powerful.

Tom looked on concerned and winced when his small son punched me. "Is that the best you can do?" I said.

At that, Steven screwed up his face and did his best imitation of Hulk Hogan. But even with sound effects, he was still a little boy, and his punch had no punch.

Then I asked Tom to come over and stand next to his son. "I just want to see how tall you are. Steven, stand next to your daddy and see how tall you are." The difference between a three-foot boy and a six-foot man was, of course, dramatic.

I next asked Tom to lift the boy up into the air. By now, it was obvious to both parents what I was saying, and Tom hoisted his small son all the way up to the ceiling.

"Whoa!" Steven cried, enjoying every minute of this.

Then I asked Tom to pick up Ryan. "I just wanted to see if your daddy is strong or not," I said to Steven. "Is he strong?"

Steven nodded vigorously.

"He is strong, isn't he? And what about your mom? Can she pick you up?"

Honey came over and picked up first one and then the other boy. She couldn't lift them over her head like Tom, so she hugged and kissed them instead.

"You see," I said to Honey and Tom, "I don't understand how these kids give you such an impossible life."

Just at that moment Ryan started to play with one of the table lamps. This time his mother stopped him with a calm but firm no.

"You did very well, just then," I said. "You see, he *is* manageable." And then I went on. "Let me tell you my idea. Steven, come here a moment. Stand up on this chair."

He climbed right up on the chair.

"Dad, come here. Are you taller than Daddy?"

"No," Steven said, after checking carefully.

"Let's see, Steven, if we can find something higher. The radiator. Stand up there." Steven climbed up on top of the radiator, which was about three and a half feet off the floor. He liked this game.

"Let's see if you are taller than Daddy now."

His father walked over and now Steven was about a head taller.

"And are you taller than Mommy, too?" Honey walked over and stood next to Tom.

"You are taller than both of them!"

Steven liked this best of all. "I'm taller than all of you!"

"But that's not true," I said. "That is his feeling. His feeling is that he is taller than you, but he certainly is not."

I long ago developed the only mathematical theorem in family therapy: If a preschooler is taller than either of his parents, he must be standing on the shoulders of the other parent. I was trying to demonstrate this theorem to Tom and Honey.

"For instance, you can pick him up so easily." I gently scooped Steven off the radiator with one arm.

"And you can do this." I hugged him and sat down, pulling his arms across his chest and holding them tightly so that he couldn't wriggle out of my grasp.

"Can you move?" I asked. Steven wiggled but couldn't budge. I gave him a squeeze and he curled up on my lap, smiling like a contented kitten.

"So, you are a *little* boy. How old are you?"

"Five!" he said, holding up five fingers, perfectly willing to be a little boy.

"I want to show you something. Go to the corner there and bring me the doll. I want to show you what a funny doll it is."

Steven ran over to the corner and brought back the doll that looked like a prince. Actually, it was reversible. It could be a prince or a frog. I wanted to show Steven how the doll could be transformed from a frog to a prince, and I wanted his parents to get the message.

"Kiss the doll, and I will show you what happens. It's a very funny doll, because if you kiss it"—I pulled the prince's costume over his head—"it becomes something else."

"It's a frog!" Steven was delighted.

The frog that could be a prince was a metaphor for Steven's metamorphosis from a little boy to a monster and back to a little boy again. This was a dumb show presented for the benefit of Steven and his parents.

"Something happens to Steven that made him believe that he is taller than both of you—but he is not."

Tom leaned forward; and Honey, for the first time, seemed totally focused on our conversation.

"It's very important for you to be grownups besides being

parents. You are taking care of the children but not yourselves. You said you were jailers, but I think you are prisoners.

"You have a girls' night out," I continued. "Do you have a spouses' night?"

Tom shook his head. "No," he said quietly.

"How long do you think your marriage will last?"

Honey shrugged and said, "I don't know." She chewed her lower lip.

"Not long, I can assure you, if you don't start making time for each other. Then, Honey, you will have two kids and you will be busy all the time, and you will have *no* time to be an adult because you will be just a mom."

At that point Ryan came over to ask me to help him with the frog-prince doll. It had gotten stuck as a frog.

"You need to find ways to make the children small. You are absurd parents, because you think that these little boys have a power that they don't have."

"But you can't ignore them," Tom protested.

"I am concerned for you as a couple," I repeated. "You don't need techniques for dealing with the kids. What you need are techniques for having fun with each other."

Tom said wistfully, "I think we've forgotten how."

"It seems that both of you have become prisoners of the kids."

At that I got up and shook hands, and we said good-bye.

After the session Dan Farragut and I talked about the family and about how to continue treatment. We were pleased with the consultation. I felt the pleasure that comes when I know that some shift has occurred in the way in which the family experiences life together. I was especially satisfied with my work with the children. I liked them, and they liked me, and together we had challenged the notion that they were impossible. But I told Dan Farragut that I was concerned about the emptiness in the Wardens' marriage and suggested that he should stop having family sessions focused on the children and instead should meet with the couple alone.

Four months after my consultation with the Wardens, Dan called to give me a progress report. Tom had stopped avoiding

Honey and the children and started becoming more of a hus-
band and father. He and Honey had begun to talk more, and
Tom took over a good deal more of the supervision of the boys.
Honey felt displaced.

The more involved Tom became with the kids, the more he
and Honey were confronted with their differences. They argued about when to send the boys to bed and how much responsibility to give them around the house.

Along with their increasingly contentious disagreements
about the boys, Honey and Tom also began to quarrel about
their relationship. They argued about where to go out together. They argued about spending time with friends. And
they argued about sex. At times it seemed they argued about
everything. Helping them get the boys under control and move
closer together as a couple had set them on a collision course.

Within four months Honey moved out of the house, leaving Tom with the children, and started talking about a permanent separation.

I had considered the possibility of a separation, but Honey's
abandonment of the children was totally unexpected.

I was upset because I felt that I had contributed to this
unhappy turn of events. Maybe I should have let sleeping dogs
lie. I tried to convince myself that a separation might be good
for both of them, but I couldn't stop thinking about the children. Since Dan was continuing to see both spouses sepa-
rately, I suggested another consultation.

When they entered my office, the radical restructuring of
the Warden family was evident in some highly visible changes
in all four of them. The two boys, Steven and Ryan, hadn't lost
any of their restless energy, but for most of the forty-five
minutes we spent together they played by themselves on the
floor. Let off the short leash their parents used to keep them
on, instead of running wild, they just stopped straining. They
were free to play, and their parents were free to talk.

Tom seemed less like the gloomy, intense man I'd met four
months ago. His hair was shorter, he'd replaced his dark-
framed glasses with lighter wire-rims, and he no longer
seemed so anxious about what the boys were doing. It wasn't
that he didn't care. It was that he seemed to trust them.

Honey looked fresher and much prettier than I remembered. Her long blond hair was lustrous, and her face was
relaxed. She wore dark slacks and a black turtleneck.

Perhaps the most surprising thing about the Wardens was the absence of overt animosity between Honey and Tom. Usually when couples separate, they suffer violent spasms of alienation. I wondered why that wasn't so with Tom and Honey.

Honey spoke first. She seemed anxious to explain herself. "Last time we were here, your words made a big impression on me. I was doing everything—I could see that, but I didn't know how to stop. You were right, I didn't trust Tom. I didn't think he was willing to spend more time with the boys, and I was afraid if I pushed him he'd lose his temper and take it out on them."

No longer did her eyes intently follow the boys. Even when their play got noisy, she didn't get distracted. But then she didn't look at Tom either. She looked at me with troubled eyes.

"But after we left here last time, Tom started helping out more, without my having to say anything. Unfortunately that's when the problems got worse between us. We're just two completely different people. His ideas about discipline—well, they aren't my ideas. And as for doing things together, we tried, but it didn't work out. No matter what we did, we'd always end up arguing."

Tom listened without saying anything. There was none of the usual wrenching conflict between two people coming apart. It was almost as though these two were already divorced.

Honey continued. "For so long, when things weren't right, I tried to change myself. If he didn't want to have anything to do with the kids, I did it all. When he wanted to help out more, I let him. But I couldn't make it work. I couldn't change myself."

And so she left.

Tom's version of what happened wasn't much different from Honey's. The main difference was that he was bitter about her leaving. He felt abandoned and rejected.

When he switched from talking about the marriage that was coming apart to discussing the boys, Tom brightened up.

"Both boys have gotten a lot better. I'm a little stricter than Honey, and so I don't let them get away with a lot of stuff she used to. But I remembered what you said, too, and I give them plenty of time to play on their own."

He'd also begun to give Steven more responsibility. Before, the boy's room was treated like a toxic dump. Steven messed it up, and so they had taken the mattress off the box springs and put it on the floor, and taken out everything of value. Their message to him was: "We give up. Do what you want." But after Honey left, Tom changed all that. He put the bed back together, gave Steven an old desk to work at, and even put the computer in Steven's room. Steven responded not by destroying anything but by starting to keep his room neat.

When Tom told me this, I said, "How do you explain that?"

"I don't know," he said. "Maybe he just needed to be trusted." Maybe Tom was speaking for himself too.

After Honey left, father and sons were more at ease with each other. The hidden conflict between the spouses that set up the jarring currents was no longer operating.

Tom was philosophical about the breakup of the marriage. "These things happen," he said. "People stop caring for each other." He spoke without sadness, as if hope had expired.

In fact I sensed that Tom was hurt and bewildered by Honey's leaving. Anger and hurt had become resentment, and then bitterness, and finally despair. They'd both tried and failed to get through to each other. Now they'd given up.

As Tom said, these things happen. But something else, something ominous, was also happening between Tom and Honey. Their hurt and anger toward each other had become invisible again, as it had been before. Unseen and unresolved, it was again being played out in the arena of parenting. In taking over, Tom pushed Honey away and encouraged her abandonment of the children.

To Tom I said, "Your anger at her for leaving you becomes a force that pushes her away from the kids. And the kids need her."

He didn't say anything.

"Honey," I said, "you are still the mother of these kids. You love them and they love you. You're part of them forever, and whatever he says doesn't change that."

This was a very hard session for me. That these things happen didn't make me feel any better about being partly responsible.

There was no putting back together what had come apart, no epiphany, no breakthrough in this painful meeting. Having lost the glue of concern for their children, the couple now faced an emptiness between them that had long been hidden. The one thing of any consequence that I said to Tom and Honey was to remind them that no matter what happened to them as a couple, they would never cease to be parents. But even in that I was wrong. A year later Honey was living with a man with two children of his own, who felt that Stéven and Ryan were too disruptive for his sons, so Honey stopped seeing her children. It happens.

The therapy of Tom and Honey illustrates the dialectic between couplehood and parenthood. Couples need to nurture their marriage in order to function better as parents. Conversely, when facing breakdown, they must protect their parenthood from the corrosive effects of marital conflict.

Love, even sympathy, died long before the Wardens came to therapy. But the pathways of pain are capricious. The animosity between Honey and Tom was submerged and reappeared in the form of impossible behavior in Steven and Ryan. Once Steven got an official diagnosis—"hyperactivity"—the focus on him maintained his symptom and masked the difficulties in the couple.

Was therapy with the Wardens a success or a failure? I don't think it's possible to measure life in such narrow terms.

In individual terms, Honey moved out of a very unhappy relationship with Tom. One can hope that her new family will give her an opportunity to be a fuller person. It seems clear that the new family unit of Tom and his two children is a happier and better-functioning unit than before. The children's symptoms have subsided as well.

But even if we accept the possibility that divorce may be better than two parents continuing to make each other's, and their children's, lives miserable, the idea of a mother forsaking her children chills the heart. Honey's departure was a profound and wrenching upheaval. Her absence left a large empty space in the boys' lives. I hoped it wouldn't be permanent. And yet, even when one parent breaks contact with the children, a family is not destroyed by divorce. Rather, it changes shape.

Nevertheless, my response to the breakup of the marriage

was a sense of regret. I know it isn't my job to "save" families from separation, but I am biased in this direction when young children are involved. There is unfinished business with the Wardens. If I could, I would invite both family groups for a network meeting, trying to help them reconnect Honey and her boys. I always hope for happy endings.

9

A Father's Rage

I want to tell you a story about a man who hit—and did not want to hit—his children. Reports of family violence call up a certain stereotype: urban poverty, unemployment, drunkenness, brutish men. But it doesn't always happen that way.

Violence is an ugly form of power in the face of which we all feel threatened. The violent person is seen as powerful and menacing. In fact there are two forms of violence. Violence to achieve a goal might be called "coercive violence." But there is another form of violence, "pleading violence," in which, as we saw with Philip and Lauren, the victimizer perceives himself or herself as a victim. In families where there is child abuse or spouse battering, violent men—and sometimes

women—often experience themselves as helpless responders
to the other person's baiting.

In these circumstances the desperate and uncontrolled at-
tacker pleads for understanding of his or her impossible plight.
Regardless of our emotional response to such a distortion of the
facts, punitive control of this kind of violent person may only
increase the feeling of victimization—and the likelihood of further violence.

———◆———

The Farrells were an ordinary middle-class family from Vermont. Carter Farrell was in his early forties. After graduating
from college and working in Philadelphia as a probation officer for a few years, he returned to his native Vermont to
work as a hunting and fishing guide. For two hundred dollars
a day he would take tired men with jangled nerves from the
city into the woods and streams of Vermont to do what he
never tired of doing. However, guiding is a chancy occupation.
Only the most popular guides make a living at it. Carter
lacked the easy, affable manner that might endear him to
people who crave conversation as part of the package to restore their spirits. But his great skill at fly-fishing the Batten
Kill and Mettawee rivers, and his unfailing ability to locate
deer in the fall and wild turkeys in the spring, made him
highly sought after by serious sportsmen and -women.

At the time I met the family, Carter had retired from
guiding and taken a job as a commissioner in the Vermont
Department of Fish and Wildlife.

Carter's wife, Peggy, was an elementary school teacher
whose experience and good sense made her a perennial choice
every time a principal's job opened up in her district. Her
answer was always the same: "I'm a teacher, not an admin-
istrator." And so, once every five years or so, she avoided the
mistake that a lot of people make of trading in a job they love
for one with a fancier title.

Peggy and Carter had three children, a girl of eighteen, a
boy of sixteen, and another girl who was eleven. Robin was a
senior in high school, Keith was a sophomore, and Tippi was
in the sixth grade. They were nice kids, but Carter and Peggy
had problems with them.

The Farrell family was referred to me by their therapist,

Kate Kennedy, for a consultation. They'd come to her a couple of months previously for discipline problems and then gotten bogged down. Kate, a former student of mine, felt that a consultation would be helpful and convinced the Farrells to come to New York over a weekend.

The Farrell family filed into the room and filled it up. The father, tall and intense, led the rest and sat in the corner chair, farthest from me. He wore blue slacks, a red polo shirt, and a long mustache. Next came his wife, a small, attractive woman with a round face, who sat next to her husband. Her skin was fair and she wore her reddish blond hair cut short. A muted peach-colored blouse set off her gentle features, and contrasted with her husband's strong colors. She was followed by the children, who sat in a row next to their mother. The two teenagers sat at the end, as far away from their father as possible.

I began by asking the parents, "Maybe you can tell me why you've been seeing Kate Kennedy for—how long is it— two, three months?"

"It must be about two months, I think," Mrs. Farrell said. Her voice was mild, not weak but restrained. She was a pretty woman, soft, subdued, and in control.

"Robin and Keith were having trouble," Carter explained. His voice was more forceful than his wife's. "Problems at school and problems at home, getting along."

He was a lean, hard-muscled man with reddish brown hair. In profile his sharp nose and intense look reminded me of a hawk.

"We were having problems with discipline," he said, summing up the situation as he saw it.

"When you say 'we,' you mean both of you?"

"Yes." He nodded.

"With whom, these two?" I asked, pointing to Robin and Keith, the eighteen- and the sixteen-year-old.

"With all of them, really," he said. "But primarily these two. Discipline is the main problem—or lack of it, really." He was a stern fellow, patriarchal rather than paternal, and a great believer in rules and regulations. He glanced at his wife and sighed. "We never have devised a good disciplinary program. We just sort of handled it on an ad hoc basis. For any particular situation that arose, why, we did *something*."

Something about this couple's blend of formality and amiability made me want to cut to the point. "Who is the sheriff in the family?"

Carter and Peggy looked at each other in bemused silence. Most parents like to pretend that they share the power, even if that's blatantly untrue. Then Carter said, "I suppose I am."

He got no argument from his wife. And so I asked her, "And are you a deputy sheriff, or are you the attorney for the defense?"

She smiled a small, rueful smile. "Probably—history has been— attorney for the defense." Her husband shifted slightly in his chair. She sat very still.

"And are you a competent or an incompetent sheriff?"

"If I were competent, we wouldn't be here," he said, shrugging slightly.

"So the family has an incompetent sheriff, and a—competent or incompetent attorney for the defense?"

"Unfortunately, I suppose, a very competent attorney for the defense," she said.

"Wow, you *are* in trouble," I said. "This is the worst arrangement that exists."

They laughed and exchanged embarrassed smiles.

They were polite and friendly, but they were approaching me with caution. I knew their problems were serious. Kate told me that the father had fits of rage and sometimes got violent. But they were playing it slow, well-mannered and well-controlled.

I had tried to cut through the formality with a whimsical metaphor, and they had admitted something that would have been very hard to say in plain English.

Then I turned to Robin and Keith. Robin was small and pretty like her mother. She wore a denim jacket over a blue shirt. Her brother was tall and bony, like his father. He had his mother's reddish blond hair, only his was long and parted in the middle. He wore a dark-blue nylon windbreaker over an old white T-shirt. He had the big hands of a man but still looked almost feminine, in that androgynous way of some teenage boys.

"Is Mother always on Father's back, trying to protect you?" I asked them.

Robin said, "Yes." Her brother nodded.

"That means you must not be learning how to deal with your father—because she's doing your job."

"Well—" Robin began.

Her mother broke in. "That's what I've tried to tell you. If you have a problem with your father, instead of coming to me about it, talk to Daddy."

"I see that it is like that," I said. "Because just now Mother became your translator."

Robin nodded. She looked young for her age, but she was quick and perceptive.

"So she's helpful like that."

"Well, she only does it with Daddy," Robin said. "But that's because—"

"No," I said. "She just did it with me."

"Oh," Robin responded.

"I was talking to you, and she interpreted me to you. Does it bother you, my accent?"

"No." She smiled. "I think it's nice."

"Do you need help to translate?"

"No," she said, still smiling.

I smiled, too, and then turned to Peggy. "Mother, relax."

"I apologize," she said and laughed, seeming not to take offense.

I like it when something like this happens to me in a session, this first immersion in the family's way of being. Mother just told me that I had broken a family rule: I contacted the children without going through her. Perhaps in families where there is a violent man, a strange man has to be checked out before he is admitted. So Mother was the gate-keeper. Where was Father?

Now I moved to explore the father's isolation, proceeding on the assumption that the counterpart of a mother's overinvolvement would be the father's underinvolvement—that enmeshment and disengagement were part of a mutually reinforcing pattern. If I was wrong, they would correct me.

"So," I said, going back to Robin, "Mother does a good job of protecting you. What kind of trouble do you get into?"

"Well, Daddy and I don't get along, and that causes a lot of trouble." She spoke with a strong New England accent, and with the certainty of one who has thought about this. "My father and I don't have any communication at all. Except for like 'Please pass the salt' or something—but we can't talk about anything serious. And we usually don't agree on things."

' "Like what?"

"Like anything."

"Like Russia? China?"

She gave me a small, twisted smile, the kind teenagers reserve for adults who ask them to explain themselves. "No, when I say serious things, I mean things that concern me. My problems. Like schoolwork, or with my boyfriend, or *anything*."

"What kind of brute is your father?" I asked, responding to this very polite family with blunt language. I was challenged by the disparity between the image of violence that Kate had described and the pleasant, polite family I was seeing.

The father sat forward, listening carefully to what the daughter he loved but didn't know how to talk to would say.

"Brute?" she said. She sighed. This wasn't easy.

"Is he a primitive kind of person?"

"No, it's not that. He's just real—he's kind of closed up around people. For a long time I don't think he liked to be that involved with us. He's not a bad person. That's just what happened."

"He just doesn't understand people?"

"No, I think he might be scared of people—not physically, but just—I feel like he puts up this barrier for people—well, because they're new, or he just might not be interested in them."

"I see," I said. "Keith, how do you see it?"

"Huh? I'm not sure exactly what you're talking about." Keith was less articulate than his sister and clearly uncomfortable with this conversation about feelings. So I tried to make it easier for him. "Are you having trouble with your father?"

As I spoke to his son, Carter leaned back and rested his elbow on the back of his chair.

"Well, yeah, because we're just two different people," Keith said, as though stating a regrettable but, after all, inevitable fact. "And usually teenagers and fathers just don't get along."

"That's not true," I said. "There are teenagers who *do* get along with their fathers. You are saying *you* don't get along with your father."

Keith nodded.

"And what about your mother? Do you get along with her?"

"Well, yeah," he said, as though it were a strange thing even to ask.

"Why? I thought teenagers didn't get along with their mothers."

"Oh, no," he said. "I can talk to her."

"Can you talk with your mom about things like girl-friends?"

"Sure. I can talk to her about anything."

"Why? That surprises me. When I was your age I talked with my father about these things. Because he had been an adolescent before me, and my mother had never been an adolescent male."

I was beginning to challenge the mother's centrality, but I was doing it with the logic of simple-minded truisms. The logic of my statement was unassailable, making the challenge to the mother invisible.

Then I turned back to Keith's mother. "So how is it you have this insight into young men growing up?"

"I don't know that I have an insight," she said evenly, defending herself against my insinuation. "But I like to let the children know that they can tell me how they feel and that I'll listen, and care, and understand."

Very quickly the father had been identified as the problem in this family. His children couldn't talk to him, and his wife took up the slack. The logic of my questions was to track the father's isolation and the family's anger at him. The logic of my emotions made me protective of the father, the underdog. It's almost a reflex. When one member of the family is an outsider, I gravitate toward that person, hoping to bring him or her back inside the family circle.

"Tippi," I said, turning to the eleven-year-old, "Robin said she's been having a lot of trouble. Keith there has difficulty in talking with your father. What about you?"

For the last few minutes she'd been leaning forward on her

elbow, looking down, her mind elsewhere. Now she looked up abruptly, surprised and pleased to be asked her opinion.

"Well, I don't have any difficulty talking to either of them." Her accent was even heavier than her brother's and sister's. "But I don't really talk to him," she said, gesturing toward her father, "about things like boyfriends and stuff. I don't guess there's any reason," she said and shrugged.

"And do you talk with your mom?"

"Mm-hmm," she answered. Her expression said, Why on earth not?

"Carter, how is it that you manage to talk with Tippi? Apparently she's the only one who feels you can understand her. How did you manage that? How did you succeed in that?"

"Because I realized, when she was still young, that to have a good relationship it needed to start early." He spoke slowly and deliberately, a man measuring his words and controlling his feelings. "So I spent quite a bit of time with Tippi even when she was still a baby."

If he'd known how to ask his older children for their love, if he'd let them know he was open to them, they might have met him more than halfway. But he was too proud or shy to send them any signal they could recognize, and so it never happened.

Something about Carter touched me. He was a gentle man, humble, reticent but longing for contact. He was clearly troubled by his relationship with his children, but he presented himself as calm and unconcerned, friendly but unemotional. One of the themes of Argentinean tangos is that a man with machismo doesn't cry and certainly doesn't let others see him if he does. They must have similar tangos in Vermont.

"Carter, I have a wild guess. I have a feeling that Peggy runs interference between you and the kids. Is that the way it is?"

"That is true . . ." he said hesitantly. "I'm not sure exactly how you mean that. She has been the interceder—the go-between. I don't think that she intended to keep me from the kids, or vice versa. I think that was her idea of how best to handle the fact that I didn't relate all that well to the kids."

I was surprised that he defended his wife. But Carter was an honorable man. He still believed in chivalry. I was concerned that unless I could free this man, he would go the way

of the hero of *Billy Budd*, Melville's tragic tale of decency
blinded by principle and tongue-tied frustration that turned
to violence.

I said, smiling, "They are your children?"

"As far as I know." He smiled back.

"In any case you raised all of them?"

"Well, I raised Tippi; she raised the other two."

"So they are *her* children." Then I returned to Robin, who
seemed so perceptive and so honest. "So you have a one-parent
family?"

"No, we belong to Daddy. It's just that we don't have as
close a relationship with him as we do with Momma."

"How did that happen, Peggy?"

"I'm sorry?"

"How did that happen? You have three kids, and in my
book three kids are a handful, and they usually need two
parents. How did it happen that these two have only one parent?"

"Well, that question is not easy to answer." She spoke
slowly, under control, like a professional helping person, anxious that I get it right. "One reason is that when Carter and
I were young and first beginning to raise a family, we had
very different ideas and feelings about how to deal with the
children. And rather than working out our differences, I think
I took it upon myself to decide how to deal with the children,
and to do what I knew was right."

I felt stymied, because I knew that logic can't change a
story the family knows to be true. But then absurdity came to
my rescue.

"When did you divorce Carter?"

"Pardon?"

"When did you divorce your husband?"

This time she knew what I meant, and was silent.

My question was like a gypsy fortune-teller's: intuition
cloaked in ambiguity. She could have responded any way she
wanted. She might have said, "I don't understand." She might
have said, "That's crazy."

After a very long minute, she said softly, "About ten years
ago."

Again there was silence.

Then Carter turned to face his wife and said, "Longer ago
than that."

They looked at each other without saying anything. Then
Peggy lowered her eyes.

"Whom did you marry, Peggy, the kids?"

She didn't answer right away. Finally she said, "I don't
know. I think I'm still single."

A strange answer. Her fantasy, maybe. She was in fact
very much a mother, very involved with her children. But
underneath she felt lonely, deprived, and unappreciated. She
was alone.

"What happened to you, Carter?"

"With respect to what?"

"With respect to Peggy."

"I don't understand the question," he said in a voice edged
with hostility. The more I probed, the more he resisted. Maybe
he was afraid to go where he felt me pushing him, or maybe he
just wouldn't be pushed.

The Farrells came to therapy for their children. Now, fifteen minutes into the session, we were deep into the emptiness between the spouses. Carter was ready to explore his
inappropriate disciplining of the children, his out-of-control
temper, his violence, maybe even his loneliness. But there
were limits. A man doesn't open his bedroom door for the
perusal of strangers.

"Well, the question is simple: She divorced you ten years
ago—what happened to you? When did you decide you would
not invest energy in changing Peggy—in trying to help her
understand you?"

"That question is based on a much too simplistic idea of
what the relationship was at the time."

"I don't know. Tell me."

"Because, I think, the basic problem arose from my concept of a father's proper role in the family." He spoke with
slow, deliberate control. "It had always been my feeling that
when the kids got old enough, we would start doing things
together—the kids and I. I would become actively involved
with them."

This is a common assumption of fathers, though not always stated so openly. Man is the provider, woman the nurturer. Carter thought fatherhood began when the children
were old enough to behave and to join him in his activities.

"That means you lent her the kids when they were young,
and when they were older you were going to take it over?"

"No, not take it over so much as become part of it. Because up until whatever age this was going to occur, my role as a father was to work and pay the bills—"

"And to let her do the parenting."

"Right. As far as raising the kids and worrying about doctor appointments and nighttime feedings and spankings, and that sort of thing . . ."

"It was her job," I said. Then I asked Peggy, "And you accepted that?"

She furrowed her brow. "I suppose I did for a period of time."

"So you were really a one-parent family. Mother took care of everything. Peggy, why did you accept such a strange arrangement?"

"I didn't know any better," she said with feeling.

"You didn't know how to say, 'Carter, I need you'? It's four words."

She didn't answer.

"He had one function and you had another one?"

Carter nodded. Peggy didn't. "Until Tippi was about three or four years old and I started working, and then I had many functions."

"Did you ever ask Carter for help?"

"Yes," she said softly, and chose not to elaborate. She did not, it seemed, want to criticize him too openly. Not here. Not now. They were alike in that respect.

"And does he help?"

"As we've gotten older he's become more helpful." This was not a ringing endorsement.

"Do you think they need him?"

"Yes, desperately."

"What will you do to give space so that this very tall fellow begins to be able to talk with his dad?"

One of the reasons parenting remains an amateur sport is that as soon as you get the hang of it the children get a little older and throw you a whole new set of problems. In the early years of their marriage, Carter and Peggy's rigid version of the traditional family worked, sort of. But when the children got older and he tried to become involved, there was no room for him.

"Are you very angry at each other?"

Carter said, "No."

"You're not angry with her?" It was hard to believe, but I knew by now it was true. The house rule was: No open acknowledgement of marital conflict.

"No," he said, trying to keep the anger he felt now at me out of his voice.

"I understand that you had been kind of angry at the kids?"

"Yes," he said, and his jaw tensed visibly.

"At whom were you angry—Keith?"

"On occasion, yes. And Robin. And Tippi."

"What Kate Kennedy told me was that you hit Keith—or you hit all of them."

"I hit them, yes."

Slapping the children was part of his idea of acceptable discipline. This was not uncontrolled violence; it was "instrumental." He slapped them to achieve a purpose. But he had also hit them when out of control. He had done wrong and he knew it, and he hated me for bringing it all up again.

"And when you hit Keith, was it Keith alone that you hit?"

When a child's misbehavior infuriates a parent, the real anger is often at the other parent—especially when the two are in conflict over how to deal with the children. My question was an invitation to expand the view of the problem, to explore Carter's response to the children in the context of their being Peggy's children.

He looked puzzled, and so I repeated the question. "Did you hit Keith alone?"

"Yes," he said, meeting my eyes.

"You're certain you weren't really hitting Peggy at the same time?"

"No, I hit myself." Carter was an intelligent man, proud and guilt-ridden, bound by rigid values. He saw himself as at fault and was willing to pay; he wasn't about to blame Peggy for his mistakes, or to let me do so.

"That, I know. What I don't know—"

"No, I did not hit Peggy."

"When you hit Robin, did you hit her alone or did you hit Peggy at the same time?"

"No," he said. *"I did not hit Peggy."*

He understood, but I wanted to make sure everyone else did. So I asked Keith. "Do you understand what I asked your father?"

"Did it have any effect on Momma?"

"Yes. I asked if he was angry at your mom and he hit you instead. Because whenever he deals with you, he deals with Mom as well, since you are her children. What do you think?"

"Well," Keith said, "they're adults, and usually whenever they're mad at each other it seems to me they can talk it over."

Keith's parents didn't go around yelling at each other, and so, he assumed, they must be reasonable. This was the myth his parents had taught him. Once you know the family folklore, you don't need to ask questions. But knowing the dangerous extremes the father could reach, I couldn't leave this story unchallenged.

"Carter, I understand that you left home because you were feeling too angry. You left the family for a few weeks?"

"No," he said, "I didn't leave because I was too angry. At the time I left I wasn't angry, but I realized that the frustration caused by my not knowing how to properly discipline the children had gotten out of hand, easily to the point where I would hit them."

"Which incident is clearest in your mind?"

"The clearest incident," Carter began, "is an incident that happened with Keith." Going back to this wasn't easy.

"With Keith? Okay. So why don't you three," I waved my arm to indicate Keith and his parents, "talk a little bit about this incident."

With a couple like Lauren and Philip, where there was so much volatile reactivity, I discouraged confrontations to avoid escalating their anger. Here it was different. Anger was submerged. By the time it surfaced, it was already out of control. It was essential to uncover the conflicts that triggered violence.

"First of all," Peggy said, "I was not around when it began. I came in when I was called onto the scene." Nobody, it seemed, wanted to bring back that awful moment.

"Okay," I said, trying to sound reassuring, "maybe the three of you can piece it together."

"Which incident is he talking about?" Keith wanted to know.

How many incidents had there been? Could they be separated, or were they really one long incident with interruptions, like a string of sausages?

It was his mother who answered. "When Daddy came upstairs with some cigarettes that he said you had gotten into."

No one else was ready to speak.

Then his mother said slowly, "As I was told about the situation by you and other people—Robin and Daddy—you were very surprised when he came upstairs with the cigarettes in his hand and pushed them in your face, because you didn't know what he was angry about, or what was going on."

Now Keith remembered. "Well, all I know is Robin and me were talking, and it was at night and it was right before I needed to go to bed. We were talking. And Daddy comes storming upstairs and took out a bunch of cigarettes, and me and Robin just looked at each other, real puzzled. And he started smearing 'em all over my face and he grabbed me by the neck and he pushed me up against the wall and he was yelling all kinds of stuff. But I couldn't understand it—I was just about in a state of shock. And I didn't know what in the world was going on. He was choking me, and I couldn't breathe at all— well, hardly. And Robin was crying over there, and I can remember Momma coming. But I really didn't know what in the world was going on. It was a weird incident."

Recalling the attack, Keith showed neither anger nor fear, only bewilderment. It was as if his father were more alien than brutal, a man whose ideas and moods were unrelated to anything anyone in his family could understand.

"Continue talking. Because I just want to see how you dealt with that."

Peggy said, "When I came upstairs, I saw Carter with Keith up against the wall, and I started pulling on his arm and told him to let go. And he pushed me away. And I stood there and made sure he let go of Keith. And when he let go, and Keith went into his room, I asked Carter what was going on, and he went downstairs and didn't say anything to me. I had to get the pieces of the story, mostly from Robin. She was the one who was the observer in the situation."

"What did you tell Mom?"

"Well, I was just there with Keith when Daddy came upstairs. He didn't say anything. He just took the cigarettes out

and smeared them in Keith's face and started choking him.
And put him up against the wall. And he was saying, 'Well,
you haven't learned at all, have you? When are you going to
learn to stop stealing from me?' And Keith kept saying, 'I
didn't take them,' but Daddy kept on."

Robin told the story simply and without embellishment,
recreating the pain and humiliation of the attack. Listening
to her, Carter fought the urge to look away. His eyes drifted
but he forced himself to look at his family, a proud man determined to face the truth.

And Robin continued. "I don't remember if I went downstairs to get Momma or if I just started yelling for her, but she
came upstairs. And I was away from Daddy, and Momma
grabbed hold of his arm and told him to stop. And he just kind
of flung his arm to push her away. And then he let go, and
Keith went into his room. And Tippi was crying in her room,
'cause she heard all this going on."

Father struck son, and two wounds opened, one between
father and son, one between husband and wife. Both were
unhealed.

After the incident Carter went to his room and packed a
suitcase. Then he told his wife that he had to be away on
business for a week. He said good-bye and left. When he came
back after a week, nobody talked about the incident. It was
buried.

Carter's violent explosion frightened everyone in the family and created the need for some kind of decisive action, a
ritual of punishment and atonement. And so he left. He
walked away. That was his view of the options. The family
understood and were afraid to say anything.

I looked at Carter, a good man who could not bend. I felt
that it was imperative to help him and the family question the
house of values they had constructed on a subterranean fault
line that could erupt again at any time. By now I was sure
Carter would never hit Peggy, but he was in danger of hurting
the kids or himself.

Carter seemed glad to have a chance to explain himself, to
get somebody to understand.

"What happened was I found a carton of cigarettes up in
my closet that had been opened. Someone had taken a package and tried to glue the carton back together so I wouldn't

know one was missing. Now you remember that you had taken cigarettes of mine in the past, and so I assumed it was you. In addition to the fact that you were stealing cigarettes—as I thought—what really made me angry was to think that you thought I was so stupid that I wouldn't know how many packs of cigarettes there were in a carton. That's what really made me so angry— the insult to my intelligence."

When Carter thought his son took him for a fool, indignation swelled up and drove him into a blind rage. As Carter spoke, his wife and daughter listened with their heads down.

Carter continued. "And when I came upstairs with the cigarettes, I was going to say something—I don't know what, I can't remember. But when I got upstairs, and you and Robin were standing there talking, my anger became so great that I couldn't say anything. I *could not* say *anything* to explain to you."

Something important was going unnoticed here, and I said to Robin, "Ask your dad to explain why he became so angry."

"Why did you get so angry when we were talking?"

"The fact that you two were talking had nothing to do with it. I was angry because someone had come into *my* room, into *my* closet, and stolen something from me."

"I think your father is wrong," I said. "I think he was angry when he saw both of you talking."

"No," Carter said hotly. "The fact that those two were talking had absolutely nothing to do with it."

I repeated my point. "I think your father is wrong."

"Her father is *not* wrong!" Carter looked me straight in the eye, and I could feel his fury.

"Carter," I said firmly, "you are only a father. I am an expert. Later on you will understand what I am saying."

"Perhaps," he said evenly.

I was pulling rank. I felt sorry for Carter—I pitied his isolation, his impotence—but I was frustrated by his certainty and his righteousness.

I turned to Keith and said, "Why didn't you ever ask your father why he became so irrational?"

"Usually—I have lied to him before—and at the time he thought that I was nothing more than a liar, as far as I could see. So I figured there was nothing I could do."

"You figured he was right? Or that he was crazy?"

Keith smiled and shook his head. "He's not crazy."

"He's not crazy? So why couldn't you talk to him?"

"Well, usually, I can't really talk to him about anything like that, anything serious."

"You mean he's heartless?"

"No, he's not heartless. He's just . . ." Again the boy looked perplexed. The impossibility of reconciling the father's strange, stubborn ways with known categories wasn't easy.

I was increasing the emotional intensity of the session. I didn't like the bland logic that was protecting a dangerous and irrational act.

"What about you, Robin? Didn't it surprise you, what your father did?"

"I never thought he would hit Keith."

"Couldn't you ask him, 'What happened, Dad?'"

"No, because for the next few weeks I really hated him. I didn't even want to go near him."

"Did you hate him too, Keith?"

"I think so."

"Do you understand what happened, Peggy?"

"No," she said, and there was a lot of feeling in that one little word.

"Did you ask your husband what happened?"

"Yes," she said, "We talked about it afterwards. He told me why he was so angry."

"And did you understand?"

"No, not really."

And so it remained buried. The event, the anger, the guilt, the fear, the hate, the love—all of it. I felt Carter's isolation.

I got up and asked Carter to bring his chair away from the family and next to mine. He did so without hesitation and sat down. I looked at the distance between him and the family and saw that it was not enough. So I asked him to move his chair even farther away, well outside the circle of the group.

Then I said to him, "I understand what happened to you, but it seems nobody in your family does."

"What happened?" he said, curious and wary at the same time.

"What happened to you—" I said, and then got up and moved his chair still farther away from the group, "—that's what happened to you."

He looked at me, and then he looked at his children and his wife, and it was the look of a lonely outsider looking in.

My voice became soft and yearning. "You are an excluded man," I said, putting words to what all of them now could see.

Carter and I talked for several minutes, just the two of us. I was aware that we were talking so softly the rest of the family had to strain to hear. "They are all so round and beautiful," I said. "You are the square peg. You are alone." Then I raised my voice for the family to hear. "So you become brutal because there is an invisible barrier between you and them. They create in you the feeling that they are a unit and you are excluded."

Carter Farrell saw himself as strict, a practitioner of old-fashioned standards. What he didn't see, or didn't fully appreciate, was his rigidity. His wife was an armchair psychologist, protecting his children from their father's incompetent authority. Each was sincere, and they polarized each other into progressively more extreme positions.

Instead of coming together they drifted apart, leaving the mother close and connected to the children and the father outside, raging in pain. When he went upstairs, angry, to talk to his son and found the boy and his sister in animated, friendly conversation, he felt overwhelmed by a sense of rejection and isolation. Feeling shut out and unable to talk to his children, he erupted in a flash of violence.

I asked Carter to rejoin his family, and he moved his chair back to where it had been before, next to Peggy's.

"Why can't you get close to your children?"

"The question is, Why don't I feel that I can get close to my children?" He crossed his legs and leaned back.

"Yes." I wanted to give him room to reenter his family, but he was not an easy man to talk to.

He folded his arms across his chest. "The answer is because of the lack of groundwork that was laid with the children when they were young."

"Carter, it's now. It's going on now."

"Okay, I understand the question. The reason I don't relate to them now, personally—get involved—is because of the antagonism I feel from them."

"Of course."

"I have made overtures, attempts, to let them know that I do understand the problems they're going through. I've been through those problems. I do understand them."

"So why are you so helpless?"

He gave me a look full of hurt and anger and guilt—and I was never more aware of the tangled nature of human emotions.

Beneath his guilt Carter felt the righteous rectitude of the cheated and misunderstood. I was asking him to put aside the bravado of the rooster and the penitence of the guilty to face his helplessness. Only by admitting need and loneliness could he be a full person and a full member of the family.

And then I asked Robin, my "cotherapist," in the family, "Why can't your dad be . . . your dad?"

"Well, after so long of not having him—"

"It's not true you didn't have him. You had him in a particular way."

"But it's very scary to try to accept him with what's happened so recently, because how are we to know it's not going to happen again?" As Robin spoke, her voice took on some of her mother's practiced patience.

"Well, it will happen again—if that's his position at home," I said, pointing to where he had been sitting outside the family circle. "If he needs to knock to enter."

"Peggy, how is it that he became the excluded one? Why can he only act with irrational force to become a father? How did that happen?"

"I think it's a very simple matter of a lack of skill. Because he cares, and he wants to have a good relationship with the children."

The fault was Carter's: He was ineffectual. We had to get away from explanations that focused on Carter's flawed character, and toward an understanding of the tragic flaws in the chemistry of their relationship.

"Talk together about how Carter feels excluded. Who excludes him. And about how that can be changed."

Now Peggy turned to face her husband. "Do you remember this morning when Tippi asked you if you could pick her up a little early from school? So she wouldn't have to go to the class she didn't have her homework for?"

"Mm-hm," he said, wondering what the point was.

"And you said, 'No, Tippi, I'm sorry, I can't help you out.'"

"Mm-hm."

"That was a very good communication with Tippi. Because you let her know how things were, but you also showed her that you cared about how she felt."

"And how did I do that?" he asked.

"When you said, 'I'm sorry I can't help you out.' You let her know you realized that she had a problem—and that you cared that she had a problem—but that this is the way things are. And that's different from the way you very frequently deal with the other children—and others of us, from time to time.

"Like last night, when Keith said he didn't have the dishwasher detergent. And you said something very mean. You said, 'Just because you *want* dishwasher detergent doesn't mean we *have* it.' And I feel like those small distinguishing remarks tell the kids you don't care."

Peggy spoke to Carter like a patient teacher to a slow learner. She wasn't preventing Carter from talking to the children, and she didn't exclude him from the family, but she was the interpreter and judge of their contact. Yet I felt that Peggy was open to change. It was time to bring in the reserves. I moved to the children as helpers.

"Keith, change seats with your mom," I said. Like his father, he readily complied. Keith sat up straight, and his father, sitting next to him, leaned forward, facing me.

"Carter, as long as Peggy takes the position of translating the children to you, they will not know how to talk with you, and you will not know how to talk with them. Talk with Keith."

"I don't like you wearing those pants," he said. This must have been on his mind. It was almost as though he was determined to demonstrate his intolerance.

"Why not?" Keith asked.

"Because they're torn, and I think you should think better of yourself than to go around school wearing a torn pair of pants. I don't want people thinking that my children have to wear ragged clothes."

Keith sat listening to this sudden criticism without complaint, but his eyes lost focus, as though he were enduring yet another meaningless lecture.

When his father finished, he said, "So you're saying when

I wear torn pants it makes you look bad?" Like most adolescents, Keith could smell hypocrisy a mile away.

"It makes me look bad, and it makes you look bad."

"As far as you can see. See, I like the way I look. And maybe I like whatever people think of me when I wear these things."

"Is that the only pair of pants you have to wear?"

"It's not the only one I have to wear, but it's the best."

"Those are the best pants you have to wear?"

In the sixties my son's long hair drove me crazy. I knew how Carter felt.

"Oh, yeah, but I've got a lot of those dressy things that I don't really like to wear to school."

"So you'd rather go around wearing rags and have people think whatever you think they think of you than wear nice slacks and have them think you're a nerd because you wear good slacks to school?"

Keith nodded.

The boy and his father had run out of lines.

"That's the end of the conversation," Carter said. "I have no way to understand that."

To Carter his son's ways were written in a foreign tongue. He understood the boy's I-don't-care style of dress as well as he understood Greek. But I didn't want to leave this interchange as a failure of communication. I wanted them to realize that they had talked. Agreement isn't necessary for good communication.

"You see, this was a perfectly good conversation between two cultures. You and your son belong to two cultures that see things differently. It happens that in this crazy culture in which these kids live, ragged pants are in and dressy pants are out. We are old-timers; we don't understand that. He needs to be able to do something to explain that to you. But Peggy is the translator. So they go to her. Meanwhile you remain the square peg and cannot enter.

"Now, Keith, it is your job to explain yourself to your father so he can understand you. And you will need to help him to accept your torn pants."

I got up and went over to Keith and asked, "Would it be better if you tore them more to show your knees better?"

Hoping to detoxify an unnecessary struggle for control

with a rigid father, I was playfully trying to expose this ragged style for what it was: a harmless teenage affectation.

Robin giggled. Her mother smiled. Keith sat straight and ripped his pants more so that they really showed his knees. If he was embarrassed he didn't show it. He had his father's ability to stick his neck out.

"That's it," I said. "*That's* it!

"Carter, can you understand that aesthetic? I can't. It's crazy. But that is how these kids think. Your son is a member of an alien culture that thinks knees are beautiful. Who knows?" I said and shrugged.

"Can you explain to your father why that's beautiful?"

"Well . . ." he began.

"Please," his father said.

How could a fifteen-year-old explain the complex dictates of the adolescent dress code to a father, especially a father too rigid to tolerate his son's need to experiment with becoming his own person? And yet Keith tried.

"It's kind of like it shows that you don't have anything to prove. That you know you're not any better than anybody else. Because you see all these kids always bragging about their Jordaches and whatever. But me and this little society I hang around in—my friends—we just can't stand kids who like to shut out people because they're not as good as them. They're always talking about how expensive their clothes are, and such as that."

"So the people that wear Jordache and jeans like that shut you guys out because you don't wear them?" Carter asked.

Amazingly these two were getting through to each other. First the son was able to say what many adolescents cannot put into words—namely that growing up is about inclusion and exclusion. Now, equally surprising, the father was demonstrating an openness to his son.

"Mm-hm," Keith nodded, not quite used to the strange sensation of communicating with his father.

"Carter, what was your uniform when you were fifteen? How did you show that you belonged?"

There was a long pause. Then Carter turned to face his son. "I didn't. I didn't belong." There was real sadness in his voice. "I didn't belong in the sense that you belong. So I *don't* understand." Not fitting in was an old story for him.

"You did not belong?" I asked.

"No," he said, quietly.

"That's a pity. Belonging is very important. You were a loner?"

"Yeah," he said, trying to keep his voice steady.

"Did you ever get a group?"

"When I was eighteen, I suppose."

"How was that? Tell Keith."

Again there was a long pause. "I don't remember exactly how it was, but when I was eighteen your Uncle Jared, and Jamie, and Raymond and I just started hanging around a lot together. We enjoyed each other's company. We were interested in the same things. We had the same off-the-wall sense of humor. We had the same irreverence for society, and old people, and institutions. We just fit together well."

As Carter talked about growing up and the struggle to belong, Peggy listened with obvious compassion.

I turned to Keith. "So that was his torn pants."

Keith nodded thoughtfully.

For Carter it was a revelation to realize that his children could be similar to him in some way; that Keith and he shared the same irreverence for conformity and institutions.

I turned to Carter and said, "When Keith explains it, it's very clear, but he doesn't usually try. They go to you, Peggy."

"And you accept all of that, and so you are a single mother."

I was trying to broaden the focus from Carter's irrational actions to make it a mutual problem with mutual responsibility, but she felt blamed, and she fought back. "I don't really accept it. I deal with it the best I can."

"But," I said, "he feels excluded. He remains outside."

"Only because of his choice."

"No. It's a combined effort. It's not true, Peggy, that it's all his doing. You're all doing it. Robin, you exclude your dad. Keith, you exclude your dad. I don't know about you, Tippi. Do you talk with him or do you think he's just too square?"

"I'm not sure what you mean by square."

"Like I don't know what's happening," Carter volunteered. With Tippi, it seemed, he felt no need to be defensive.

"Tippi, do you think you can teach him?"

I was challenging the "correct way" of doing things. In a

rigidly hierarchical family, I was putting the youngest child in charge of her father's education.

"On my own?"

"Yes, on your own. Who else can help you?"

"Keith," she said, looking at her big brother.

"Both of you? Talk with Keith. I think you would be a good teacher because I don't think you would quit. Maybe both of you can imagine some way of helping your dad enter into the eighties. You know, he got stuck in the fifties."

Tippi said, "I don't know how to come up with a solution." Then she turned to her big brother and asked, all earnest, "Do you know any way to teach him how to be hip?"

Keith grinned. "That would be pretty difficult," he said. "Maybe we could just every now and then update him on what's going on."

"But it's . . ." Tippi was truly exasperated. "It's like you could tell him that," she said pointing to Keith's torn pants, "was cool, and he'd know that that's what you were saying, but he wouldn't exactly understand *how* it was cool and *why* it was cool." As far as Tippi was concerned, her father belonged to a different species, *homo adultus*, so the possibility of real shared experience was an *im*possibility.

"So you'd say a shirt with a hole in it is cool, and then he'd get a fishnet shirt. Is that what you're saying?"

"No! I'm saying like why would he *want* to get a fishnet? Because he doesn't hang around people with holes in their shirts or torn pants. It's cool to us 'cause it's accepted. That's like the girl in our school with the blond streak? It looks retarded because nobody else has a blond streak. But if everybody else had it except you, you'd probably get a blond streak like that to be accepted. And if he hung around everybody that had holes in their pants, eventually he'd probably get a pair of pants and put holes in them."

Tippi was still young enough to speak openly of the need to conform. Some day she would ask questions like, What is the meaning of life? But now all she wanted to know was, Does this look okay?

"I want you young people to help your father understand people in the eighties. But you will need to learn how to teach him that, while remaining sensitive to his authority. For him, being an authority is important. Can you do that? It's a hard trick."

Keith nodded. He was willing.

"Yeah? Tippi, what about you? Do you think that you can teach your dad?"

Tippi grinned and nodded. Young and innocent of bitterness, she liked the idea of bringing her father up to date. I was touched, and Carter was smiling.

Then Keith said, "Well, that's the way Mom is with us. We can talk together."

"Yes, I know," I said. "But that is what closed Father's door."

Then I said to Robin, "Your father was educated with a very different idea of respect and authority. Can you understand that?"

"How he's different? Yes, I can."

"But you didn't."

"No, because I didn't realize at the time that he was so left out, and it was our fault, too."

"It's so easy to see. I could see it in the way you walked into the room and sat down. You three kids sat down next to Mom, as far away from your father as possible. Mother sat between you and him, like a protective barrier. It was just so simple."

"I felt like he did it by choice," Robin said, echoing her mother's thoughts.

"He doesn't have any choice," I said. That, of course, was not quite true, but I wanted the children to see their role in this. They already saw their father's.

"I think he's in pain," Peggy said. "Your father becomes frustrated and furious when you don't talk to him. Can't you see that?"

Robin nodded, and her eyes filled with tears.

Only then did I glance at the clock and realize that nearly three hours had gone by. "We will stop now. It's four o'clock."

The Farrells seemed a little startled, too. For three hours we'd been deep into the family's pain, and now it was time to stop. They had to go back to Vermont. Carter and Peggy had to go back to work, and the kids had to go back to school. It was time for the session to end, but I didn't want its momentum to stop.

"I would like to give you three kids a task. See if you can put your heads together and come up with a plan to help your dad connect with you. I don't know how, because I don't know your dad, but I know that he feels alone. He grew up as a loner. And in your home he's still a loner. Can you think what to do to help him? Can you do that?"

All three of them nodded, Tippi most enthusiastically. Then we said good-bye.

Carter and Peggy had very different ideas about how to raise children and, instead of finding a way to come together, they pushed each other farther apart. When Peggy saw Carter picking on the kids for every little thing, it seemed natural to defend them. When she did, it was natural for Carter to feel resentful. And so a pattern was set in motion in which mother and children grew closer and father became increasingly alienated.

In some families this pattern of polarization between parents would lead to a lot of arguments. But Carter and Peggy weren't like that. They kept everything inside. As a result, resentment festered and turned to bitterness. Their divorce was an emotional one, the kind that doesn't show up in the usual statistics.

Carter's unbending sternness masked a personality that feared and despised weakness. He denied loneliness and uncertainty in himself, and he attacked violations of his strict moral code in the behavior of his children. Peggy didn't agree with him, but she could not or would not challenge him directly.

Within this value system there was no flexibility and little room for growth. With time the structure of the family took a destructive spin. Peggy, the good mother, became the fulltime teacher, source of all inspiration and understanding, while Carter, who could not challenge Peggy's goodness, saw himself reduced more and more to an outsider looking in, neither a father nor a husband.

And so the Farrells became a caricature of the traditional family: Women nest, men hunt. "When the children get older," Carter and Peggy thought, "there will be space for Carter to become involved." Meanwhile Peggy's job as a mother expanded to the point that there was no space for her to be a wife. "I am still single," she said, denying her role in the family, while in fact she was more and more a mother.

The violence that erupted in the Farrell family was a product of confusion and loss blocked from expression by closed channels of communication. Opening those channels released the pressure and made violence unlikely to recur.

Carter's need to deny and deflect his anger made the whole family prisoners of rage. With access reopened Carter moved toward his wife and children, and toward acceptance. Peggy moved out from between him and the children—toward him. The children did what children do more often than their parents expect; they met him more than halfway.

PART FOUR

REMARRIAGE

Almost nowhere in family life are triangles more notoriously troublesome than in stepfamilies. Stepparent triangles begin innocently enough, but can become very troublesome indeed. Perhaps the biggest mistake stepfamilies make is trying to model themselves on the traditional nuclear family. Anxious to heal old wounds and impatient for a new order, stepfamilies sometimes rush things that must take time.

Parenting works best when it's done by a balanced team, but "balanced" doesn't always mean equal. With stepparents it's advisable to let the biological parent take the lead. That's because a stepparent enters into a family that already has established rules. What usually works best is for the biological parent to enforce the rules. He or she is the only one with the moral authority to discipline. The stepparent should begin as an assistant parent and should be given time to ease into a full partnership.

The most difficult role in a remarried family is likely to be that of stepmother. Custodial fathers often turn over the care of their children to their new wives as soon as possible. After all, mothers take care of children, right?

Stepfamilies have to go through the same processes of accommodation and boundary making that new families go through, but with one big difference. In first-time families, parents have time to forge a bond before they have to deal with children. Stepfamilies don't have that time.

10

The Second Time Around

Stunned by the jumble of griefs that is divorce, some people retreat to quietism; others advance on new relationships, hoping to find happiness the second time around. Unfortunately, though, when it comes to blending children from previous marriages, the second time around is the *first* time around. Whether the new partners are widowed or divorced, stepparent triangles often prove their undoing.

Triangles? Who thinks about triangles when two wounded veterans of previous marriages are lucky enough to find love again? We think most naturally of a twosome—the couple, or perhaps the merging of two small families, each with a piece missing. Remarriage does, of course, mean recoupling, but it also means much more than that.

Stepfamilies are rich with possibility—for competition and conflict, jealousy and resentment, and for love reborn. The sadly familiar rivalries that spring up between stepparents and stepchildren, and stepsisters and stepbrothers, are only the dark side of what can be a set of mutually satisfying new relationships.

Families are richer than we know, and nowhere is this more true than with stepfamilies. What it takes to turn this wealth to advantage is respect for the integrity of each of the many new relationships. While it's fine to want to be "one big happy family," most happy families are made of many parts, distinct subgroups that need time alone to share confidences, argue and make up, solve problems, work on projects, and play together.

Stepparents need to honor the prior claims of loyalty between parents and children. Not doing so can be a big mistake, one on which many stepfamilies founder. As a therapist my job is to worry about avoiding mistakes or resolving them after they occur. But over the years I've become increasingly aware of the positive possibilities of family life. Stepfamilies can be difficult, but they can also be wonderful.

————•·•————

Unlike most families who wouldn't think of calling a therapist until things have gotten out of hand, Ron and Marci called for a consultation early into what was for both of them a second marriage.

"I called on the advice of a friend," Ron explained. "She knew you were going to be in Los Angeles for a few days. We don't have any serious problems yet, but we want very much to get off on the right foot," he said. Intrigued by this unusually precautious request, I agreed to see them.

I traveled to L.A. with the usual East Coast prejudices about this city that continually reinvents itself. In Ron and Marci I met the contemporary California couple I'd expected to meet. He was a studio musician who played in clubs between recording dates. She was a once-hopeful actress working as a secretary in one of the large aerospace technology companies.

Marci sat down, and her little daughter, Heidi, five years old, sat next to her, along the wall to my left. Ron and his daughter, Denise, who was twelve, sat next to each other along the adjacent wall. The effect of the seating arrangement was to portray two small families joined at right angles through the parents.

The four of them seemed young and fresh and relaxed. With his thick mop of black hair and crew neck sweater, Ron reminded me of the singer Paul Simon as he appeared in a concert I had attended. His shoes were high-top black sneakers. His daughter, Denise, had shoulder-length blond hair and wore a short pleated skirt that made her look like a little girl, but her precocious insouciance made her seem more like her father's pal than his twelve-year-old daughter. Marci had a round face and short, curly, honey-colored hair. It was a nice face. She wore an off-white jacket over a black T-shirt and jeans, and high heels that matched the jacket. Her little girl, Heidi, wore a pink-and-white dress that made her look even younger and more doll-like. She was quiet and polite, and my impression was that, of the four of them, she was the most shy.

Ron began by saying that he and Marci had just come out of unhappy marriages and wanted to make sure that they were doing right by each other and the girls. When I asked him how many years he and Marci had been married, he smiled and said, "Six weeks." Only in L.A., I thought.

Ron and Marci's decision to see a therapist this early in their marriage, long before they ran into any real problems, seemed appropriate to the famous therapeutically oriented California life style. Perhaps the sunny climate induced a sunny vision of the perfectibility of relationships. Nonetheless, what Ron and Marci were facing was serious. Preventive family therapy may have seemed like a California cliché, but in fact it made sense.

Ron was impatient or uncomfortable, I wasn't sure which, when I asked about his first marriage. Californians, I learned, look to the future, not the past. In Ron's case this was less a Pollyannaish confidence in the future than an adamant elision of history, especially painful history. But I pressed him because I wanted to know what happened, and because I wanted to know what kind of emotional baggage these two people were bringing with them.

Ron married young. His wife sang in one of the clubs where he worked. After they had Denise, she quit singing and went back to work part-time in a talent agency, taking with her the habit she'd picked up in the club of drinking a little too much. Ron tried to talk to her about her drinking, but she didn't want to hear it. She was unhappy about giving up her singing career, and she blamed him. "Whose idea was it to have a baby, anyway?" she said one night after three or four glasses of Chardonnay. It seemed that the only time they could talk was when she'd had one or two drinks. Before her first drink she was tense and irritable. After two or three she frequently became angry and abusive. Things got better, and things got worse. About these years Ron would say only, "Let's just say it wasn't easy." After nine years they called it quits. Denise went to live with her mother, but when the drinking got worse Ron sued for custody and won.

Marci, too, married young, but her marriage lasted only three years. "We thought we were in love, but we never really knew each other. I tried to make it work but he didn't, and we never really had a chance."

Marrying under the influence of infatuation, Marci and her actor-husband had the illusion that their feelings would transcend their differences. They found out that among the remedies for romantic idealism, few are as effective as matrimony.

Perhaps it's no longer necessary to dwell on the fact that people who get divorced don't necessarily suffer from some character flaw or failure of nerve; they haven't necessarily "failed" at anything. Divorce can be a courageous step to correct mistakes and get stalled lives back on track. Still, despite our familiarity with divorce, the average person thinks of it as the end of the family and has a limited understanding of divorce as a stage in the life cycle of some families—a stage that requires families to change shape. Divorce is not an ending; it is a transition.

For Ron and Marci both, uncoupling had been a time of loss and liberation, and much confusion. Unlike some newly divorced people who need time alone to heal, Ron started dating almost immediately and went through a series of relationships before he finally met Marci. He was relieved to be free but hurt too much to be alone, and love is a wonderful bandage for emotional wounds.

Marci was more wary the second time around. At first she didn't feel like seeing anyone after her divorce. Considering what a mistake the marriage had turned out to be, she was surprised how hard the divorce hit her. Maybe the loss she mourned was more an idea she had about herself and "family" than the actual reality of the relationship.

The two girls listened to these stories they'd heard before as though it were ancient history. Somehow their parents seemed to have protected them from the wounding process they themselves had gone through.

"So, Heidi," I said, "now you have a big sister and a daddy. Wow!"

"Two," she said in a small voice.

"*Two* daddies," I said, and she laughed.

Ron and Marci may have thought they were merging two families into one, but it would be more complicated than that. The formation of a stepfamily isn't really a "blending" of families, which suggests a kind of fusion or distillation and a loss of individual identities. Rather than one combined unit, the new family is a complex amalgam, consisting of a number of pairings, each with its own shape, each requiring a boundary to allow the sisters and spouses and stepparent-and-child pairs to function. I would be exploring these pairings for the next hour.

I started with Heidi. Since she was the youngest, talking with her about the serious business of family reorganization could be done with a light-hearted tone.

"How is it to suddenly have a big sister? Is she bossy?"

Heidi shook her head no, giving the polite answer.

"She's not bossy?"

This time Heidi laughed and nodded emphatically, "Yeah, yeah!" Pointing playfully at Denise, she said, "She tells me what to do."

"And it works," Denise said in the same playful spirit.

"Older sisters are like that," I said. "They think they have all the answers. Is it easy to have a big sister?"

"Mmm. . . . No."

They were sisters, and they weren't sisters. They would be friends and they would be rivals, but for now the whole thing seemed like fun.

"And your mommy now is much busier than she was before?"

"Yeah, but the only thing I don't like is she doesn't give me any more attention. She gives *Ron* all the attention!"

Ron and Marci both laughed, a little embarrassed, and

Marci said, "You *wicked* man." She had a deep, purring voice
and a warm, understanding manner.

"Do you kick your mom and say, 'Don't give him attention'?" I asked.

Heidi laughed, delighted with this idea. "No way!"

Heidi's cuteness was contagious, and I couldn't help becoming a little childish myself. "You can kick her in the shins
and say, 'Hey, hey, I am here.' Did you do that?"

She shook her head.

"Try it, sometimes it works. Or step on her feet."

This time they all laughed.

"Maybe you could kick Ron."

"No way! I would kick my mom."

"*I* get to kick Ron," Denise said in a sugary voice and
poked him in the shoulder.

The two girls naturally claimed priority with their own
parents. The new mates were friendly intruders, but intruders
nonetheless. Each child would lose a little of the exclusivity
she had with her parent. This letting go would be a little
easier to the extent that they formed ties with their new sisters and stepparents at the same time.

"Denise, let me do something. You and Heidi change seats
for a minute."

They had been seated as stepfamilies; parents protecting
their children. I wanted to explore the possibilities and difficulties of changing.

Denise got up and sat down next to Marci. Heidi sat beside
Ron.

"You know why I did that, Denise? So Heidi can kick Ron,
and you can try that look you use on your dad with Marci. You
have a beautifully seductive look, and it works on Ron."

"No, this works," she said and gave him another little-girl
version of the artful vamp.

"This is what works for my mom," Heidi piped up. She
crossed her arms and stuck out her lower lip in an exaggerated pout.

Everybody laughed.

"Try it on Ron," I said.

Heidi mugged for Ron, but he didn't melt the way Marci
did. "It only works on my mom," she concluded.

"Marci, does Denise try her seductiveness on you?"

"Not really. She pretty well saves it for her dad."

The girls were learning that their tricks worked only on their own parents.

Unlike most of my cases, Ron and Marci weren't stuck with serious problems, they just wanted to make sure that, as Ron put it, "they got off on the right foot." In most cases I am a challenger and a breaker of patterns. With families in transition, families in the process of creating new patterns, I see my job as like that of a harbor pilot who guides incoming vessels through obstacles that are familiar to him. My job is not to challenge but to support and guide.

"Well, it's a big job you two have. Look how easy it is when you marry for the first time. You have time to work things out before the kids come. So when the kids come you are already a strong unit, and they cannot do the kinds of things that these two kids are trying to do to you."

"Divide and conquer!" Ron quipped, and everybody laughed.

Heidi kicked Ron playfully.

"I think, Ron, if you keep Heidi sitting in that chair, she will develop a relationship with you." He laughed.

"A very hurting one," Denise joked.

Heidi, pleased with all the attention, started kicking Ron harder.

"Probably Ron will find a way of defending himself," I said. "But I don't think he can defend himself from you, Denise, because your style is so smooth. You've been together for two years?"

"Yes," Denise answered.

"How was that?"

This time Ron answered. "Well, it was really busy, because I was working nights, and unfortunately we've been through two relationships together—with people who thought they wanted children, and then when they got in the middle of it they found it was easier to bail out. We went through two experiences that were—"

"Terrible," Denise put in.

"*Très tragique*," Ron said dramatically.

"*Veddy*," Denise agreed. These two had their lines down.

"Your dad said *we* went together through two very difficult relationships. How were you involved?"

"Well I was with him, of course, so when they kind of got together I was part of it. She was like 'Oh, my little darling,' and I was like, 'Uh-huh, yeah, sure.'"

"For how long?"

"Allegra was a couple of years," Denise said.

"Well, Allegra and I were together for . . . a year and a half—"

"And Candice," Denise added. She didn't want him to lose track.

"And Denise was with us the last half. And Candice—we were together about two weeks." He laughed.

"No. It was a month and two weeks," said the scorekeeper. She had stopped being charming and was now earnestly reminding her father of what he had put her through. In her mind she had first priority.

Even if by today's standards these two girls seemed precocious, it was probably more due to the way their parents relied on them for companionship than to the famous California glibness.

"Marci, be careful," I said.

"Be real careful?" she said, laughing.

"She will sabotage you."

"Oh, she tries."

All this was said in a playful tone, and the kids thought it was a game, and their parents and I knew it wasn't.

Children of divorce do a lot of scary thinking. They have seen their parents stop loving each other. The possibility of abandonment terrifies them. Competition with new family members is therefore serious business.

"Do you think you will succeed with Marci, Denise?"

"Verrry much."

"Do you think you'll get rid of me?" asked Marci.

"No, I don't want to do that. I just have to get to your weak spots—and then . . ." She laughed, glancing sideways at Ron to see if she'd overstepped herself. "But I'll only do that when I'm mad or something."

"Okay, let's make another set of pairs," I said. "Denise, change seats with your dad."

The two girls had been sitting between their parents. Now as Denise moved next to Heidi so that her father could sit next to Marci, she said with feigned horror, "Oh, no!"

Ron sat next to Marci and said, "Interesting concept."

"So, Ron and Marci, how will you manage this very complex set of relationships?"

Ron said, "We spent a lot of time talking about how to pull us all together as a unit."

"Before you married?"

"No, after we were together."

Marci said, "We kind of went into it thinking 'Sure, you have a child, I have a child, this will be real easy.' We both love children, what's the problem?" She shrugged, poking fun at her own naive optimism.

When they were dating Ron and Marci honored each other's love of their children. With characteristic California optimism, they had no doubt in their ability to forge a brave new family. What they were finding out was that the children, those innocents, could act ingenuously to undermine the necessary compromises. They resisted changes in the patterns they had already established with their natural parents, and they did what they could to get around their stepparents.

Ron said, "We're feeling each other out right now, actually." He turned to address himself to Denise, apparently looking for her approval as much as telling her how it was. "We're establishing some rules to get some kind of family order."

"Ron, if you can, look at Marci and continue talking with her. Let the kids entertain themselves." Then I asked the girls to move over to the couch, and I got up and sat down like a barrier between generations.

Ron continued. "We're establishing some rules, some kind of basis and foundation, and learning to know each other, and what are our good and bad points. We believe that fulfillment and self-expression can coexist with cooperation and mutual understanding." He looked at me for approval. "How does that sound?"

"It sounds like a chapter of a book." We both laughed.

"We're writing it every day," he said.

"Tell me in more everyday terms," I said to Marci.

"Well," she said. "As events transpire we try to talk and discuss together and decide what we're going to do with the situation—you know, what our goal is."

"Bring it down two notches to reality," I said. Ron said, "Okay, when the kids don't clean up their room . . ."

"That's it!" I said.

Everybody laughed. Life, we all knew, wasn't "events transpiring"; it was getting after the kids to clean up their rooms.

Permissiveness often becomes a special problem for divorced parents. Children exploit inconsistencies between households, single-parent families are understaffed, and divorced parents are often demoralized and depressed. Denise's mother floundered after the divorce. Work took all her available energy, and she came home so stressed and tired that she took a couple of glasses of wine to relax. Two became three, and then four, and then she slipped into a loose befuddlement and out of the role of mother. Not only was she lax in supervising Denise, she also relied on her daughter to cook supper and straighten up—some mornings even to help her dress for work.

Marci was the mother-in-charge when she was married, and she continued in that role after her divorce. Ron, on the other hand, had never been much of a disciplinarian. Ron didn't take to drink, but he, too, was a little lost after the divorce. It's difficult to assert parental authority when you are confused and lonely.

Now Marci and Ron were faced with the task of coordinating two different styles of parenting. This isn't easy even in first marriages, in which parents are inclined to follow (or rebel against) the traditions they were brought up with. It doesn't get any easier the second time around, when parents and children have already established a set of rules and rhythms.

I asked Marci, "What difficulties are you having with Denise?"

She hesitated for a moment, reluctant to complain. Nobody wants to be a wicked stepmother. "Probably the biggest difficulty is getting her to be responsible for her own things. I don't think I should have to clean up after her, because I think she's old enough to do that for herself."

Marci and Denise were having a harder time than they expected bringing their relationship into sharp focus: It still seemed blurry and undefined. Denise had imagined a friendship like sisters; Marci had imagined there would be no doubt about who was in charge.

"What's your style? You like to be nice?"

"I like to be nice, but sometimes I end up being a nag—and I don't like that."

"Ron, what is your style?"

"Calm and explosive," he said, joking instinctively.

"Are you similar or different from Marci?"

"I think in the beginning I felt a lot of guilt because Denise and I had been apart a long time, and I wanted life to be very beautiful and rosy and every second to be 'Yeah, we're together.' Which was in a way real good and in a way not realistic."

"It doesn't work, does it?"

"No, it doesn't. At this point I try and get her attention by talking calmly, by trying to make her understand what I'm trying to get across to her." Ron had a lot to learn about twelve year olds. "If it doesn't work that way, if she starts picking apart my words or turning things around, which she sometimes seems to do, then I lose my temper and have to calm down. I still haven't got to the point where I can just stay calm and reasonable. I tend to get a little angry and yell."

"Welcome to the world," I said.

"Yeah," he said, and laughed.

Ron subscribed to the popular view that parents should rely on sweet reason in their dealings with their children. Reason, they believe, will give them the moral authority to be in charge. Maybe. But sometimes it's being in charge—taking charge—that makes it easier to be reasonable.

"What do *you* think of his parenting style, Marci?"

She hesitated, then looked at Ron. They both laughed.

"It's okay, honey, I can take it."

"I think it's still being developed. I don't see it as something that comes real easy. He parents when he has to; he'd probably rather not—I don't mean be a parent, I mean parent."

"When he's having a hassle with Denise, do you step in, or not?"

"I usually stay out of it until he comes to a point where he's not sure and seems like he needs some talking to or some feedback."

Marci was a smart lady. She knew intuitively not to rush into the role of mothering Denise. When kids resent being told what to do by a stepparent, they say, "You're not my mother!" They're right.

"Right now you're careful not to take over the discipline with Denise?"

"That's right. She's Ron's daughter; I let him do it."

"And you think with time you will develop a relationship with Denise and be more comfortable?"

"Mm-hm."

Then I asked the girls to come back and sit down with the adults. I moved my chair over toward Heidi. She was sitting up very straight, very grown-up, in her pink-and-white dress, with her feet not even close to reaching the floor.

"Let's start with you, Heidi, okay?" She smiled shyly.

"You said Mommy doesn't give you enough attention. That's one thing. What else is different?"

"That's the only thing," she said.

For all her precocious charm, Heidi was still young enough that her mother was her whole world, and though Marci loved her, though she was at the center of Marci's world, Heidi was not *her* whole world.

"I bet your mommy has a very soft shoulder. Do you like to put your head on Mommy's shoulder?"

Heidi nodded and smiled.

"What about Ron? Have you ever tried to do that with Ron? Go and test his shoulder."

She shook her head.

"No? Not yet, huh?"

"When I get used to him," she said.

"Well, I suppose six weeks is not a very long time. Can you try his shoulder and see how soft it is, Marci?"

Marci cuddled up to Ron and put her head on his shoulder. "He has a *real nice* soft shoulder," she said.

To which Heidi said, "I guess Mom gots a soft head, too."

We all laughed. Heidi wasn't so shy after all.

"Denise," I said, what are the difficulties of the new situation for you?"

"Well, I'm having to change a lot—*a lot!*"

"How?"

"Well," she began, and glanced over at her father. "Say I wanted to go out to a movie or something, right? He used to go, 'Oh, fine.' Just 'What time will you be back?' But now 'I've got to meet the mother, I've got to do this, I've got to do that. You might not be able to go because we might not have time,' and this and that, and I rarely even get to go."

"Whom do you ask?"

"My dad *and* Marci. Both."

"And your dad also says you cannot?"

"Well, see, what it is—well, last time he said I can't because he didn't know who was going, and he didn't want me
to go to a—*drive-in movie!*" She spoke in that tone of mock
alarm teenagers use when they want to belittle their parents' concern. "He used to let me go all the time, but now he
doesn't."

Denise looked over at her father to see if she was having
any effect on him, or perhaps to see if she was in trouble.

"So he has changed," I said. "Why did he change?"

"I don't know, probably because of Marci. He has to act
like a father and everything."

"You mean Marci is influencing him?"

"Yes!" She giggled.

"And what does she say? 'You are too soft'?"

"I don't know. . . . 'You should be more fatherlike,' maybe."

When they were together, Ron had let Denise do pretty
much what she wanted, hoping, perhaps, that indulging her
would earn him absolution. Now all that was changing.

Denise remained good-natured while complaining. Still, it's
no small thing for a child suddenly to find the rules changed.

"And you cannot influence him? You know, before you did.
I saw your look. You have a look like—you don't remember
but there was a great actress called Greta Garbo, and she had
that look, that anguished, longing look of '*How can you hurt
me so much?*' You have it perfect."

"It doesn't work all the time," Denise said matter-of-factly.
This new family in formation had the same strains that other
families had, but they hadn't developed any of the bitterness
and animosity that makes openness impossible.

"And does it work with Marci?" I asked.

"Never," she said.

"Of course not. You need to try new things with her. It's an
opportunity for you."

"Try some new looks," Denise answered, falling back on
the jokester pose.

I said, "You will need to learn new things."

Denise went back to being serious. "I used to be able to do
a lot of stuff and not be treated like a little kid."

"So you became older than your age because your dad was
so flexible?"

"I guess you could say that. I think it's because—well, my

mom was a Hollywood agent, and she didn't have much time to do things, so I'd get up and cook breakfast and dinner before she got home."

"You cooked breakfast and dinner for your mom? So you were a strange animal."

Denise laughed.

"You acted like the mom of your mom. That means you were your own grandmother."

At this Denise dissolved in giggling.

"I guess you could say that."

"And now you are here, and Marci has more time?" I said, being careful not to criticize her mother. "Marci is more managerial?"

"And has kind of taken everything away, so I can't do much anymore. And they say I have to act like I'm twelve, and it's kind of hard when I think I *am* acting like twelve."

"No, no. You're acting twelve plus."

This she could accept. "Yéah."

"But that was your training. Now you have changed families—that's tough."

"And the big change was I used to be able to go everywhere with my dad. Now I'm not able to go *anywhere* at all."

"My goodness. So in a very short time you moved through three families. The family of your mother, then alone with your father—no, when you were with your father you had . . ."

"We went through two relationships."

"I love the way you say 'we' went, because it makes you and your dad always a team. That's something that can be a problem for you, Denise. Because your dad now wants to team with Marci, and Marci wants to team with your dad. And you will find yourself—"

"And I'm left out in the rain."

"But you can join Heidi, who also feels left out in the rain. So you can be together."

"Yeah, but it's pretty difficult, because she's seven years younger, and I'm seven years older."

"Yes," I said. "It will be easier for her than for you. You will have a tougher time."

Denise laughed, happy to be sympathized with. "Verrry tough time."

"It can be nice. But it will take you time before you know

that what's happening to you is good for you. I like the fact that Marci is saying, 'I am the responsible one.' And when you were with your mom sometimes mom used to say to you, 'Denise, be responsible. Take over.' It's a big shift."

"Pretty big," Denise agreed.

At that point I got up and invited Ron and Marci to move back and join the girls. "Okay, you can come and join this group. It's a nice group, you know."

"I think so," Ron said. Marci agreed.

"It will be difficult, but you are nice people, maybe you can make it."

Ron looked at Marci, and Marci looked at Ron, and they smiled. "*Why not!*" he said, affecting a British accent.

Then I said, "The nice thing about Denise is that she is so bright, and she understands. Emotionally she does not. But she has a good head, and that can help a lot."

Ron looked at his daughter and smiled, the proud father.

"Marci, you will have to find a way of entering into a dialogue with her."

Marci nodded.

I moved from talking about Marci and Denise to Ron and Heidi. "Ron, are you usually so intellectual, or not?"

He smiled and rolled his eyes, flattered but not quite sure what I meant. "I never really thought about it."

"You talk in such a highfalutin' way."

"*Artiste,*" he said. "I don't know." I was embarrassing him.

"Do you play? Do you play with Heidi?"

"A little bit," he said uncertainly.

Ron's wisecracking might be taken for play, but it wasn't. It was a verbal adult trick that masked a real difficulty in giving up control.

"Heidi," I said. "He doesn't know how to play. Will you teach him?"

"He has to learn by himself," she said, still playing at the role of Momma's pet.

Marci said, "He can't learn all by himself."

"You will need to teach him, Heidi. He's stiff, you need to soften him up."

"Yeah," Ron said to encourage her.

Ron accepted my point about the need to become more playful, not only to enable him to get closer to Heidi, but to enable him to get closer to the childlike part of himself. His learning to play with his little stepdaughter would be her greatest gift to him.

I turned back to Marci. "Probably, Marci, you and Heidi will need to help these two people that you have taken into your heart to be younger—her to be younger, and him to play."

Marci said, "Well, sometimes we get real serious. Life is tiring and hard and real serious, and I think we need a lot more lightness."

"And who is the one that introduces humor when you're having a hassle, that makes you see that the situation is difficult and absurd?"

Ron said, "I don't know that we've accepted that yet." He laughed. "Maybe we should."

Marci agreed.

"Your family is very new. I think you are wonderful people, and I wish you the best of luck on a bumpy road. You know, I can identify the areas of difficulty, but I don't know if that does any good."

Then it was time to go, and we said good-bye.

Like most people in second marriages, Ron and Marci came together with two separate stories expecting a complementarity they didn't find. They had to construct it.

Initially confident in their ability to unite two fragmented families, the first frictions disabused them of the illusion that two plus two could equal one. Each of the six subgroups in this new family would need a boundary to allow relationships to develop and flourish. Because new ties don't replace old loyalties, the pairings between the girls and their natural parents would need special respect.

For all their laid-back manner, accompanied by such attractive smiles, Ron and Marci were very much animated by the anxiety that haunts everyone who's been through a divorce—namely, that they might not make it a second time around.

Having "failed" once, remarried parents often feel a tremendous pressure to create a happy family. But Marci and Ron were not so insecure that they were reluctant to exclude the children from any of their own activities. They would not be one of those families driven to the kind of stuck-togetherness that is a hedge against loneliness as well as intimacy. Their respect for their own rights—and the children's autonomy—would make them honor the boundary between generations that allows children time to be children and gives couples time to be alone.

Children may be the most important and vulnerable members of the family. In fact, it could be argued that the family is an institution for raising children. Nevertheless it's important to remember that the life of the family depends on a strong couple bond.

Ron and Marci came together less encumbered than some couples in second marriages, because the ghosts of their previous marriages were such unhappy ones that they locked them out of their minds. This made it easier for them to make a fresh start.

11

The Stepdaughter's Habit

When we think of the story of our lives we sometimes overlook the fact that family life is a compound set of stories. In this case one tale is a remarriage, another is a child's stalled advance on adulthood, and a third describes the connection between the couple's differences and the child's problems, making this the story of a triangle.

Studies of stepfamilies have shown the critical importance of strengthening the bonds between remarried partners and not letting the clamorous needs of children drown out the intimacy of the new marriage. That's why it's so crucial to create a boundary around the couple, to protect their privacy and give them time to work out their relationship. Every new couple needs shared loving time alone together. Making re-marriage work is like succeeding at any other activity: You have to put in the hours.

———————◆◆———————

The Fischers were a nice middle-class family whose daughter was a drug addict. They had other children, all grown up and successful—parents are quick to tell you that when there's one child with problems—but Stephanie, who was twenty-five and living at home with her father and stepmother, was ad-dicted to cocaine.

I first learned about Stephanie and her family from Adri-enne Simon, a talented young family therapist who'd been working with the Fischers since Stephanie had entered a drug and alcohol rehabilitation center. Adrienne asked me to meet with them because she was having trouble interrupting the parents' overinvolvement in Stephanie's life. That her par-ents' interference was blocking the daughter's recovery is of course an interesting way of looking at addiction, and one that only a family therapist would entertain.

It was true that the intrusiveness of Stephanie's parents thwarted her autonomy. However, Stephanie's irresponsibil-ity made it almost impossible to support her right to inde-pendence. The goal of our consultation was twofold. I wanted to challenge Stephanie's position of victim, and charge her with responsibility for herself and her addiction. At the same time I wanted to counter her parents' rescue and control op-erations.

Harry Fischer was tall and athletic, the model of a well-dressed businessman. Surprisingly, he started the session. He wanted me to understand that this was a second marriage, that his first wife and Fay's husband had died. There was something else he wanted me to understand as well. "I'm a hands-off kind of person. Fay is a hands-on person. Maybe that's how some of our problems got started. I let things hap-pen and then deal with the consequences. Fay likes to attack it while it's happening. She fights me on that, and when she fights me I resent it." I admired his conciseness and candor.

Fay Fischer, a handsome woman with gray streaks in her

hair, spoke forcefully and directly. It was time to get to the point, she said. They'd done everything they could, but Stephanie kept making a mess out of her life.

Stephanie was quick to respond to her stepmother's complaint. She was anxious for me to hear her side of the story. "Well, I screwed up a little," she admitted, "but I'm also not given any privacy, and I resent that. They want to know everything." She was apologetic and resentful at the same time.

Stephanie had an angular face like her father's, but her pallor contrasted with his healthy color. She wore a dark gray wool suit with a long skirt, dark stockings, dark eye shadow, and a dark, reddish brown shade of lipstick. I wondered if she knew what she really looked like, if she actually thought of herself as tragic. She dressed so carefully and sounded so whiny.

"They manage to know everything about you?"

She smiled a tight-lipped smile and shook her head ruefully. "Some way or another, they do."

"You should be more skillful than that."

"I should be," she said, abashed. "They're so involved in my life that it's holding me back." Stephanie at twenty-five was still locked in the adolescent debate with her parents. "They don't let me do *anything* without interfering."

Addicted families tend to hold on tenaciously to their way of doing things. Resistance to a broader view is often enormous. Guilt is so clearly located in one person. The parents have been at the receiving end of the child's destructive behavior for so long that it is nearly impossible to explore that child's competence. You almost have to start with acknowledging the parents' pain and risk losing the identified patient, or join with the patient and risk losing the parents. Could I find a middle ground?

"I don't know if you know about families, Stephanie. It's always a two-way street. That means if they're involved in your life, you're probably skillful in attracting their attention to your life."

"Probably," she snapped, and strode over to jerk a Kleenex out of the box.

"Do you think you need somebody to protect you?"

"No! I can protect myself very well," she said. The black high-heeled shoe she dangled on the end of her foot twitched a little faster.

"Then how is it your parents are so involved with you when you don't want them to be? It seems like a contradiction." Mr. Fischer leaned forward on his elbow. Mrs. Fischer crossed her legs and pulled her jacket closer over her shoulders. I could sense them thinking, "This guy is going to blame it all on us."

But I continued speaking to Stephanie, "At your age most people have a closetful of secrets."

"Are you asking everybody?" her father interrupted. "Or are you asking her?" He spoke with broad gestures. "I could tell you why we're so concerned, but I'd rather she tell you. She seems to think she deserves privacy—"

"I *do* deserve privacy. Everybody deserves privacy."

"Let me finish before you jump in," Harry said. The statement was flat and final and closed the discussion.

"All right, I won't talk." Stephanie took out a hard candy from her purse and sucked on it aggressively.

"This is typical," Harry said wearily. He shrugged, as if to say, You see what we have to put up with.

Shamed into silence, Stephanie turned away from the conversation and concentrated on dangling her shoe.

They were in familiar territory. It was the well-known dance of the irritable, concerned father and the irresponsible, rebellious daughter. Each knew unerringly how to provoke the other. In such an emotional climate I try to prolong the dialogue beyond the usual threshold of endurance, searching for something new, something beyond bickering—some opening for uncertainty and hope.

"Stephanie, what happened just now between you and your father?"

"We fought. As usual. We just don't get along."

"That's not all of it. You just had a squabble. Why? What did you feel your father did?"

"Talked down to me." She sounded like a petulant teenager. "Which is typical." She got up abruptly and went over to the Kleenex box on the table and yanked out three tissues. Again the same gesture—bitter, defiant, misunderstood.

"Okay," I said. "They think you're sixteen, and you behave with them as if you're sixteen. Are you twenty-five away from home?"

"I am."

"Then why are you sixteen at home?"

Stephanie pushed a strand of hair out of her face and said nothing. She had screwed up too many times to deny it, and too many times to feel the full weight of it.

Fay had had enough. My questions seemed out of step with the tragic reality of the last two years. "May I just interject something?" She looked at Stephanie, and her voice grew strident. "I think we've exercised up to this point a feeling of you're now mature enough, handle your own life, and let us live ours. But—"

Automatically I stood up and gestured for Stephanie to move out of the seat between her parents. This has become a reflex response to the crossing of boundaries; it is a concrete metaphor for autonomy. But unexpectedly Stephanie got stubborn. "I'm perfectly comfortable here."

"No, no. You're not comfortable there."

"Yes, I am. I like couches. I don't like chairs."

"Yes, but I don't want you to sit between your parents at this moment."

"Well, that's okay. I really want to sit here." Stephanie folded her arms and crossed her legs and glared at me. No one said anything.

Finally Stephanie broke the tension by getting up and moving.

How did we get into this? I was trying to release Stephanie, but she felt bossed around and resisted, and suddenly I was a player in the Fischers' drama of defiance and control.

"I think there's something Stephanie does that makes you believe that she's sixteen, fourteen—and you become controlling, and she resents you tremendously."

Harry responded to the word *controlling.* "We're not controlling her. We're just trying to keep her from doing the things that she has done—because we get involved in it, too. If you get a summons on the door and the summons says you have to appear in court—"

"That's *my* business! Not yours."

"Well, it's *our* home," Fay said with rising anger.

"I'd be very happy to get a post office box," Stephanie replied.

"Fine, then get it," her father said. He was ready to let go.

Fay wasn't. She launched into a tirade, using words like *selfish, irresponsible, thoughtless, rude,* and *dishonest,* each one hammering away at what was left of Stephanie's pride. Once or twice Stephanie tried to defend herself—"I'm just as law-abiding as you are!"—but gradually she sank into sullen, silent dejection. Instead of wrong, she became wronged. You could see it on her face.

Once this would have been Harry's cue to enter, stepping in to protect Stephanie from Fay. But since Stephanie's addiction the old coalition had weakened, and Harry had retreated to inaction. Unwittingly I took Harry's old role. "Fay, how old is Stephanie when you talk to her like this?"

"We've tried to explain," Fay responded. "We've tried over and over! She charged thousands of dollars on my credit card and she doesn't even have a job. But when we try to bail her out—"

"Let me bail myself out!" Stephanie shot back.

"Beautiful," I said. Stephanie was now asking to be treated like an adult, and I wanted to support that.

Stephanie did all the things her parents accused her of. What they didn't realize—what most parents of troubled children don't realize—is that the way they expressed their concern only perpetuated Stephanie's irresponsibility. Nagging doesn't make anybody more responsible. It only makes them defensive.

I went on. "An adult lives with the consequences of what she does. You'll never become an adult if they're always standing by to rescue you."

Again this was a familiar gambit. I was joining with Stephanie in challenging her parents, but in joining I was suggesting that she become autonomous and responsible— which was, of course, precisely her parents' request.

The drama of coming of age is usually portrayed as a variation on the theme of the myth of the hero. It is that, and it isn't. Young adults like Stephanie who remain psychologically enmeshed with their families have a harder time making friends, holding jobs, and falling in love; some seem unable to do so at all. When this happens we tend to blame the young adult, the failed hero.

In fact, Stephanie's problems started way back when she was twelve, when her mother died and her father remarried. This story of drug addiction turned out to be a more involved tale, one complicated by remarriage and triangles.

Harry and Fay were both in their fifties when they met, and each of them had recently buried a spouse. Both mourned long and happy marriages. Finding each other marked the end of mourning and loneliness, and the beginning of hope and happiness.

Ironically, that very hope carried the seeds of trouble. The new marriage would be haunted by the previous ones. Those marriages had been so happy that cherished ghosts were kept alive in the form of expectations that would cramp and squeeze the new partners.

Fay had two adult children and three grandchildren. Harry had one married child and Stephanie, who was twelve when he remarried. The extended family included children and grandchildren, all of whom had to learn how to build new connections. They each saw the new spouse in the dead parent's place, but they also saw the widowed parent's new happiness.

For Stephanie, however, the situation was different. She still had strong and fresh memories of her own mother, dead a year. To her, Fay was an intruder.

Harry and Fay remarried in hope, just as every couple marries in hope. They would merge their lives and families and futures. They'd re-create what they lost. They'd be a family.

But Fay entered a new family, born of loss, with a husband who gave the best part of himself to his work and a stepdaughter on the brink of adolescence. Coping with your own adolescent children is hard enough. Taking over for someone else is harder still. A stepparent has to earn the moral authority to discipline. That takes time. Fay, who took to the task of mothering with more enthusiasm than sensitivity, didn't have time, because Harry turned over the job of dealing with Stephanie the minute she moved in.

Fay needed to create a significant relationship with a stranger, who was her daughter, sort of, as a way of demonstrating that she loved her husband. Stephanie, on the other hand, felt no obligation to love this intruder. On the contrary, she would have been happy to remain in sole possession of her father. Harry was pushing two strangers into a forced intimacy, while he stood back and criticized the process.

Feeling cheated out of the happiness she thought marriage meant, Fay became increasingly frustrated and angry. As time went by she displaced more and more of her need for engagement and control onto Stephanie, who responded as adolescents do to an excess of unwanted adult scrutiny. Lines of battle were quickly drawn. Stephanie asked her father to intervene on her side—"Fay's always picking on me." Harry found himself impaled on a triangle, with both women he loved vying for his loyalty.

Slowly the tension between the three of them took over their lives. Fay was distressed by Stephanie's rudeness, her language, her friends, her school performance, the way she kept her room—everything. Harry was consumed with anger, all unexpressed, about Fay's constant criticism. Stephanie felt that everything she did was wrong. Like her father's, hers was an intensely private nature. When she came home from school she wanted to retreat to the sanctuary of her room. Fay's questions felt more like prying than caring, and thus the step-mother who only wanted to love her became a force against which to rebel. Stephanie started staying out late on school nights and when, at sixteen, she took the car for a joyride without a license and crashed it, the crisis seemed sadly pre-dictable.

Stephanie became a symbol of divided loyalties. She re-minded Harry that he owed loyalty to her mother's memory and to her as his daughter. Fay insisted that Harry declare his primary loyalty to her. Stephanie resented Fay's every re-quest and demanded that Harry stick up for her. Harry got mad, first at Stephanie, then at Fay. Feeling mistreated, Fay increased her pressure on Stephanie, who, in turn, increased her rebellion and her appeal to Harry to side with her. So Stephanie became the focus of a stalled merger.

Conflict eased during Stephanie's four years away at college. But they all dreaded summers. When she finished school and returned home to live, the old patterns of blame and resent-ment flared up again. Stephanie got a job but she began to drink, then do drugs. Then she was laid off. These few facts summarized the story of Stephanie's false start on adulthood from her father and stepmother's point of view. To them, she was a disappointment.

The job Stephanie got in banking was, from her point of view, pretty special. But the pressure to perform awakened her inner doubts. After work she joined her coworkers for a few drinks to unwind and compare war stories. After a couple of margaritas her stomach unknotted and a warm relaxed feeling washed over her. The numbness made it easier for her to laugh and joke, and feel like she belonged.

The first time Stephanie saw three of her fellow trainees using cocaine she felt a shudder of dread, like driving by a bad accident and seeing people trapped inside one of the cars.

A week later Stephanie's supervisor took out a small envelope and said, "Shall we clear our sinuses?" as though using cocaine was the most natural thing in the world. Stephanie was afraid to say yes, but more afraid to say no. So she said yes. To herself she thought, Just this once.

After that Stephanie started going to happy hours and doing a little cocaine regularly, just to relax. Sober, Stephanie was a worrier. She worried about how she looked and what people thought of her, and whether or not she had what it takes to make it in banking. But when she was high she stopped worrying about everything; she even stopped worrying about her parents' worrying about her.

At home her moods alternated between irritability and withdrawal. Fay saw this, saw her runny nose and red eyes, and told Harry that Stephanie was using drugs. Harry couldn't believe it. Finally the weight of the evidence became overwhelming, and, confronted, Stephanie confessed.

"Yes, I've done a little coke," she admitted. "But I don't really have a problem. Just leave me alone." Tears were shed and promises made.

But then Stephanie couldn't bear it. She started going to clubs with names like Bogart's and Cagney's and waking up with a headache in the bedrooms of men she didn't recognize. By then she was finding it harder and harder to face work. She usually had to smoke a joint or take a Quaalude or a Nembutal to calm her nerves—"the cocaine jangles."

Things got bad, and then things got worse. She was fired from her job, and they refused to give her a recommendation. She grew pale and thin. The clubs she hung out in now were tougher places with tougher men. No longer did she get high to feel good, now it was just to stop the craving. The craving was a wild, voracious thing inside her. Only if it were fed would it sleep. Hungry, it woke up and drove her mad.

One morning when she got up, Stephanie couldn't breathe through her nose. In the bathroom she blew her nose and out came a bloody mass of nasal tissue. She was scared. How had her life gotten out of control?

Two hours later Fay was checking her into a drug treatment center. Fay talked to the woman at the desk, while Stephanie filled out form after form. Stephanie smiled while the woman explained the program, but inside she was yelling and kicking and howling.

Alone in the small room where she was taken for detox, Stephanie lost track of time. No sooner would she drift off than someone would come in and take her blood pressure and temperature. She vomited a lot, and she didn't always make it to the toilet. Once or twice the doctor came by to give her some Librium. Later she would tell friends that detox was like having a bad case of the flu. But it was worse, much worse.

When Stephanie was in Phase Two her parents started coming twice a week to special meetings for family members of people in recovery. When they were supposed to share their experiences, they talked about her in the third person, as if she weren't there. She wasn't. Her mind was on vacation. She made it through detox and she was making a start on recovery, but she just couldn't deal with her parents' self-righteous recriminations.

It was Adrienne, one of the staff psychologists, who insisted that Stephanie and her parents begin family therapy even while Stephanie was still at the center. This was very much against the traditional approach to recovery, according to which forcing recovering addicts to deal with their families was the last thing you wanted to do.

Viewed in isolation, Stephanie's problem was addiction. Viewed as a member of a family system, her problem was still addiction. The family didn't make her take cocaine, and her parents weren't responsible for her addiction. Stephanie became an addict not in her family but outside, under the influence of a boss and coworkers who used cocaine to escape. But family members can participate in the maintenance of an addiction. In the jargon of addiction treatment, they are codependent—addicted to a relationship that supports addiction.

Family therapists see each member of a system as reinforcing the behavior of others by his or her feedback. Each one is the cause and effect of the others' behavior: They are stuck to, and with, each other. From this perspective family members may be part of the problem, but they can also be part of the solution.

My first objective was to help Stephanie realize that autonomy and responsibility go hand in hand, and her parents to realize that when their demands became respectful they would be helping their daughter grow up. The second objective would be to help the spouses let go of their preoccupation with Stephanie and start getting involved with each other.

"Fay, can you sit on this comfortable couch next to your husband, because I want to talk with both of you." She got up without a word and sat next to Harry. "How can you help each other let Stephanie grow up? It's very difficult, but you must think, What is the minimum we can do?"

The key word was *minimum*. But it was almost impossible for the Fischers to understand that sometimes less is more. They were committed to doing their best, and to the idea that more is better—even when it's more of the same.

"Minimum?" Harry picked up on that. "*I* would do less. Much of what I do, much of the way I behave, is created by Fay," he said, dragging his words out phrase by phrase. Turning to Fay, he went on. "If you left it to me, I would let her seek her own level. I would treat her like water, and water has to seek its own level." He gestured broadly to show what he meant. To his way of thinking, Fay was trying to make water run uphill.

Harry sounded tired, discouraged, and unwilling to argue, as though he'd used up pity and anger. "If she wants to destroy her life, I would almost let her do it. But you won't allow that to happen. You say she must get help. We find a place that will help her. We take her there. She goes. But then she turns around and resents the fact that we're trying to help. We—"

"Can I say something?" Stephanie just couldn't stay out of it.

"Not really," Harry said in the same monotone.

I went over and sat next to Stephanie and whispered to her

that this conflict was between her parents: "Let them settle it."

She yanked another tissue out of the box and wiped her nose. She said, bitterly, "He just repeats himself, time in and time out."

Any conflict between two people in this family triggered the third to get involved. This detoured the original discussion and kept them from getting anywhere.

"Let's see," I whispered to Stephanie, still very close.

"We have to let her find her own way," Harry went on. "That's what I'm trying to tell you. I'm willing to come to therapy and discuss it, but if she ends up in jail, she has to go to jail. If that's the way it has to be—"

This was too much for Fay: "If only I didn't have to see it!" Then she turned to me. Nothing changed in her face that you could put a finger on, but she suddenly looked ten years older. "I've gotten to the point where I'm losing the drive. It's taking a physical toll." She looked worn out, but her voice lost none of its sharp pressure.

"Fay, Fay," I said, showing my concern. "How did you become so overresponsible?"

"How? Because my husband's way has been—by his own admission—to see it all and just sit back and let it happen. I have not lived that way, ever."

"But look what it's doing to you."

"I know. It's devastating. And it's had all kinds of repercussions."

Harry's powerful passivity provoked Fay's control, and vice versa. One was the extension of the other. "Fay, you are a very responsible person, and you married a man with a slower tempo. You take two steps to his one."

"I know," Fay said. "We each march to our own drummer."

"That's right. But there's more. He's an expert at waiting: If he waits just a little bit, you take the initiative. It's totally predictable. He waits, and you step in."

Fay laughed. "I understand exactly where you're coming from." She wasn't ready to give up. "Very objectively speaking, I have regard and respect for everything you've said—"

"But?"

"But," she went on, "when subjectively involved, I feel my blood seething, and it is very difficult." According to Fay, it was Stephanie's abuse and Harry's neglect that drove her. It was them.

So starved for understanding and sensitive to criticism were the three of them that any direct comment about their role in the family sorrows—even one that might turn out to be constructive—felt like an ice cube on a sunburn. My insistence that both Fay and Harry polarized each other felt like an attack, and it made Fay defensive. In her exasperation there was little room for reason, and no desire to pursue it.

I went over and stood in front of Harry: "How can you engage Fay so that she won't feel so alone?"

I was pulling apart the family triangle at all three poles. First I had encouraged Stephanie to be more responsible. Now I was asking Harry and Fay to focus on each other.

"Maybe you should begin to think what you and Fay can do for each other. I think you're spending way too much time on Stephanie. She needs to learn to rely on herself. You've done everything you can do for her. Can you begin to think how to help Fay relax?"

"With great difficulty," he said. "Maybe."

The hard, heavy years had worked him over, too. He had his own grudges. He could almost forgive his daughter for putting him through hell. She was sick. But he was having a hard time forgiving Fay for the sin of demanding more from him than he could give.

Fay had an innate anxious energy. She had put this energy to use as a mother, and now she didn't know what else to do with it. Harry's failure to respond to Fay's fretful complaints only made her more fretful and more complaining. She wouldn't stop mothering Stephanie until she got it right, and she wouldn't get it right until she stopped. Stopping was the hard part: Trying to stop something usually doesn't work. What works is starting something else. Unfortunately, Fay wasn't able to start becoming more involved with Harry because he wasn't there for her.

After the consultation I advised Adrienne Simon to concentrate on boundary making when she met with the three Fischers together: She should talk to the couple and keep Stephanie out of the conversation. If they tried to focus on

Stephanie's problems, she should redirect them to their own lives. I also suggested that she meet with Stephanie alone to help her resist the highly charged entanglement with her parents.

Adrienne concentrated on helping Stephanie to take more responsibility for herself and to begin to differentiate from the family. They considered practical matters, such as how to apply for a job, how to dress with style without being provocative, and how to behave on an interview. They even discussed how to ask a man to use a condom.

Stephanie stopped using cocaine and sobered up. She still lived at home, but she began a serious campaign to get a job. With less reason to worry about Stephanie, Fay and Harry became more involved—and more irritated—with each other.

When Adrienne again met with the three of them together, she found them repeating their old destructive patterns. Fay criticized Stephanie in a loud, shrill voice. Stephanie protested. Harry watched, fuming silently on the sidelines. Fay grew louder and shriller. Finally, exasperated, Harry lashed out at his daughter: "Let's not forget that the basic problem is Stephanie. She refuses to get a job and just sits around doing what she does best. Nothing. What the hell *do* you do all day?"

What was she doing? She was living suspended, exhausted, silent and dulled. Scarred by her failures and an addict's own private vision of hell, she watched television, read a little, and tried to keep from thinking about the white powder and the hot wind blowing through the cold, empty places inside her.

Stephanie talked about coming home from a job interview very excited that it had gone well. When she shared her excitement with her father, he said flatly, "When you get the job, let me know."

Like many young people who retreat to their families after an unsuccessful start on independent adulthood, Stephanie was wounded and fragile. She was disappointed in herself, anxious for her parents' understanding, and highly sensitive to their criticism. It's called shame.

Stephanie longed to hear her father say that he loved her and was proud of her. The fact that her behavior made it hard for him to say these things did nothing to diminish her longing to hear them. Maybe she wanted to say, Forgive me, forgive me for failing you. And maybe her father wanted to say, I love you. But neither of them knew how.

The counterpart of Stephanie's shame was her parents' guilt. If children are their parents' report cards, then Harry and Fay hadn't yet passed their final exam. She made them feel like failures, and each of them reacted to this sense of failure in his or her own characteristic way. Fay with a pushy intrusiveness, and Harry with a withdrawn bitterness.

Adrienne had a clear picture of what was wrong in the Fischer family, but she had trouble getting them to hear her. She'd grown too close. She felt their frustration and their pain, and she was caught in the grip of her sympathy. And so she requested another consultation.

I greeted the family in the waiting room and led them into my office. Fay and Harry looked the same, but Stephanie seemed different, brighter. She was wearing a blue silk shirt and a short black skirt. The ribbon in the back of her dark hair matched her shirt. Her face had lost some of its pallor, and when she smiled her cheeks got cheerfully round.

I noticed that Fay had a cast on her arm. "Did your husband break your arm?" I asked jokingly.

"No, I don't hit," Harry said. His tone was sardonic. "My weapon is silence."

"How do you do it?" I asked.

"You build a little wall," he said, slowly and evenly. "And then you get behind the wall, and you part from the scene." He spoke without apology or sorrow. "Then you're in your own little world, and the rest of the world doesn't bother you."

Harry kept his world small and manageable. Within the confines of the business, he was absolute master. At work, he controlled chaos. At home, he avoided it, or shut it out. When Fay tried to claim his attention, he shut *her* out.

Fay agreed. "He puts insulation around himself and hears only what's on the periphery. Therefore he doesn't have to relate—facially, verbally, or any other way."

"And what happens to you?"

"It bothers me greatly—because there's no sharing of a life." Fay spoke with increasing agitation. She was feeling her pain and showing her anger.

I got up and walked over to them. "Can you say, 'I want to be in your world'?" I asked her.

"Oh, no. I have verbalized it, but he won't let me in."

Harry slowly shook his head. Fay's small, rapid gestures showed her agitated irritability, just as Harry's broad, slow movements showed his implacability.

I sat back down. "I don't know why, but I'm thinking about those whales trapped in the ice in the Arctic."

The papers were full of news about the two whales trapped in the ice, and the joint efforts of the USSR and the United States to save them. The world was in a self-congratulatory mood. I don't know if the image was prompted by Harry's immobility or by my own feeling of futility.

"Well, they must have a decent relationship," Fay said, "or one would have killed the other by now—and there'd be only one whale."

Fay said this without any sign of rancor. Behind the nagging wife is a lonely woman. Unfortunately the husband who responds only to the nagging traps himself, and his wife, in a pattern of hounding and evasion. And there is no trap so hard to get out of as the trap you set for yourself. I wanted Harry to think about this.

"What happens to Fay when you get behind your wall, Harry? Does she feel lonely?"

"Oh, she's very lonely." Fay leaned forward, resting her chin on her hand. She was anxious to hear what he would say. "Extremely lonely. It's a matter of wanting to do things, and to share. I'm not always willing to. She will share with me what I enjoy, not necessarily happily. But—"

"So you succeeded in training her."

"She's not trained," he said in that even, insistent way of his, and I felt the weight of his resistance. "It's not a matter of training. She just submits. She's just decided that she can't move the immovable object, so she might as well try to work with it the way it is." This man was wonderful at making admissions that were really denials.

"How were *you* trained?"

"How was *I* trained?"

"This technique, this passive resistance—"

"It's not a technique. I wasn't trained." Again I felt his resistance. "It's just the way I adapted."

"How did you learn this wonderful, and sometimes not so

wonderful, approach to life? You wait. And you are able to outwait anybody. You learned to become a whale. You must have learned that very early in life."

"Yes, I did. I was pretty much on my own as a young person, and I learned to protect myself."

"Is that why you came to therapy? To see if you still need all this protection?"

"Oh, I'm sure I don't. I don't need protection—except from what I don't want to be involved with."

"If you don't need it and you still use it, you're stuck in a time capsule."

"I'm stuck. Those around me are stuck worse." The defense rested.

Harry defeated every attempt I made to get him to move. With him, I felt, it was impossible to win. So I let go of the struggle. If I didn't fight, he'd have no one to resist. "Any attempt to produce change will need to be done very cleverly. Harry can't know when you want him to move, or in what direction. If he does, he'll outsmart you every time, and defeat himself."

Fay, who at last felt understood, said, "You know the expression, your foot's in cement? I always say to him that he puts his feet in cement." Agitated and anxious now, she spoke rapidly, first to Harry and then to me. "You put them there deliberately and you refuse to make an attempt to reprogram yourself and get the hell out of that cement. Yet he's not happy about it."

"But that's not the problem," Harry said. "That's just the way we are. The problem is Stephanie. Her way of life, the things she's done." His voice was low and weary and matter-of-fact. "And it causes tremendous problems between Fay and me."

"How does Stephanie cause problems between you and Fay?"

"I will explain it to you," he said softly, patiently, like an exasperated parent trying to remain calm while explaining something to a child who isn't getting it. "Fay is a doer. I am a not doer—in this instance—and I'm willing to let things happen. Things go from bad to worse, and I do nothing, until I get to a point where I'm desperate and then I'll try to do something." He paused between each phrase, controlling the conversation and compelling our attention. "Stephanie has been in trouble for a lot of years now, and as a result it's created tension in our home—between Stephanie and me, between Stephanie and Fay, and between Fay and me."

This was an old story. Harry and Fay felt controlled and defeated by each other. But when things got hot, they turned their attention to Stephanie. She was their cross and their excuse.

"Stephanie, aren't you going to jump in?" I asked.

She folded her arms and smiled. "I'm trying to stay out of it."

Harry wasn't ready to settle for that. "You can't stay out of it, Stephanie, because you're right in the middle of it. You're *it. You are it.*"

"I get blamed for everything that goes on." She had her father's wry smile. It was a smile that said, I know what these people are up to. "And all their problems, basically, I'm blamed for."

"Basically, most of the problems we have are as a result of the things you've done."

Stephanie gave up on her father and turned to me. "They're very busy in my life."

The three of them were so locked into a pattern of blame and recrimination that the least bit of anxiety triggered another round of chasing each other's tails. They reminded me of a carousel that used to come to my village every summer. I remember watching, fascinated, as a wooden leopard chased a wooden horse. Each time the man turned the crank the chase resumed, always without progress.

"Let me tell you, Stephanie, that parents never abandon their children. They continue trying to rescue them. Even if they'd like to stop, they can't. And Fay is the one who takes it upon herself to keep this family together. She is a person with tremendous energy."

"Oh, you overestimate that," Fay said. "I said before that there is a lack of resiliency at this stage of my life."

"Do you know that Fay is at the end of her rope, Harry? Do you realize that?"

"Kind of." Harry shifted uncomfortably. "She's been desperate, for quite a while I guess."

There was genuine concern in his voice, but Fay didn't hear it. "When I see things," she said with rising exasperation, "it's right under our noses! You can't pretend you don't see. Stephanie says she's going out for a while—and then she walks in two days later, *drunk*. Well, the bells ring in Harry's head. I mean it's like, Where have we gone? We're back to square one. He can't deal with it, and Stephanie throws the blame on everybody else. She wants 'space.' She forgets she doesn't know what to do with her space properly. And maybe if she filled her space properly she too would be happy." By now Fay was really wrought up. "First she tells you she's got a job—then she tells you she's not going to go to it for a couple of weeks—someone out of a job for *one year* and then she gets a job and is not willing to start—with thousands of dollars of debt on her head—bounced checks, fraudulent checks—and still is not willing to take a job and start paying this off—it's inconceivable!"

This strident reminder that the problem was Stephanie was a reaction to my attempt to confront the conflict between the spouses. Fay's tirade sounded mean, unless you knew about the hell Stephanie had put her through—unless you knew that the one thing more frustrating and painful than trying to change Stephanie was trying to change Harry. But suddenly I knew where to go. If Fay was hopelessly in need, and no therapist came to her rescue, her despair might activate Harry. For the next half hour I concentrated all my energy on bringing out Fay's pain and hopelessness.

"Fay is like Moses striking the rock. But the rock will not give water just because she hits it. *It will not happen*." My voice began to rise and fall like a preacher's. I enunciated slowly and got up to drive my message home. "I don't think anything will change. This is a family of very stubborn people. You'll cling to your own ways until something cracks. But the thing that will crack is Fay. You two have evolved protective techniques of projecting responsibility. Fay doesn't know how to protect herself."

I hammered away at them, preaching doom, predicting failure. "Stephanie doesn't take responsibility, and Harry doesn't take responsibility. It's lucky they have Fay. Somebody in this family has to be responsible. So it's Fay. But she will crack. Because she's pushing against impossible odds. She's a doer, and she wants things to happen, and she hopes things will happen, but things won't happen, so finally *she will crack*."

But Fay, the doer, could not accept such helplessness. "Well, when I broke my arm and went to the doctor, he put a cast on my arm, and gave me medicine, and this week I'm going to start exercises—I have a prescription—and I hope to fulfill the prescription, and hopefully my arm will get better. We came here wanting the same thing. Here's my problem, now you are objective, you are not involved, and you are a learned person. What is my—what is our—prescription?"

I was saying, Accept helplessness. Her retort was to help me become a better rescuer. Remembering that sometimes less is more, I said, "I think I told it to you."

"Then I missed it."

Harry hadn't. This was one of the moments in families when things suddenly shift. It doesn't necessarily involve some dramatic action or big speech. It can be as quiet as turning on a light in a dark room. You could almost see the light come on in Harry's eyes.

He, who was in many ways the most stubborn of the three, was finally getting the message. "He said, very simply, that Stephanie and I will go on doing what we have learned to do."

"But that's so negative!" Fay said. "I can't accept that!"

"You're asking his advice and telling him you won't take it."

"No! That's not a prescription of what to do. That's a prognosis. I don't want a prognosis. I came for a remedy."

"Well, he's telling you that you *can't* help."

"But she's a savior," I said. "She's a rescuer. She'll never stop."

Then a thought occurred to me. "Do you know the myth of Sisyphus? Sisyphus was a Greek condemned to push a boulder up a steep hill." I stood up. If I was going to play the storyteller, I might as well do it right. "And through all eternity he had to push that rock until he got to the top of the hill. But every time—"

"It came down and killed him," Harry concluded. Now he was actively trying to help.

"No."

He tried again. "It blocked the entrance to the cave."

"No, no, much worse. Every time he got the rock to the top,

it rolled back down to the bottom. And Sisyphus had to go back and push the rock all the way up again. This is hell. And it happens every time. That's Fay, and it's hell for her. She's got to push this rock," I pointed to Harry. "She's got to push that rock," I pointed to Stephanie. "And she thinks the rocks will move, but every time they roll back. I don't think you understand this, Fay, but this is your hell. So now I will say good-bye to you. I hope someone will save you." I got up and shook her hand.

It wasn't easy to be so blunt, but I felt that I had to be tough to provoke this family to change.

Harry was sitting on the edge of his chair. He was smiling. He got it. I said good-bye and left with a sense that Harry knew what needed to be done.

The following week Harry took Fay for a two-week vacation to Florida. While they were gone Stephanie found an apartment and moved out of the house. She was on her way. So were Fay and Harry.

Harry had long seen Stephanie's irresponsibility and the futility of Fay's constant intervention. He'd seen it, and hated it, and refused to be any part of it. What finally penetrated his thick wall of protective isolation was the realization that his own stubborn refusal to enter the fray kept it going.

Fay and Stephanie were both ready to change, too. Fay was frustrated and exhausted. Stephanie was tired of getting picked on and, even more important, ashamed of the behavior that provoked it. But these two were so locked together in love and anger that their interactions had become stylized. They were so exquisitely sensitive to each other that the slightest movement from either one set them both spinning in the same old, cruel circles. It was Harry's change, his willingness to move toward his wife, that broke the cycle.

This is an important truth about families. Significant change can be initiated by a sudden shift. The full knowledge of a fact sometimes enables you all at once to see many supporting but previously unsuspected things. It's not a matter of trying harder. It's a matter of trying something different.

But there is a second important truth about families. Change must be worked through. You can initiate change with a sudden shift in attitude and action. Keeping it going long enough to help the rest of the family adjust to the new rules takes work, takes time.

The working-through process in the Fischer family was kept on track by Adrienne's continued involvement for the next six months. That was two years ago. Harry and Fay still call her occasionally when they feel the need to discuss something—usually Stephanie—with a compassionate, wise adviser. Stephanie keeps in touch, too. She has a steady live-in boyfriend and is once again holding down a responsible job in banking.

PART FIVE

AGING

As I suppose becomes a man my age, I am familiar with death. He walks two steps behind me. He has stooped shoulders and favors his left leg, giving him the same ungainly walk I have. Maybe that's why he is invisible as he walks in my shadow. I encountered him often during my medical studies and during the war. But we really got acquainted when I was fifty, when my father died. My father had had a mild heart attack about ten years before, but since then he'd been living a normal life. So his stopping the car on the side of the road and making my mother a desperate widow was unexpected. He was, and then he wasn't.

When the numbness of grief wore off, the specter of death caught up with me and introduced himself. We talked about priorities. About walking slowly, accepting more—in myself and others. My children and my wife, brother, sister, and mother as they are, not as I might wish them to be. I stopped on the road to pick a flower, and this time looked long, getting richer on small moments. I found death wise and helpful.

We continued talking for several months; then he disappeared. Once again I began to hurry. My hot temper, which had cooled, flared up again. Goals that had been postponed became urgent imperatives: a book I hadn't written, my impatience with my job.

Death came again and took my friend Fundia, so angry at having cancer, so bitter about having been singled out so young. I remembered back to 1948, when we were both in the Israeli army. Death knocked, but we beseeched him to go away, and so he passed over Fundia that time. Somebody else died. That time.

Death, which sometimes seems so sudden, comes to most of us by degrees.

After my sixtieth birthday I began to notice that my body was becoming a stranger. Once when I was at the Franklin Museum of Science in the "Life in the Future" section, I stood under the electronic sensors of a tactless machine that said, "Stand still. You are five feet six inches." Not me! I'm five eight. I moved out and tried again, standing up straight and tall. The same mechanical voice said, "You are five feet six inches." Where had I lost two inches of my self?

Feelings like that, feelings of loss and diminution, have become familiar to me. The maddening inability to remember names, the loss of quickness and flexibility, even waking up to discover I'd dozed off—all are elements of aging. Small deaths. They make me familiar with the process of being diminished, a process that ends with turning into other people's memories.

I met death again when Pat's mother died. She was eighty. One day she wasn't feeling well, and we took her for a routine examination. It was cancer of the pancreas, fast and fatal. She accepted the indignities of hospital care with characteristic resignation. She was spitting blood, so an examination of the lining of her stomach was scheduled. I can still see the young doctor urging her to bend her neck back, farther and farther, while he forced a long, rigid tube down her esophagus and into her stomach. The doctor was in his own world, a world of science and medicine. The patient had shrunk to the lining of her stomach.

After that came exploratory surgery, then more tests. Why can't doctors respect death?

Pat's father felt betrayed. He'd expected to die first. His world began to shrink. He retreated into sleep, woke up to a world not of his liking, and went back to sleep. "You know, Sal," he explained, "I'm tired. I just don't feel like waking up." But he did. His was a long dying—almost three years.

Death came late for my mother. Before sinking into a coma she responded to some medication by growing confused. She spoke to me as if I were still her little boy, and I was. I kept vigil at her bedside. Death sat with us, knowing he could afford to be patient, and we talked some more. I had to be away for a day. Mother stalled death. She was waiting for me. I spoon-fed her half a boiled egg and some water, opening my mouth in synchrony with hers, just as she'd done for me when I was small and helpless. Then she went to sleep and didn't wake up. But she stayed with me. I still have the urge to call her whenever something important happens. Her phone number is still on my Rolodex. Now Pat and I are the oldest generation. There is no one ahead of us, no one to shield us. We are the carriers of history—the only link between our parents and the future.

After my mother's death we began a research project on

normal families who had a member with serious or terminal illness. We had read about the Co-op Care Unit at New York University Medical Center, where patients are admitted with a caring partner. Pat and I were fascinated by the concept. Was it really possible to find in the United States models of hospital care that took relationships into account?

We interviewed families in the hospital and later in their homes. At first when we came to their homes we felt like intruders, but the families received us with tremendous generosity. They showed us their family albums, photographs of themselves when they were young, their children, and their grandchildren. They shared with us their pain, their anxiety, their uncertainty, and their denials of death. Each of them knew death was living in the house, but they felt the need to hide that knowledge from the others. Our coming to see them allowed them to voice their anguish and to communicate with other family members through us.

We discovered that families coped best when they found the flexibility to shift functions and transfer power. There came a point when other family members had to take over and the patient had to let go. This was a moment of crisis, since now everyone had to recognize that the process was irreversible. That the person who had been so strong would never be strong again.

We also met many families who began to mourn at the point of diagnosis. In these families there was more denial of death and determined avoidance of the illness as a process. It was important in these families to make it clear that the patient was alive, though changed—that the future existed and was very precious. A dying father could still help his daughter who was having trouble with math.

Over the two years we worked with these families we learned that death is a process during which the family has to reorganize as the strength of family members and their functions change. We learned great respect for these families and for their ability to become a family with a sick person, and then a family without him or her.

For most people the road to death is aging, a slow process of turning inward and letting go. But just as some people can't face death, others can't face life. For them, aging starts early.

But any force with such powerful possibilities can go powerfully awry. Now I will tell you a strange story about a miscarriage of complementarity.

———◆•◆———

At sixty-eight, Emilio Rivera had been in bed for seventeen years. A man who suffered the burdens of life in the form of aches and pains, he used and abused a progression of analgesics—aspirin, Bufferin, Advil, and Darvon, before moving up to Empirin with codeine.

Few things remind us of our essential separateness the way pain does. When somebody tells us he or she has a headache, we cannot know what that headache feels like. We only know our own headaches. Each of us responds to pain in our own way; it is one of the experiences that separate us from each other. No matter how much we love each other, we do not share each other's pain.

The family therapist who encounters pain faces a quandary. He or she cannot say "Your husband is causing your lower back pain," or, "Your wife is producing your headaches." Pain is hard to account for with a theory that claims people are so connected they maintain one another's problems. Anger and fear and anxiety fly around families like sparks, jumping the gap from one person to another. Pain ends at the surface of the skin.

Physical pain does not yield readily to interpretations about family organization. So when we deal with families in which one person has pain, we think about individual treatment approaches.

Going to a doctor, however, may not be the answer. Physicians are notoriously dismissive of pain. They say things like, "It will pass," "That's only your body responding," or "You just have to live with it." If your back hurts or your ankle aches, the orthopedist will deal with the presumed cause and give you vague assurances that the pain will disappear when the problem is resolved. The chiropractor will manipulate your bones and hope that the pain will disappear. If these experts cannot find some *thing* to treat, or if pain lingers, you may indeed just have to learn to live with it.

Today there are special management pain-clinics. They offer relaxation techniques, bioenergetics, drugs, and hypnotism. But they are not interested in family organization. Family therapists don't know pain management, and pain-management specialists are not interested in the family. So a man like Emilio Rivera—who has been afflicted with pain for thirty years—falls between categories. Usually such people do not come for family therapy, or if they do, they leave because they are not happy with the direction the treatment takes.

When he was still young, Emilio became afflicted with a vague, undefined sensation of migrant pains in his body, for which he spent seven years visiting as many doctors and healers as there were in the rural part of his native Costa Rica. Failing to find a solution, he began to prescribe his own cure in the form of whatever painkillers he could put his hands on. Soon he was taking massive doses of analgesics, and soon after that he became addicted.

Some people say that a hypochondriac's fondest wish is to come down with a real sickness—some certifiable ailment to vindicate his or her worry and justify his or her complaints. When Emilio was found to have a mild case of asthma, the heart went out of him, and he took to his bed. From that time on he declined into premature old age, tended selflessly by Dolores, who was both wife and nurse.

In bed day after uneventful day, he hid from the aggravations of life and drifted into a vast, almost terminal calm. Emilio's wife and children responded to his invalidism with alarm and sympathy, and then irritation, and finally resignation. Their lives went on.

When the family moved to New York, Emilio was able to overcome his addiction to painkillers but still found it necessary to remain in bed for most of the day. He lived in a restricted area of his apartment in a state of semi-invalidism. And so the story of one person with pain became a story of a family organizing itself around that pain. When a family adjusts itself to support one person's infirmity, it's not always easy to know when that support ceases to be necessary.

For sixteen years Emilio and his family had been in a state of accommodation that permitted him to function minimally without pain. Then, in the seventeenth year, the director of a geriatric unit in Brooklyn, where the family lived, became aware of the family's sorrow and approached Emilio with a great sense of mission. Like Rip Van Winkle, Emilio was an oddity and a great challenge.

Before long a van from the hospital came at ten o'clock each morning to take Emilio to the geriatric day-care center. There he was engaged in the endeavors such places organize—more designed to fill time than to be productive. At two in the afternoon Emilio was returned to his apartment, where he immediately went back to bed.

The family was pleased. Emilio's mornings at the center gave Dolores a few hours for housecleaning, free of Emilio's demands. For the rest of the day their activities remained exactly as they had for many years, Emilio watching soap operas in Spanish and Dolores caring for his needs while complaining about the need to care for him.

How Emilio occupied his mind in those long afternoons in Brooklyn, where the shadows come early and the darkness comes late, no one knew, and after a while they ceased to care. Then the devil threw a monkey wrench.

One day Emilio made a remarkable announcement. The long days and empty evenings had bred in him a restless longing to return to Costa Rica. He felt a nostalgia for old friends and for his earlier self, as he had been before the curse of his sickness. And so, he announced, he would return to the town where he was born for a short visit.

What prompted this mysterious awakening of the spirit no one knew, but the whole family was alarmed. How would he manage? What if he became really sick? His wife and children had grown used to him as a dependent, bedridden invalid. This totally unexpected plan was difficult to understand and even more difficult to accept. They admonished him to stay in bed, and when he refused to listen they summoned the family doctor to dissuade him from his foolish plan. But Dr. Montoya could find no reason why Emilio should not go to Costa Rica if he wished. It might do him good. This assessment only aggravated the family's distress.

Emilio's family had been tossed around a lot before drifting into the calm of his invalidism. When the children were young his drinking and moodiness made him unsafe to be around.

Then he quit drinking and became even more morose and emotionally unavailable. They stood by and watched helplessly as he went from doctor to doctor and faith healer to faith healer, hoping to cure what he first called the sadness without reason and later called illness. And then, when his drug habit took possession like an evil spirit, they suffered the usual hell of families struck by the plague of addiction. Now they were very much afraid of anything that disturbed the fragile peace. Having lost faith that things might get better, they settled their hopes on things not getting worse. And so, greatly alarmed, they contacted me, and I agreed to meet with the whole family to discuss Emilio's startling plan.

After forty years of living and working in the United States, I still feel a special pleasure working with Hispanic families, with whom I share echoes of my own experience in rural Argentina. Like Emilio, I can remember from my childhood visits to local *santeros*. I remember that one cured my sister of a digestive disorder, making complicated measurements of geometric shapes imagined on her small body, until she was pronounced cured. And she was. I know that the Costa Rican and Argentinean cultures are really different, but with the passing years I feel a kinship with all Hispanic people.

It was raining the day of our meeting, and the family was a few minutes late. I waited with mounting curiosity to see this man, who after so many years had suddenly decided to get out of bed. When they arrived I saw a healthy-looking young man in his twenties chatting amiably with his mother. Trailing a few steps behind was the father, looking frail and tentative.

Emilio Rivera was a tall man gone to seed, with sloping shoulders and a large, rounded stomach beneath his freshly ironed white *guayabera*—one of those large, loose shirts worn in the tropics. He shuffled into the room with his chin tucked down, leaning a little forward as if he were heading into a wind.

His wife, Dolores, looked like one of the mournful women in Garcia Lorca's dramas of Spanish tragedy. A black kerchief covered her white hair. She was somber, dignified, upright, wrinkled, and a little hard. Her eyes were dark and she kept her lips pressed tightly together, almost as though she were making an effort not to complain.

The third member of the group was their son, Dion, a robust, beefy young man with thick black hair and the beginnings of a beard. He smiled a lot and chewed gum aggressively. Emilio and Dolores sat next to each other in two chairs along the wall near the door. Dion spread himself out on the couch at right angles to his parents. His sister-in-law, Mariela, and brother, Rafael, would be joining us as soon as they found a parking space.

I thought we might as well get right to the point, and so I said to Emilio, "I understand you're planning a visit to Costa Rica."

"Yes, just a visit," he said, glancing at his wife.

"I don't say nothing," Dolores replied, shaking her head. "Everybody is mad. Nobody wants him to go." She looked over at her son on the couch, and he nodded agreement.

Just that fast the lines were drawn. Emilio, with his plan to visit Costa Rica, on one side; the rest of the family, with their fear of the consequences, on the other.

Emilio's wife and son took turns pointing out the dangers of a trip to Costa Rica. How would he take care of himself away from the watchful eyes of the family? Emilio protested in the monotonous benign way that had become his trademark. They argued with the tired pessimism of a family who had long since given up hoping to make each other understand.

I found the situation profoundly absurd. They insisted that he was too sick to be well. He argued feebly that they should let him try to be independent.

"Mr. Rivera," I said, "how old are you?"

"Sixty-eight."

"Well, they talk as if you are a child. I don't understand. Why do they do that?"

"Well, because they love me so much, they act that way."

"It's out of love?"

"Si, out of love."

"I don't understand. Is Mr. Rivera an adult or is he a child?" I had made contact with the enemy, and it was a formidable one. I feel comfortable working with anger, stress, and anxiety; but love troubles me. Love is a mine field of guilt, loyalties, demands for reciprocity, accusations of defaulting, and claims of unfairness. But through the years I have developed some strategies to defuse this explosive device.

"Mr. Rivera," I said, "They have put you in a cage. They protect you, and it's out of love, so you cannot be angry, because it's out of love."

My challenge, I knew, was too puny to make a dent in the ironclad organization of this family. But I knew I was aiming in the right direction, and I had at my disposal my knowledge of Hispanic culture with its powerful value of male autonomy. The joust had just begun, and I was prepared to use the mace and chain.

Mr. Rivera's son spoke for the family. "You're absolutely right. We *are* overprotective. But we're overprotective for a reason. If we don't watch out for him, he won't take care of himself. In the past he was free, and he chose ways of Darvon, he chose ways of aspirin. If we don't watch him, he may take the Darvons, he may take the codeine—he can do anything."

"Señor Rivera, your family is very protective. At sixty-eight, they treat you as if you are either too young or too feeble." I got up and shuffled a few steps like a decrepit ancient and amplified my point in Spanish, "*Don Emilio, ellos lo tratan como si usted es demasiado viejo para vivir.*" (They treat you as if you are too old to live.) As I moved to Spanish I honored him, calling him Don Emilio, the title of respect.

"She loves you, and he loves you. And you love to be loved. But to me it is a jail. It's a pleasant jail, because it's a jail of love."

"Well he's been given the chance to move many a time," Dion said, leaning forward. "He's chosen not to move. With his illnesses, his back, his headaches, he doesn't move."

Dion, the son of immigrant parents, with feet in both cultures, was used to serving as a conduit between his parents and the gringo culture. The good son, he spoke for his father, but silenced him in the process. I, however, had already chosen sides. The trip to Costa Rica seemed like a fresh step out of Emilio's life of invalidism. It was worth the risk.

"Do you really want to go to Costa Rica, Don Emilio?"

"Yes," he said with conviction.

"For how long?"

"That depends. A short time. A month, two months. I told them to give me a break, to be myself, eh? And to live my own life." This he said with real feeling.

I liked this man. He reminded me of certain *hombres* from my childhood, simple, cunning, friendly, resigned to life's designs. I remembered Don Chas in San Salvador, who used to tell my father: *"Mauricio, siempre me toca bailar con la mas pesada."* (I always get stuck dancing with the fattest partner.) Emilio, too, was playing the cards life dealt him. He was too self-absorbed to see himself as an exploiter of his wife and children. He was just playing the only cards he held.

"Emilio," I said, "you will need to convince them that you are responsible. You will need to convince your wife and your son, who love you a lot, that at sixty-eight you are a person who can be a month in Costa Rica without their surveillance." And this, I knew from experience, needed to happen in the session. He would need help. "Can you convince them?"

"I told them, but they don't seem to like the idea," he said meekly.

Emilio protested in character, nothing inappropriate for an invalid, sincere but a little feeble. He had used the power of passivity for so long that he knew all its many variations.

His son feigned fatalism: "I'm convinced, let him go. Either he will kill himself doing the wrong things or he won't." His wife said that she was not convinced but could not stop him. Then she proceeded to try, listing his past mistakes and repeating how worried everybody in the family was.

Emilio had grown lethargic with irresponsibility. Now he was almost comically ill-suited to act as his own champion. I would need to help him. "If they continue to think that you cannot live without their protection, they are making things very difficult for themselves. It's a jail for you; it's also a jail for them."

My second therapeutic sally: Your jailers are in jail with you. The power of systemic thinking lies in such shifts of perspective. The tenacity of conviction is shaken. First: The family helps Emilio remain sick in bed; in that way, he is controlled by them. Second: The family is in bed with him; in that way, they are controlled by him. Now I urge the (feeble) patient to (forcefully) convince the family that he doesn't need them. Later will come the variation of trying to convince the family that they don't need him. Later.

"You need to convince your wife that you are a man who can spend a month without her loving protection and control."

"She's hard to convince," Emilio said in a whiny voice.

"No, Emilio, I think your voice is too soft."

Now Dolores spoke up. "He's weak. He spends the whole day in bed. He don't go no place."

"I can't," he protested. How could he demonstrate his strength without invalidating his weakness? "The main thing about me is my weakness," he said, shrugging his shoulders tragically.

"What weakness?" I asked.

"Physical weakness," he answered.

"Uh-huh . . ." I felt like a bugler sounding reveille to wake the dead, so I changed the subject. "Where would you go in Costa Rica?"

He would go, he said, to stay with friends in the rural countryside, far from the noise of cities. He spoke with enthusiasm and nostalgia for old friends and for a time before things had gone wrong. Avid for the sights of Costa Rica, his voice became the voice of the man he was.

Dion wanted me to know how isolated his father would be. "It's so far into the hills that the public cars don't even want to go there."

At that point there was a knock at the door. I went over to open the door and was greeted by Emilio's older son and daughter-in-law. We shook hands and they came into the room and sat down on the couch next to Dion.

They looked prosperous. The daughter-in-law, Mariela, had dark red hair, cut short, and gold hoops in her ears. An attractive woman in her late thirties, she wore an emerald green satin blouse and black wool slacks. She worked as a paralegal and carried herself with confidence. Her husband, Rafael, a pharmacist who offered advice and remedies to the family, wore a brown leather sports jacket over a blue silk shirt. His wire-rimmed glasses gave him a look of serious purpose.

I said to them, "We're talking about the fact that your father has a very soft voice and has trouble convincing anybody that maybe he is a responsible grown-up person. He convinced your brother-in-law, but he says you are very difficult to convince."

"That's true," Mariela said evenly.

"He convinced me," Dion was quick to add, "that he *wants* to go. And I'm convinced that we should let him go to learn his lesson. That's my feeling. But, that he can really take care of himself, keep control of his asthma and maintain his hypertension at a certain level, I'm not convinced."

Again I felt the family's stubborn resistance. Rather than argue with Dion, I turned to his brother. "I think your father lives in a cage. In a cage of protection, a cage of concern, a cage of love—but it's still a cage."

I went back to my first metaphor. In order to engage the newcomers, I would have to retrace steps we had already taken, before we could go forward. Therapy takes repetition. The trick is to repeat the same theme with several variations.

"This is a problem for the whole family, and unless all of you change, he will not change. He did a good job of convincing you that he's incompetent and that you need to protect him. He did his part. But you do your part, by keeping him in a position where he doesn't need to make any effort. I think it's a serious family problem. And I don't think you will change. I think you are stuck in that position. See, love can be control also. He has trained you to do that."

"What would you suggest we do?" Mariela wanted to know.

"He would need to convince you," I said.

Emilio said nothing.

I was trying to convince them that it was a two-way street. That was hard for them to see. In families it's always a two-way street, and it's always hard for family members to see that.

To make matters worse, I seemed unable to elicit from this man a sense of pride. I tried to make him my ally for change— "You need to convince them." But he refused to join me. Calling him a weakling did not make him indignant, and saying that his family kept him in a cage only made him say that they loved him. Love is hard to argue with.

"It's like a Catch-22," Dion said. "If we let him go on his own, I'm willing to bet money I'll end up on a plane within five or six weeks having to bring him back.

"He needs to start by doing something *here*. Get out of bed. Walk around, move around."

"Go to work," the older son added.

"Yes, go to work," Dion agreed. "Do something. But the minute he gets home—zoom, beeline to the bed."

"And the minute he gets into bed," I said, "there is a system of helpers. You are part of his going to bed. You are in cahoots. Don Emilio, they make you a cripple. And you tell them to do that. The family and you are in a system that makes you an invalid."

I repeat. I move to another level and repeat. I change my tone of voice and repeat. I have developed a large repertoire of saying the same thing. When I was an analyst it wasn't so obvious. I had time on my side. Now, to break a logjam of seventeen years, I needed the magical intensity of the shaman or the boring repetitiousness of the obstinate, or both.

"How would you break that?" the older son wanted to know.

"With great difficulty," I said.

This made him angry. "Well, *how*? I keep hearing this, but I don't hear how it's done."

"Become less helpful," I said.

"In other words," Dion said, "don't do everything for him?" Of the five of them he seemed the least stubborn.

"Let's be honest," the daughter-in-law said. "He won't move. Then the pressure is on my mother-in-law. She ends up doing everything. It's not fair."

A small movement forward. A hole in the seamless construction. Mother is protected by overprotecting father.

"She has her own illness," I said. "Her illness is being overly helpful."

They considered him to have a problem and her to be stuck with it. I wanted them to see that the problem was both parents.

"Your mother is made of iron, and your father is made of cotton."

Dolores nodded and the children laughed.

"If your mother would not be iron, your father could be copper, or bronze." Their laughter made me feel that this metaphor struck a nerve. "If you begin to convince—not your father, but your mother—that she's wrong, maybe you can change both of them. Your mother is tough like nails."

"I'll be honest," Dion said. "I cannot sacrifice my mother for him to learn a lesson. If we stop taking care of him, then she'll be stuck. Again, I'm being overprotective, but it's for a reason."

Thrust, counterthrust, en garde. But I thought the story had opened up. Now we were talking about the children's loyalty to mother and disrespect of father.

The rigid structure of the Rivera family resembled one of Buckminster Fuller's geodesic domes, where every module depends on connecting modules to prop it up. As long as all the elements remain in place, so will the whole edifice. Perhaps I could loosen some of the connections.

So I said to the children, "You don't let your parents negotiate their proper balance. They have a well-oiled system. He makes her work for him and she is happy to work for him."

Now Rafael spoke up. "So you're saying everything is all right? Everything is perfect?" His anger took the form of mockery. "He's happy that she works for him and she's delighted to be his slave? Is that what you're saying? She suffers because she likes it? It sounds like a television program." They all laughed. It was a big joke.

But I didn't laugh. I felt like I was back at square one.

"It's not a joke. Because you are participating in a situation that is very tragic. A sixty-eight-year-old man is made very, very old, and he doesn't have any freedom. He wants to go to Costa Rica for a month. And there is a tremendous amount of concern that he will not survive. And he says that he can do it, and nobody believes him."

Again it was Rafael who answered. "Well, because last time he tried to manage his own affairs, he did a lousy job. What you have to understand is that we have given him his due respect as the head of the house, as a man."

"No, I don't think so." I played the elder, my challenge solemn.

"We do. We let things go and then we end up holding the bag. He has spent—and you can ask him," he said, turning now to confront his father directly. "How many doctors did you go to? How many fortune tellers and *santeros*? How much money did you spend, going from charlatan to charlatan? Did anybody say anything?" Emilio simply listened. He'd heard this litany too many times to show his shame. "Has anybody said anything about you bouncing from doctor to doctor, looking for the cure that doesn't exist?"

"The issue," I said, "is not really whether he goes to Costa Rica. That is something you will decide. The issue is, can you be more respectful and less helpful, instead of loving and overly helpful?"

For a moment all five of them were silent. Then Dion spoke up. "In other words, be less involved with them? Let them live their lives? That went to its biggest test when my mom was operated on and came back home, where she would depend on Pop to do for her. He helped a little and then he stopped."

Emilio helped the way husbands unused to helping do— badly—and Dolores responded the way wives used to doing everything do—by criticizing.

By now the mood had shifted. We were no longer arguing about going or not going to Costa Rica, and we were no longer talking about who was right and who was wrong. We were talking about a family pattern, something they were all involved in and where there was less concern about who was at fault.

So, in this different mood, I tried again. "You're very aware of your father's dependence on your mother, but you don't see that your mother is dependent on his depending on her." Again I emphasized the complementarity of the helpful and the helpless. But with repetition the point was becoming more familiar, and the family's reality less certain. Don't be so sure things are what they seem I was saying, and I thought they were responding.

"She keeps him an invalid. She spoils him by waiting on him hand and foot. I think Mrs. Rivera is really very stubborn—as stubborn as Mr. Rivera. But nobody notices her stubbornness. You notice his stubbornness being a patient, but you don't notice her stubbornness being a nurse."

Now it was Dolores who protested. "Everybody thinks I stop him," she said, shaking her head and looking hurt.

Dion jumped to her defense. "*He* thinks that. I wish the doctor could only come to our apartment."

"If it had not been for my mother, my father and mother

would not be together," Rafael said. Mariela agreed. "He doesn't even appreciate all that she does for him." Until now she had been silent, like her mother-in-law. Dolores's silences were loaded with criticism, yet they were maintained as silences, and they carried more weight than the words they suppressed. Now I was challenging the power of silence, and it was time for words. Rafael continued, "Her purpose was to keep the family together, ever since we were children."

I challenged a family icon and blood spilled. Memory of silent and rowdy battles, and mother always the glue, the protector, the weaver.

"The question is," I said. "how are you going to help your parents now, so that you don't have a father who is an invalid and a mother who is tired."

Dolores was raised in the mode of acceptance. Life is hard. You suffer, but you accept it. Look at the husband fate served up to me, she said.

In challenging her view—the whole family's view—I risked hubris. Here was a woman who did everything for her husband (it's not unknown), and I was saying that she was as much a part of the problem as he was. My challenge was to the pattern, but to her it felt like criticism.

"In the morning I get up at six o'clock. I pray. I make breakfast for him. Then I tell him to get up. 'Leave me alone. I can't move. I can't get up.' I don't touch him. I don't do nothing." It's him, not me, she was saying.

"Do you dress him?"

"No!" she said indignantly.

"Do you prepare his clothes?"

"Si. I wash them, and iron. And if something is broken, I fix it. I lay them out for him."

"Do you make lunch for him?"

"Of course."

"Then you go to bed and watch your soap operas?" This I said to him.

A martyr to his health and his nerves, Emilio craved the sedative of routine. And so he took to his bed, a voluptuary of illness. If his quiet afternoons were given over to the stupor of television, well, what could a sick man do?

Dolores felt trapped. She sought comfort in resignation and prayers. It was the same for all her female friends, as it had been for her mother. It didn't occur to her that there was a choice. If there was anger it had to be muted. Anger is a sin, like pride, gluttony, and sex. Happiness is not to be expressed, because it may attract the evil eye or make somebody put a curse on you.

Each day at four o'clock Dolores made Emilio a snack. Then dinner at six. She ate alone in the kitchen, standing up because she never had enough time to sit down.

"Don Emilio, when the kids come, do you eat with them?"

"No, I don't like to eat at the table. I eat in the bed."

"Sometimes on Sunday do they say to you, '*Papa*, come and eat with us'? '*Veni, come con nosotros*'?"

"Many years ago. But I refused, and they don't bother me any more."

His exaggerated version of the inaccessible father had inspired their protest and then earned their contempt. When Emilio's sickness removed him emotionally from the family, his wife and children tried to pull him back. They wore themselves out trying to coax him back to life. Then they gave up.

"So, Emilio, you eat dinner, and then what happens? Your wife does the dishes?"

"Well, no, because we have a ma-cheen."

"And who loads the dishes?"

"Well, she does it."

"So she's your maid."

"Yes, my wife has been good to me every time. During my seventeen years I was in bed day and night, she took care of me." Was this what his pride had come to?

"You've been in bed seventeen years?"

"Yes, of course I was in bed seventeen years."

"Do you think that you could be in the *Guinness Book of World Records*?"

It was so farcical, I couldn't resist. But you don't challenge absurd lives with irony. The Riveras would need to defend their reality by investing it with meaning. We construct theories to defend our beliefs. Our lives don't have to make sense, we make sense out of them.

"No, you have to qualify to get the record." He said this matter-of-factly and then proceeded to describe the rules for establishing world records, as though remaining in bed for a quarter of a century was the most natural thing in the world.

Was there no provoking this man?

It seemed unlikely that these two people would change. Emilio was proud of his record in bed, and Dolores certainly seemed resigned to her loyal, concerned protectiveness. I said this to the children, and I added, "They are too old to change."

Emilio protested. "Excuse me, *señor*. We haven't done these things on purpose."

"Of course you have done these things on purpose. It's not unconscious."

"Everything I have done, eh? doesn't come from within me."

"It comes from within both of you. You made a bargain seventeen years ago, and the bargain was that she would be your maid. And you accepted the bargain. So you are condemned to be an invalid. And you, *señora*, are condemned to be a nurse. And you, children, are condemned to support your mother so that she can take care of your father—in support of that absurd kind of bargain."

"The problem with her, eh? is that she is all heart," Emilio said.

"What?" I said. His thick accent made it sound like "all hurt."

"She is all *hart*," he repeated with emphasis. "So if she don't do for me, she would do for everybody."

"It's an absurd system," I said. And then to make sure that Emilio and Dolores understood, and to give it power, I explained it in Spanish.

Dolores answered in Spanish, protesting her innocence. She has tried to get him to move. She waits for him to do things, and then when he doesn't, naturally she has to.

"Why don't you ask him to help you?" I said.

"Why I have to beg him?"

"Because you need him." I turned again to the children. "Everybody knows that he is selfish. But nobody is telling her, 'Why don't you let him help you?'"

"Yes," Mariela said, "and he has complained about that."

"He is a man of honor," I said in Spanish, invoking

the celebrated Hispanic value to provoke Emilio's pride, "and he would like to be able to reciprocate. But she never lets him."

Dolores turned away and shook her head. Once again she protested in Spanish: He's selfish. He's stubborn. He does what he wants. He never listens to me.

Somewhere outside the sky opened, and sunlight splashed across the wall behind the couch and onto the faces of Dion, Mariela, and Rafael. Dion squinted and leaned forward. "I got on her case not too long ago for the same reason. He was frying himself some *plantanos*, and she jumped on him. And I jumped on her, and I said, 'Hey, let him do it his way.' *But*, again, he doesn't follow up."

A window had opened through which we could perceive another level of their complementarity and at the same time I got permission to explore Dolores's behavior in the marriage.

"Because he is so angry at her; because your mother is a very loving and very controlling lady."

Mariela said, "That's something he has said for years. But at the same time, I think, deep down inside, he likes it that way."

"He seceded from the family a long time ago," Dion added.

"Yes, but you see, *He likes it like that*. Again you are on *his* case. *She* likes it like that also." It was a kind of perverse irony that they were giving Emilio in his weakness credit for unilateral influence over his wife and family.

Dolores, looking both hurt and disgusted, protested in Spanish. She has always done what the family needed. She took care of the children when Emilio worked, and took care of all of them when he stopped working.

"That makes me more angry at my father," Rafael said. "Because if he has something against my mother, then he shouldn't have something against me or my brother—because that is a separate situation over there."

And now, at last the right to challenge Mother, to recognize human frailty in the icon, had been established. Rafael was making contact and challenging his father directly. The coalition of children with Mother against Mother's husband gave way to a polemic between an adult child and his father.

"But I don't have anything against nobody," Emilio said with bewildered innocence, the marvelous invisible power of the weak.

"But we've seen you do things against us," Dion said, "that have been pretty heartless. Honestly."

Now there was silence. A silence of contemplation or a pause before resuming the counterattack, I did not know.

Finally Dion broke the silence. "So what should we do? Do we let him go to Costa Rica?"

It happens sometimes in therapy that you recognize the moment that confirms your theories or justifies your therapeutic maneuvers. This was such a moment.

"As long as your father convinces you that he is a person you need to take care of, then you are in the same cage. The question is, can you leave that cage? I think you can, and when you do, your parents—both of them—will be free."

I got up, shook hands, and said good-bye.

After our session the family decided to let Emilio go to Costa Rica, if that was what he wanted. Let him prove that he can look after himself, they said. Besides, they thought, it would be good for Dolores to have a rest. And so Emilio left for Costa Rica, and Dolores went to stay with Mariela and Rafael.

On his return to Costa Rica, Emilio was briefly amazed at the quality of the light. After so many years in the shadow-world of his bedroom, the rich abundance of brightness dazzled and stunned him. In that interval he seemed to repossess himself, shed his sense of oppression and infirmity, and begin again to be a person capable of directing his own life. Then, gradually, he grew accustomed to the light. This lightness entered his spirit and came back in his letters.

Emilio's letters were full of cheery gossip. Pedro did this, Ramon did that. This one had a new grandchild, that one was still working. It was as if his heart had not atrophied—only slept.

Back in Brooklyn, Mariela was finding her spacious apartment crowded with the addition of her mother-in-law. Trouble began in the kitchen. Mariela said to Dolores, "I'll take care of the kitchen. You relax." But relaxing was not something Dolores understood, and so she did what she always did—she took over—and the two women began to argue about who would do what and who was helping whom. Rafael entered the discussion to support his wife, and real animosity broke out between mother and son.

As tension increased in Brooklyn, the family began to be more and more worried about Emilio. It's true that his letters sounded happy, but was he telling the truth or hiding his difficulties? He was so inattentive to details. How could they know if he was watching his asthma? And so after a few weeks of worrying, Mariela and Rafael wrote to the old man and urged him to come home. Emilio packed his bags very slowly, felt for the first time in two months a vague pain in his lower back, returned to New York, and went back to bed.

The director of the geriatric unit learned of Emilio's return and phoned him to offer the service of the day hospital. But Emilio said that he was not feeling well, and that when he was having pain he went to bed and the pain subsided. When the director asked him if he would like to see me again, Emilio said he would think about it. But the Riveras never called me.

In my brief encounter with the Riveras I had challenged a destructive life pattern and helped Emilio create a parenthesis in time in which he enjoyed the sun of his childhood. But conflicts sprang up in other parts of the family. Dolores and Mariela's struggles for space in a small apartment in Brooklyn required Emilio's presence in the States, where he resumed the role of patient that he had filled for nearly a quarter of a century.

The emphasis on Emilio's individual patienthood, supported by time and the medical establishment, kept the Riveras wedded to their narrow solutions, in which Dolores's martyrdom, Emilio's illness, and the children's protection of their parents in their rigid unhappiness were all necessary. My attempt to challenge their framing of Emilio's illness as an individual aberration and put it in the context of a dysfunctional family organization was clearly too little, too late, and too discordant with their perceived reality. They didn't trust me enough to continue exploring the possibility of change. I suppose that in the Riveras' collective memory I have joined the many *santeros* who didn't help Emilio.

Today it is impossible for me to remember Emilio and his family without a strong sense of the incongruous and remarkable power of the family system.

13

Death and the Gorilla Mask

Young therapists tend to shun the process of dying. To me it is familiar, so when I meet families with a dying patient, I bring with me an acceptance of death as a stage of life and certain ideas about what must be done to get ready. Above all, I want the family not to bury the sick member before his or her death. I want to help them claim the present and whatever future is left to them. Sometimes people cling to the past as a way of avoiding a future shadowed by death.

Carl was dying, but he wasn't ready. Neither was his family. Eyes fixed firmly on the past, because they were too frightened to face the future, all they could see were the bad old days, the years when Carl, a hard-muscled construction foreman known as "the Gorilla," had dominated and bullied his wife and children. They weren't yet ready to forgive, nor he to forget, and so they came to therapy hoping to settle old accounts.

Carl's family therapist was trying to help him and his family review past crimes and old hurts. As a consultant twenty-five years older than the therapist, I approached the case differently.

Carl was the last of the family to enter the consulting room and the first to sit down. At sixty-two, he looked like what he was, a big man dying. Cancer, creeping through his body, was drying up the flow of life in him. He moved slowly, a tired man marshaling his strength.

The rest of the family came in and sat down together, Edith and the two children, Alan and Kyra, both in their twenties. These three continued their conversation from the hallway, speaking in eager, animated voices, friendly and a little nervous.

Carl sat apart. He still had the massive structure of a powerfully built man, but he was pale and slack skinned. Hollow cheeks, deep-set eyes, and a shiny, smooth skull made his head appear even larger than it was. Edith was a big-boned, attractive woman, more handsome than pretty. Her curly hair was black and cut short. She sat opposite Carl, next to the two children who sat together on the couch.

Alan was a husky six-footer, with thick, curly, dark hair like his mother's, and a mustache that made him look more self-assured than he was. He wore a short-sleeved shirt and a pair of white chinos. Kyra was twenty-eight, three years older than her brother. She was wearing a light-blue maternity smock, and the first thing you noticed was a pretty woman, with straight shoulder-length blond hair and a nice face, but she wasn't soft and she wasn't shy.

I leaned back and said, "Okay, why don't we start. What would you like to happen?"

Kyra was the first to answer. She sat up straight and spoke the same way. She said they were a close family. "We're here to help—and be helped." Alan agreed: "We're very close, but we're emotional people and sometimes we clash." But when I urged him to be specific, Alan waffled: "Oh, nothing particular. We just, you know, once in a while have a misunderstanding or something." Alan was a big man, like his father, but he had an anxious, watchful look, like an animal expecting trouble and not sure from which direction it might come.

When I pressed harder, Alan complained about his mother, "the engulfing grandmother" who couldn't stop interfering with his baby.

"He's very impatient," Edith said. "He doesn't *dare* resent his dad telling him things, but he does resent me if I tell him the least little thing—'Well, do you think the baby wants a cracker or something?' It doesn't have to be anything important. He just resents me. Maybe it's a mother thing, or a woman thing."

"No, no it's not a resentment," Alan insisted. "But the thing that frustrates me is when you're always going on and on about the baby. You don't have to be so . . . so intense. You could just let the child be."

The story of a son who resents his mother's intrusiveness was familiar, but I knew it wasn't *the* story in this family. It was just a calling card. They were trying me out, opening a messy room in the house to see what I would do with the disorder.

Carl sat stiffly, like a man ill at ease or in pain. The yellow golf sweater he wore had the incongruous effect of accentuating his pallor. This was not a man who'd been outdoors playing golf lately. When I asked him how he felt about his son's complaint, Carl replied that it upset him to see Alan getting angry at his mother—but it was true, she did treat him like a baby. Then he swung the conversation around to himself. Speaking slowly, in a deep, raspy voice, he said, "Sometimes I blow up, and sometimes I leave the room. My problem is I have a terrible rage." Villain number one.

"I used to get very angry, very abusive, and very vulgar. I grew up in a mining camp and then in the Navy and then hung around a bunch of construction workers. So I am a master of profanity."

Kyra and Alan and Edith agreed: They'd always been afraid of him.

"And you, Edith?" I asked.

"Oh, no. I don't confront Carl. I try to keep under control," Edith said, her voice trembling.

"Not so good, lately?"

"Lately, no. When I talk about Carl's anger now, I get upset. I always tried to make excuses for him." Edith's face colored as she remembered those years of screaming, in-your-face tirades.

This was still the official story. They were telling me the truth as they knew it. Everyone agreed they'd come to therapy to exorcise a monster. "I am a master of profanity," Carl said. I liked that phrase, and I liked this man. He knew he was dying, and so did everyone else. Why, then, were they talking about his anger? It was probably true—they all agreed it was true—that Carl's anger was terrible; but was it relevant to focus on that now?

Carl was jocular now, but I was looking more than listening. To me, this man was clearly shrinking. He sat down in stages, like a very old man. His skin seemed larger than his body. This gorilla was dying. But the family wanted to preserve their image of him: The gorilla's chest-thumping might be the beat of life.

Now, fifteen minutes into the session, in whatever amorphous way decisions are made, I decided that my job would be to challenge the family's view of the past. It was up to me to help them construct a future, and the future had to be built on a succession of pasts and presents.

I turned to Carl: "Are you such a demanding tyrant?"

"According to them, I must have been." One of the things he was now managing was the idea that all those years when he was just being himself, his family had hated him. "I didn't realize it at the time. My father used to come home drunk and slap my mother around, and take off and—whether he screwed around or not, I don't know, but a lot of men like that did. They'd spend their money on some woman downtown or join the country club while the kids went without shoes. *I didn't want to do that*. I thought that if I stayed home at night, if I didn't drink, if I was around my children, if I was faithful to my wife, and bought them things I never had—nice things—I thought I was being a good father. When in fact I was abusing my children."

No doubt Carl was a demanding and angry father, but this story was too one sided: one villain, three victims. Life is usually more complicated than that. Besides, Edith didn't seem like the victim type. She was dynamic and energetic, a big woman, not afraid to speak up and not afraid of colors. She wore a bright green sweater with a wide gold necklace. If there was a leader in this family, it seemed to be Edith. And yet her children felt the need to protect her. I probed to see if I could broaden the focus from *Carl did this* and *Carl did that* to a father and a mother and their children playing out a more complicated scenario.

"How come you were so intimidated by this guy? You know, you seem like such a powerful lady."

"I am. But Carl was stronger than I was. It's like everybody says: They say, 'She runs the business, she runs the house, she runs the kids, she runs the car, she runs everything.' Then they say, 'But he runs her.' And it's true."

"How does he do it?"

"Well . . . I guess it was his anger."

The session continued like this for quite a while. I challenged, trying to introduce a new perspective. Edith, then Alan, then Kyra, seemed ready to take another look at themselves, but then the habitual response took over again: "I guess it was his anger."

I tested to see if Carl was a little more human than the official version. "Did you feel powerful?"

"No. But I'm sure I was a hard taskmaster, and I'm sure I did a lot of things wrong."

"Then how come Edith is such a competent and managerial person?" And then before they could plug this opening I tried to widen it, letting them know how I think things work in families, announcing my intentions. "Families have myths. They tell themselves stories—and they believe them. My job is to help you look at your story and see if it should be a little more complex."

I was pleased to be in the open now. I was challenging their truth with my variation.

And then I said to Edith, "You seem to me a very competent person. The first thing I felt about you was your level of energy." Since I wanted her to think about what I was saying, not argue with it, I turned quickly to the children. "So what was it like growing up with these two larger-than-life parents?"

"He's closed-minded," Kyra said forcefully. "Once in a great while he'd consider something that someone said, but then later he'd say, 'It's all bullshit!'"

"Do you think your mother influenced your father in any way?"

"No."

"Oh—he's totally impregnable? I'm fascinated. You say he's so powerful—absolutely impermeable to anyone else— because, you know, I never knew anyone to be quite like that."

"He was so distant," Alan said. Unlike his sister, he had a pleading tone in his voice. "It was like talking to myself. I just wished I could get through to him. Then after a while I felt like, What's the use? But I never stopped trying. The only thing I've ever really wanted in my life is acceptance from my father."

"That powerful?"

"That unachievable. We had a joke: 'It's all right, Alan, don't worry. It's all right, as long as it's perfect.' But it wasn't funny."

What did I have in my black bag for such a broadside of life? Alan's "unachievable" yearning for his father's respect touched me. I wanted to respond to him and to his needs. But I knew that was a distraction, and that this impressive array of past grievances was a way of keeping the gorilla alive.

"Have you ever seen a gorilla?" I asked.

"Yes." Edith, Alan, and Kyra answered in unison.

"You must know they're vegetarians. They just make a lot of noise."

Still defending her turf, Edith shot back, "Have you ever been around a gorilla who was going crazy like that, and confronted him?"

Instead of trying to argue, I turned again to the children. "I don't think this myth was written by Carl alone. I think the script was also written by Edith. She was the coauthor. Inside, Carl was full of weakness and uncertainty—just like the rest of us. How did she write her half of that story?"

Kyra said, "She'd try to make us be good, and quiet."

Alan added, "I never had a chance to argue with him. My

father never talked to me—we never communicated. It was always from Mom."

"You know, I love stories. I'm fascinated by how families make them up. You, Edith, you were the voice. He, the mythical despot, was always mediated by this powerful lady. So, the gorilla was a ghost that you—all four of you—kept alive."

There was a long silence. Then, speaking slowly and quietly, I said to Alan, "I think you cheated your father. One of the things children do is teach their parents—challenge them and expand their lives. You did that with your mom. But not your father. You changed your mom, because you are able to negotiate with her, get angry, talk. I don't think you helped your father."

The idea that children have power over their parents always comes as a surprise. But if I was to succeed in making Carl merely human, I would have to convince the rest of the family of their own competence. They had constructed a gorilla; surely they could also deconstruct him.

"I tried," Alan said, leaning forward. "I've always tried. But how can you express emotions to somebody when you don't get any response, when he always cuts you off?"

"How could you help your father?"

Alan paused to think, but Kyra was ready with an answer. These two were like tag-team wrestlers. "I *have been*, during the last year, by not playing his game—telling him how I feel, and if he gets all upset and angry, he'll have to work that through. And if he does something I don't like, I tell him, 'Listen, if you're going to react like that, I won't be able to talk to you.' He's like a two-year-old: You have to teach him that's not going to get over with you."

"I don't know what's been going on. We used to be so close," said Carl with the perplexed innocence of a father dealing with a daughter who is no longer a child.

Kyra's attempt to stand up to her father was a start, but it mostly took the form of telling him off and then hanging up the phone. When Kyra was telling me about changing, she was a forceful twenty-eight-year-old woman; when I asked her to talk with her father, she became a teenager, angry but afraid.

"Something is puzzling me. When your dad answered you, your voice began to hesitate, and he was just talking. What's going on?"

"I guess I'm still intimidated by him."

"But you're twenty-eight. You can talk to him. Please, continue. Don't give up on him. He needs you. You can help him." And when she started again to explain, rationalize, I said, "But why are you playing your mom's game—that you are afraid of him, when he's absolutely, here, nonfrightening? All he really wants is your approval. You're playing now your mom's game."

As I had with Alan, I tried to help Kyra challenge her father directly. I knew I was being unfair to Edith. My language ("mom's game") was accusatory. But, caught up in the plot of the session, I was by now one of the family, limited by our common history of one hour. Besides, I liked Edith, and it was reasonable to assume that she could understand that I was working on behalf of them all.

For a few moments father and daughter did talk, with no interruptions, no distractions, and no buffer. She told him that she had to be her own person, had to be honest; and he told her that all he'd ever wanted was for her to be happy. It was a sweet moment, a moment of love spoken.

And then Kyra began to talk about her mother. "Mom thought that if she got us to walk on eggs things would be easier, and I went through a period where I thought if I was perfect it would make Mom's life easier."

Edith leaned forward to speak. I turned to her and said, "You're right. If I had to face an angry gorilla I wouldn't provoke him. But if I lived with the gorilla and I saw his weakness and his pain, at some point I wouldn't be afraid. How is it that you managed to remain afraid all these years, when you know that in many ways Carl is so unsure of himself?"

"Oh, I grew up in a war zone. My father was very tough. He kept us frightened. No one stood up to him."

Through the window you could see the hazy sunshine of a hot, early autumn afternoon. But in the room where we sat talking about the sins of the father it was air-conditioned cool. There we sat, cut off from the warm afternoon, in one of those sterile rooms humming with fluorescent lights. We could have been anywhere. There we sat, hearts busy remembering, recriminations crowding out the present. They were still children. He was still Daddy: Daddy-who-stands-in-the-way.

And so it went, back and forth. They kept trying to prove that Carl was an impossible monster; I kept trying to prove them wrong. They listened, but the minute one of them felt blamed for keeping this one-sided view of the family alive, that person would jump up and prove me wrong. I felt like Don Quixote, only instead of tilting at windmills, I was tilting with memories. I wanted them to stop thinking of themselves as three helpless people ruled by a powerful, angry man. Where would that leave them when he died? And between now and then?

At one point Kyra talked about not getting a part she was counting on in the high school play and being so depressed that she went into the bathroom and swallowed a dozen aspirins. She wanted her parents to know how unhappy she was, but then she got scared and told her brother, who told Carl and Edith. "And do you know what he did? He acted totally disgusted, and he said 'If she's that fucking stupid let her kill herself,' and he insisted that my mom go out with him. I know she was worried about me, but he made her go out."

"And did she?"

"Of course. She had to."

"Would *you* have left if it was your daughter?"

"Well, no. I would have stayed with my daughter."

"Then how come you only get mad at your dad? How come you don't also get mad at your mom? For you there's one bad guy, one strong one, and everybody else just does what he makes them do. And that's not true. In this story there were at least two people."

I sensed that Kyra had given me this incident as a present, to give me space to confirm my interpretation of their family. When she said, "I would have stayed with my daughter," she was working as my cotherapist, introducing complexity into the story. But in retrospect I see that I was becoming enamored of *my* story, trapped by it, forcing the others to follow me without being sufficiently aware of their reluctance.

As the session drew to a close, I repeated and reinforced my challenge: "Everybody's focusing on how to change the monster." After Alan broke in to say, "He's no monster," I continued: "But there *was* a monster. That marriage, this relationship that they could not change, was a monster, because they were operating as if it was unchangeable. Actually, it is changeable; even now."

Alan, the one most ready to accept my revision of the family myth, seemed pleased with the idea of developing a new and more open relationship with his father. When Edith questioned the idea that Carl might accept change from his son, Alan responded by saying, "I don't mean I should change *him*, start bitching at him and all. I mean that I could change our relationship, start getting closer to him."

Kyra, too, seemed to welcome the idea of change, which she saw in her terms—continuing to stand up to her father, not letting him intimidate and boss her around.

Before she was ready to see her father, and herself, in more human, more equal terms, it seemed that Kyra needed to go through a period of angry self-assertion. Getting angry at parents may be a necessary stage in our revision of the past, like a rite of passage.

Edith was less willing to accept this new version of events. She continued to argue: Carl *was* impossible. Why did she need to hang on to the old story more than her children did? Was she fighting the implication that she was to blame for the family's unhappiness? Or did she just understand better than the rest of them that a revision of the past would leave them squarely face to face with a present she preferred not to see?

The session ended in good-natured bantering, with everyone joking about writing and rewriting stories. They agreed to meet two days later for a second consultation. When it was time to go, Carl, the last to leave, lingered a moment. He walked over to me, put his arm around my shoulder and said, quietly, "Thanks. Thanks a lot."

Thus I was astonished and bitterly disappointed when Kyra, then Alan, and then Edith called Carl's doctor to say they didn't want to come to a second session. I thought with envy of the easier life of the writer: Why couldn't *my* characters cooperate?

I pride myself on joining, a natural endowment I have cultivated with hundreds of families over thirty years. Hundreds of times I've been Uncle Sal. Why did it take an urgent phone call from Carl's doctor to bring this family back for a second consultation?

The family returned, united in a single purpose. They were going to prove me wrong. Carl, dressed in black, began: "In defense of my family, I'm going to show you how wrong you were. You see me today, an old shrunken man, ready to die. And I wanted to show you some pictures that will prove I really was the gorilla they feared. Edith wasn't perpetuating any myth. It wasn't a myth."

And then he took out a brown-paper bag holding two framed pictures, carefully wrapped in tissue paper. They were old newspaper clippings taken when Carl was a local wrestling champion, showing the gorilla-who-was: an immense and powerful man, heavily muscled, with a fierce glare.

I didn't have to pretend to be impressed. As I examined the pictures, Carl spoke, so softly that it was necessary to lean close to hear. "This is what they had to confront: two hundred and forty pounds of a person who knew what he was doing, and could do it. I wasn't afraid of anybody; and when I got enraged, I wasn't afraid of any*thing*."

Carl described how he'd used wrestling holds to punish the children, and then he stood up slowly and asked me to get up. "I want to show you something," he said. I was a little nervous, but I stood up. "If I break your arm, I'll pay for it," he reassured me. So, bent on unmasking a gorilla, I put myself in the gorilla's power.

I could have taken refuge in tradition. After all, therapy is a "talking cure," and "Tell me what you want to do" would have been an acceptable response. But it didn't occur to me. Carl was defending his family, and I would have to trust him.

Amazingly, this old man, moving slowly, took my arm and managed in a moment to make me grimace in pain. Almost instinctively I reacted like an underdog, submitting and presenting my throat to the victor. Immediately Carl released me. Acting for his family, Carl won. They were right. I was wrong.

I was hurt not so much by the attack on my person as by the attack on my ideas. A therapist is a paper tiger. His only

power lies in the persuasiveness of his ideas, and the authority the family grants him can be withdrawn at any point they
decide he's no longer helpful. Feeling extremely uncomfortable, I returned to my chair, trying to find a way to be less
vulnerable. I slowed my breathing and tried to relax my ab-
dominal muscles. I tried to sit in a detached position, avoiding
eye contact, and began to elicit some historical material. Talk
of the past is always a good antidote to the tension of the
moment.

Kyra talked about how she had met and married a man
from Belgium, a man who spoke almost no English. And she
told how this very European man came to live with her in her
parents' house. How she had to do so much for him because of
his unfamiliarity with the language and the culture. And how,
even though her family were devout Christian Scientists, he
still continued to smoke cigarettes and drink wine.

"Fascinating," I said. And then I asked Kyra, "My goodness, what did your father do to him?"

"Nothing."

"And what did he do to your dad?"

Puzzled, Kyra answered, "Nothing."

"I don't think so," I said. "I think he introduced change."

There was a pause and then Carl said, "It was hard to get
used to his ways. He drank wine and smoked, and in our
religion we don't subscribe to that. And he was a wonderful
cook, but he loved to cook fish, and I hate fish. I'd come in the
kitchen, and there'd be all this fish garbage stinking up the
place, and a big pot on the stove with fish in it, and those fish
faces with their eyes looking up at me. But he's a good boy.
Kyra loves him, and we love him."

"Alan, did you introduce deviation with your marriage?"

Alan said, "I've always introduced 'deviation' in our family," and they all laughed. Kyra leaned over and kissed him on
the cheek. They touched a lot in this family. "No, I really don't
think so," he said. "You see, at the time I got married my father
and I actually weren't even speaking. We had just had a major
blowup. I didn't even know if my parents were going to show up
at the wedding or not. My father told me my getting married at
the time was a foolish thing to do. I didn't have a secure job, I
was kicked out of the house at that time—but I was getting
married. I had a big decision to make—whether I was going to

run or whether I was going to settle down and make a commitment. So I decided this was the time. She was the woman I loved, and I was going to make it work."

We had moved from the intensity of the encounter with Carl to more neutral territory: Kyra's and Alan's marriages, other characters, other times. The family had conceded my right to ask questions, and, in turn, I was listening harder and being more open. One of the problems with having seen hundreds of families is that you become a little impatient. You think, I've heard this story before; let's move forward. You haven't. They're all different.

I leaned forward and asked Alan, "Let me ask you, in the story your family has written, do you like the chapter they've written about you?"

"Oh, I don't know. I really don't know what that would be, really. When I was younger, I had an idea, maybe. They thought I was pretty wild. They didn't like my going out all the time, staying out late."

Alan remembered how his father used to lacerate him with a look, that look of silent censure. He would like to have talked, but he didn't know how. Carl remembered Alan's I-give-a-shit shrug. He would like to have talked, but he didn't know how.

I turned to Kyra and asked, "How is it that you decided to leave?"

"My husband is a set designer. He's really very good, and there just aren't the positions around here for someone with his level of expertise. They just don't pay for it. I used to want to live here because my parents live here. But we've had to bounce around the country and make moves to increase our salary and work our way up."

"Were you concerned about what was going to happen to your parents when you left?"

"Yes, I was," Kyra said with feeling. "I was *very* concerned. I felt responsible, and I thought maybe I could change things by behaving in a certain way."

"How did you want to change things? What were the things? Was it your mother you wanted to protect?" I was cautious now, concerned that I was again in dangerous terrain.

"Yes."

"And how were you going to protect her?"

"Try to make Dad happy. Try to make things smooth."

"Quite a job."

"Too much. I quit."

And then, having talked about the years she stayed at home playing the good daughter, the peacemaker, Kyra said she'd tried to talk honestly to her father after the last consultation, and it ended in a big argument.

Carl answered, "Yeah. She said, 'Dad, you're a phony!' and I got upset, angry."

I said to Kyra, "You came here because you want to change your relationship with your parents, so that you are an adult person that can love and disagree with your father—without your mom's support. So, what happened yesterday? Talk with him."

Kyra turned her chair to face her father and said, "I haven't been around here for a year and a half. So all the things I've gone through with you have been long distance. And it isn't the same. I know I should have been more adult. I should have said that what happened in the past was misrepresented in that first session." And then she turned away from her father, searching for understanding in my eyes: "But when I was there with him, with his eyes looking at me like this [glaring], it brought back all those old feelings."

Carl interrupted to say, "But she was right. I was wrong. I did forget. I was angry when she moved away. I thought things were great. I didn't understand why she had to go."

Kyra left home in order to get out of a triangle that was preventing her from becoming a person in her own right. But at the time she didn't think much about it; she just knew that she had to leave. Then, after she married and returned home for a brief stay, she and her husband moved far away. At that point she became severely depressed. She tried to tell her father all this after the consultation, but it ended in an angry quarrel. She tried to make him understand that she had felt trapped at home before she left, but he felt attacked and got defensive. They quarreled, and Kyra was going to leave and go back home. But Edith talked to Carl, told him to calm down and apologize. Kyra stayed.

This was not surprising. In fact it was predictable. The consultation had challenged the story of the self-centered and angry gorilla and the need for a protective mother as a buffer.

But the family immediately reenacted the same old scenario. The official story was reinforced; the therapist's alternative view was reduced to a well-meaning but naive spinning of tales.

I turned to Carl and said, "Do you think you need Edith now in your dialogues with Alan?"

"No."

"And with your daughter, Kyra?"

"No. But like I say she came in pretty handy the other day, because I honestly forgot what it used to be like. All the time Kyra was living with us, I thought it was wonderful. I thought we were happy. And then she left, and all of a sudden I get the news that I was a son of a bitch. I tried. I always wanted to be close to my kids." To Carl's mind his daughter's behavior might as well have been spoken in a foreign tongue; he understood her as well as he spoke Flemish. Looking back, he knew he'd been wrong, and so now he had that bitterness as well to swallow.

Alan said, "When I was young, you were so insistent. Everything had to be perfect. I'd clean up or make something, and you'd say, 'Okay, fine, but now we have to do it right.' I never got the appreciation or recognition I needed." Like his father, Alan was highly susceptible to slights. But, unlike his father, he didn't lash out in anger. He swallowed the insults and choked on them.

Edith said, "I just wanted them to love their father."

"Well, I think you wanted the children to love me," Carl said, "and I think you wanted the children to respect me, and I think you felt you had to be the intermediary between . . . a gorilla and his children."

And then Alan said, "If you didn't want us to be afraid of him, Mom, why then was there always: 'Shh, your father this, your father that.' It was like a haunted house. It was an environment of fear."

Carl said, haltingly, "If Edith made any mistakes . . . she didn't do it on purpose." His eyes filled with tears and he lowered his head. Alan reached out and put his arm around his father's shoulder, and Carl said, "She did these things out of love."

And then, after wiping his eyes with the back of his hand, Carl said, "They were our whole lives. When we find out—or

I find out—that I did so many things wrong ... it's hard to deal with." He couldn't go on.

Now that he was dying and there was no future, he was learning one of the hardest lessons of parenthood—that children never forgive things: lapses of attention, failures of appreciation and pride, harsh reprimands that felt like rejection, mistakes made in trying to balance between being with them and letting them be. These resentments and episodes of anger stick out; the parent's embracing love is too constant to be named and so slides by unnoticed.

Edith reinforced what Carl said. "We never really had any friends outside the family, just ourselves and the children."

Kyra had slumped down to rest her back, but now she sat up and said, "I didn't used to have friends either, but now I do, and they mean a lot to me. Every time I used to have a problem, I'd call my mom and dad. Now I don't. Even if sometimes I want to—but I don't. I call my girlfriends or I talk to my husband."

I said, "One of the fascinating things about growing up is to discover that the door you always felt was closed—it's open."

Another story was emerging: of love, protection, closeness. It seemed to be a story of unfinished sentences, of almost belonging, of stammered affection, of suppressed embraces. This could remain a subtext as long as it was ignored. But when I focused on it, it became a challenge to the official story.

"It *wasn't* open," Kyra shot back. "I can tell you that." After a moment she added, "It was open but I would risk him getting angry ... and not understanding."

At that moment I stood up and walked over to where Carl was sitting and said to Kyra, "You know, when he put that hold on me I felt his power. But I am also hearing that his relationship with you was tremendously precious to him. So you had a hold over him."

"Listen," Kyra said, "my dad is fond of women—*if* they're wonderful and sweet and don't disagree—"

I interrupted, "Who trained you?"

"I don't know."

I smiled and pointed to Edith: "This wonderful lady."

Kyra and Carl responded in unison, "No." Edith gave me a hard stare and said, "You're greatly mistaken, mister. He was an angry person before I ever met him."

Everybody tensed; I felt it in the pit of my stomach. My

instinct was to retreat, but I realized that Edith was doing to me what she would like to, but could not, do to Carl; that for her, self-affirmation could come only at moments of intense anger, and that acceptance of this part of her would be important in changing their relationship. So I took a deep breath and summoned a smile.

"I like that. I like the way you stand up for yourself."

"Good," she said, angry and pleased at the same time. "I can do more of it."

Kyra and Alan laughed.

"I can see that I was wrong. I *like* what you did with me. Can you do that with Carl?"

"Yeah, I can a little more now. I talk to Carl like that, direct—but I don't say *anything* he doesn't want to hear. But I can say anything to you." Her juices were flowing now. I'd provoked her. She felt blamed and got mad—and she said so. With me she was not intimidated the way she was by Carl's anger and vulnerability. Now, having stood up to me, she became almost flirtatious. "You may be an intelligent, educated man, tops in your field. But you don't intimidate me." I was a critic she could stand up to. It was a new experience for her.

Facing me now, Edith told me about her austere, demanding father. "He was a Spaniard and a horseman. He liked to horse around a lot—and not just with horses. He married my mother when she was fifteen—he was twenty-six—and he kept her frightened and like a little girl all her life. And I married just as strong a man. I think I needed that. But now I'm a very capable person. I can do a lot of things—and I didn't need the ERA to tell me that either."

I turned to Carl and said, "Carl, here you have Edith taking me on—very easily—not letting me push her around with my ideas."

"I love it when he says my name," Edith declared. "It takes me back. Sounds *just* like my father. Exactly."

Edith was reminded of her father, and I was reminded of Nathan Ackerman, whose encounters often had this playful, provocative quality. He called it "tickling the defenses." I noticed, too, that it was Edith's honest expression of anger that released her warm (and not-so-warm) memories.

I said to Carl, "How is it that she needed to curtail this capacity with you?"

"I really think, looking back, that she was afraid of me. She was afraid of the gorilla."

Edith responded to my acceptance of her challenge, and of herself, with increased trust. Feeling validated, she used her challenge to me as a model for a demand that Carl be more considerate of her needs. Carl was confused by the sudden shift in alliances, but I felt on track. In the intensity of therapy, Carl, Edith, and I had formed an organic triangle in which my relationship with each of them affected the way each saw the other. What's more, I felt I could control that triangle.

Kyra wasn't ready to give up so easily. We invent our pasts, and we depend on those inventions to live by. I was fighting for change, but they were fighting to defend the reality of their experience. Kyra wanted to make me understand that her father had been the kind of man who has little respect for women. Her words came out in a rush. "Doctor, you don't understand: There are 'dykey bitches,' there are 'dumb bitches,' there are 'sexy bitches,' and there are 'crude bitches'—and they're all 'just a bunch of cunts.' And that's it. *That's* what we heard all our life."

Carl looked down and answered quietly, "That's when they were young and I didn't realize. . . ."

"But what about the other part," I asked, "the part of him that loves this lady?"

Kyra said, "She does what he wants. She's always acted the way he wanted her to act."

"I think he's missing a lot," I replied.

Carl said, "I know. What I don't know is how much time I have left." Edith reached out and took his hand. And Carl said, slowly, "The gorilla's gone."

And then came a moment we'd been building to, one of those moments that happen once in a while in families, when someone says something and everything shifts. Carl started it. Triggered by my alliance with Edith, he challenged the picture she'd presented to me.

Carl spoke in a low, tormented voice, "I could never understand why anybody would be afraid of me. And when she told me after thirty-two years, 'I've always been afraid of you,' that's like somebody saying your whole life isn't what you thought it was. It's a fake."

It was almost impossible not to reassure him, but Edith wanted something different. "I could never have told you because you wouldn't have tolerated it." And then, speaking in a rising voice, she began to release the weight of her anguish.

"We've been together thirty-two years, and I've been smothered. I tell you I don't want to be with you twenty-four hours a day, and you interpret that as I don't love you. Thirty-two years; it's too goddamned much! You wonder why I have claustrophobia? You were always 'so sensitive'—you were sensitive about *your* needs, not mine. You don't care about me the way I care about you."

Carl only said quietly, "I never knew that."

"They want me to talk to you, I'll talk to you!" Edith was crying now, but she went on. She was fighting for the future. "I want our life together—I don't care if we've got ten minutes or ten years—but I don't want to screw up what time we've got left. I want us to go on from here. Honestly. And I don't want us to get home and you to think I'm just speaking up because you're sick. I want to be honest."

Edith and Carl talked for another ten minutes. She talked about wanting to have some time for herself once in a while, and when Carl turned to me, smiling, and said, "See, I don't understand that: I want to be with her all the time; I enjoy her," Edith said, "*Look* at me." Her expression of feeling brought about a shift in power, releasing her and him from the old inequality. This shift made it possible to accept death. "If I don't want to be with you, you take it as an insult. You take it as a lack of love." And Carl answered, "Well, I'm going to have to change that."

I said to Edith, "He cannot change without your help. He will do exactly what he did before, because he liked the way it was. But it wasn't fair, and you need to do what you need to do."

As the session drew to a close, I summed up what I thought was the theme. To Carl I said, "You need to accept that you

are still alive, and *she* needs to accept that you are still alive."
To Edith I said, "You will need to convince Carl that you
accept him as he is, and I don't think that's easy."

Edith answered with feeling, "I know. I've been making
that mistake for thirty-two years. I was accepting him the
way he *was*. And if he's not going to be that way, I'll try to
accept him as he is now. Just because he's not the gorilla, I
guess that doesn't mean he's dead. Maybe we were keeping
the past alive . . . to keep him alive."

Carl and I talked about the death of youthful dreams. I re-
called my school days when I was a long jumper, and how
even after I stopped jumping, I was still jumping in my head,
until I recognized that the dream was dead. Carl countered,
saying, "In part of my mind I am still the gorilla, and I need
to maintain the gorilla mask because if I don't, I'll have to
recognize my dying."

Nine months later a card came, saying, "This period has been
the best of our lives. Edith borrows the gorilla mask sometimes." Six months later Edith was a widow.

Epilogue
The Silent Song

There is a song that needs to be sung in our culture: a song of the rhythms of relationship, a song of people enriching and expanding each other. The noise and tumult of everyday life often muffles the harmonies that make life together possible—the melodies of mutual accommodation and support that cement human interaction.

We are born with the capacity for collaboration, accommodation, and mutuality. Every newborn comes equipped with a well-tuned receptivity to the sound of its mother's voice and the rhythm of her movements; and the baby's needs, in turn, evoke a sympathetically attuned series of answering responses in the mother. Parent and child define each other in millions of small acts that fit together with the precision of a chemical reaction. Needs elicit responses, which in turn elicit accommodations that demand further responses. The most extraordinary thing about this continuous process is how automatically it occurs. It is the silent song of life.

But this collaborative process needs highlighting in our culture, because what we usually notice are differences and discord. We dwell on what jolts, framing difficulties, and do not attend to the patterns that make family life possible: the harmonies we take so much for granted. But these currents of cooperation exist in all families. They are part of what we experience as the family self. Young children say, quite naturally, "I belong to Mommy and Daddy." In adults this family self is felt as loyalty to the group, responsibility toward other family members, tolerance of differences, enjoyment of growth, and the commitment to avoid giving pain.

Loyalty, responsibility, tolerance, enjoyment, and kindness —these are the positive features of family life through which we expand and enrich each other. Family ties do not reduce the self—they expand it.

I've always been blessed with the capacity to look at the individual and see family connections. To see the self as being, but also as belonging. In the 1980s I went to Arizona to meet Milton Erickson. Erickson, a psychiatrist, was a teacher's teacher in hypnosis: a legend with a colorful reputation—part professional, part medicine man, part leprechaun. He had suffered a stroke that left half his body paralyzed. As I entered his consulting room, he was seated in a wheelchair, his face distorted by hemiparalysis, mouth half open, his voice slurring. But his hair was smoothly combed. He wore his characteristic purple velvet jacket and a crisp white shirt. Suddenly, in the space around him I saw the image of his wife, the person who had prepared him for this meeting with such loving care. The man, physically diminished, was completed by her. I have seen this many times: men becoming an extension of their wives' nurture, women more expanded than burdened by motherhood, children becoming their parents' parents.

I am not writing fairy tales. I know that these processes of mutual accommodation aren't always as smooth as a well-rehearsed *pas de deux*. There is pain and strain and strife in the normal course of growing up together. But we need to focus more than we do on the ways of getting along.

Ours is a society that celebrates the uniqueness of the individual and the search for the autonomous self. Differences among generations and genders are painted in polarities: parents exploit their children; adolescents struggle against their parents; women speak in a different voice, and men have strange ways of communicating. Child abuse, sexual abuse, family violence, battered women, the abandonment of the aged —these are the symptoms of relationships gone bad. But the way we characterize and address these problems rests on our tendency to perceive relationships as one sided. Blaming family tragedies on one person's cruelty and neglect is the over-simplification of a society preoccupied with individuality— and of professionals wearing blinders. I see connections and possibilities. I help families search for alternatives. I encourage tolerance of differences and acceptance of limitations. Instead of emphasizing power and weakness—villain and victim—I focus on complementarity and the construction of partnership.

When families come to me depleted from struggling with the conflicting claims of their individual selves, they implicitly make me the repository of the family self. I become the guardian of solidarity. In the heat of conflict, family members assert competing claims of injured selfhood: "You're always trying to control me!" "All you care about is yourself!" "What about me!" Strife outshouts the silent connections that make them a unit, drowning out the capacity for fulfillment through cooperation.

So I work with a double focus, moving between selfhood and togetherness, creating tension as perspectives shift. When I say to Carter Farrell, the unbending father, "You are a competent sheriff," I define his concern with authority. When I ask his wife, Peggy, "Are you the attorney for the defense?" I define her relation to authority and also the couple's relationship with each other. This shift in perspective, from the individual to the relationship, may be startling, but it is readily understood. Our connection to each other is not a new idea, only one that usually escapes our notice.

This is the hallmark of family therapy: attending to both individuality and connectedness, and knowing how to broaden individual stories by shifting to the family perspective. Once family members stop dwelling on the frustrating behavior of others and begin to see themselves linked together, they discover whole new options for relating. Perhaps this expanded view of the self is most visible when working with a couple. I say to Sarah, who is threatened by her husband's retirement, "Do you remain weak so that he can be strong?" While this seems a strange statement, both Sam and Sarah immediately recognize its validity.

Once the limits and possibilities of belonging are better understood, exploring connections can become a source of personal strength. Seeing her "dependence" as part of an old bargain with Sam, Sarah is able to claim her competence. Once the crutch is evicted from the parental triangle, Jill begins to walk. Once Carter, the authoritarian father, is able to acknowledge his own needs, he can learn from his children. Harry can be protective of his wife once he realizes that she needs him. When she stops defining herself in reaction to her parents and accepts responsibility for her own being, Stephanie is able to become responsible for her drug abuse. Once Carl, the "lonely gorilla," and his family discover the patterns that bind them together, they can stop trying to change one another and begin instead to learn to live together. Recognizing that each one of them is a significant part of the whole enables family members to be more fully themselves by being more fully together.

The family therapist can navigate between the realm of the individual self and that of the family unit because all family members recognize that they are connected, and how they are connected. With their long history in common, they recognize that in living together they both constrain and enrich each other. Life in the family does define and limit our freedom, but it also offers untapped potential for personal happiness and fulfillment.

When I see families I have a clear ideology. I don't believe that parents are cruel and children are helpless, or that husbands are logical and wives emotional, or that mothers are sensitive and fathers are not. I see a mosaic—a puzzle in which each individual self defines the others and the whole defines the self, like an Escher painting in which the end is also the beginning. The parts enrich the whole, and the whole enriches the parts.

There's a lot of talk these days about "dysfunctional families," and many people see themselves as wounded survivors: "It's their fault that I'm so unhappy. My mother drank. My father beat me." But when I meet with families I don't see villains and victims. I see people trapped in self-defeating patterns of disharmony. I know that the family has untapped resources of support, love, and caring, and that the good of the many will also be the good of each one. So I focus on helping them see the broader context of the self—the family self.

I'm not blind to the destructiveness of abusive power, and I know there are times when the weak must be protected and the ruthless controlled—by force, if necessary. But again and again, as I see families, I am amazed by the variety of resources people have and the ways they can change—that is, use their resources differently. This means accepting the possibilities and limitations in oneself and in others. It means tolerating uncertainties and differences. It also means hope—for new ways of being together. This is the song our society needs to hear: the song of me-and-you, the song of the person in context, responsible to and for others. To hear it, we need the courage to renounce the illusion of the autonomous self and to accept the limitations of belonging. The survival of the species as well as the family lies in accommodation and cooperation. A society that undervalues these capacities is a society in danger—and it may well be a dangerous society.

RELATED WORKS BY THE AUTHORS

Elizur, Joel, and Minuchin, Salvador. *Institutionalizing Madness*. New York: Basic Books, 1989.

Minuchin, Salvador. *Families and Family Therapy*. Cambridge, MA: Harvard University Press, 1974.

———. *Family Kaleidoscope*. Cambridge, MA: Harvard University Press, 1984.

Nichols, Michael P. *No Place to Hide*. New York: Fireside/ Simon & Schuster, 1992.

———. *The Power of Family Therapy*. New York: Gardner Press, 1992.